Undomesticated Women

To Brenda
Here's to staying
just about wild.

[signature]

Undomesticated Women

Anecdotal Evidence from the Road

ANNA BLAKE

Cover photo by Anna Blake

Back cover photo: Stephanie Marie Di Censo

Editors: Elisabeth Kauffman, Crissi McDonald, and Kara Stewart

Cover design and formatting by JD Smith

Published by Prairie Moon Press

All enquiries to annamarieblake@gmail.com

First published 2023

Library of Congress Control Number: 2023912560

Dedication

To Horsewomen, an undomesticated breed.

We're not like other people. We're persistent and opinionated. Generous and stubborn. Tough as twine for chores but as soft as a breath with horses. And with so much passion, we're nearly feral.

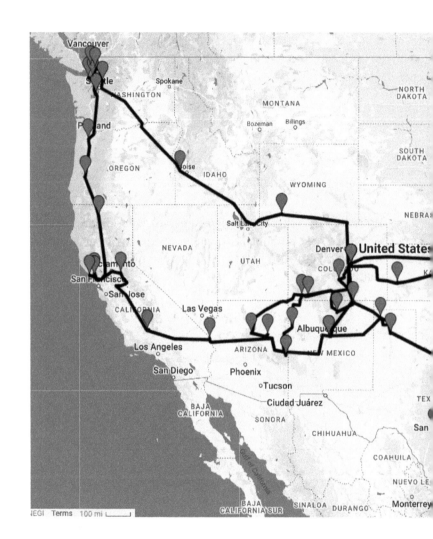

Scan the QR code for road trip photo
albums and to connect with the author

Table of Contents

Preface

My dog, Mister, and I took to the road pulling our A-frame trailer, the Rollin' Rancho. We crossed thirty states, saw two oceans, and covered 14,000 miles in eight months. I'm a traveling horse trainer/clinician promoting a kinder method of training.

Undomesticated Women is a travel memoir, a peek behind the curtain of how I do my job while sharing my bug-splattered view of this beautiful country and the reflections of a gray mare.

A little about those I name in this book. I shared stories about some brave and exceptional women because they represent aspects of the horse world I wanted to touch on. I asked permission to use their names but choosing who to write about was difficult. An apology to those not named. I didn't include each stop for the sake of page count or overlapping subjects. Every moment of the year wasn't smooth and bright, and I wanted to explore those feelings without blame. My goal was to relate my overall experience as honestly as I could, without dragging readers through every truck stop bathroom and pothole in the road.

Often people tell me I'm writing about them when I'm not. Chalk that up to humans being more alike than different. Having a common experience means we are not alone, even at our worst, and that's a good thing.

Everyone has a story to tell, and every story has as many perspectives as there are people involved. This is my story. Mister would tell you it's his.

A Strange Name for an Occupation

Face-talker

A face-talker sat next to me on the plane. It was late February 2020, and I was on my way home from a clinic in Benson, Arizona. He leaned forward and twisted toward me in the window seat. Much too close. Ignoring the book I was diligently reading, he told me his name in a volume more suited to an auditorium.

Like a lot of horse people, I'm an introvert. Not shy, but reticent. I'm not comfortable talking to strangers. Besides, it had been an intense and exhausting working weekend. I was hoping to be asleep soon.

He asked my name, maybe for the second time. The face-talker was in his fifties, wearing a blue oxford shirt tucked into pressed jeans, with laced brown leather dress shoes. Old-timers have a word for horses who give a good first impression but don't quite feel genuine. "Counterfeit" is the word, a forgery of an honest horse. The name suited this man, too. And I guess I'm officially an old-timer.

The man's shoulders blocked my view of the aisle, his knees crowded mine. No escape, so I retreated closer to the window. He probably saw himself as affable. Eventually, without lifting my eyes, "Anna."

I made it obvious I didn't want to talk. He leaned even closer but kept his voice loud, asking where I was from. After a long moment, "Colorado."

He inhaled and named every city in the state that he'd been to and what he thought about them. Introverts are notoriously lousy at small talk; we don't get the point. My eyes stayed on the page I was no longer reading. Is he that enthralled with the sound of his own voice?

After he'd exhausted his knowledge of Colorado locations and I hadn't responded, he asked what I was doing in Arizona. My pauses before answering got longer.

"Working."

Not that he was interested; it was just a launching point for him to share that he'd been vacationing and then told me everything he'd done during his visit.

My body language was pure avoidance. I didn't make eye contact and only gave reluctant one-word answers. I looked away. A horse would have wandered off to graze by now, a dog would have curled up for a nap. After no response from me at his vacation monologue, he asked what I did. An eternity of seconds passed.

"Train horses."

He immediately regaled me with his personal horse experience. Years before, he had ridden exactly once and gotten bucked off. I'm impressed. That horse had succeeded where I was failing.

I could feel his breath on my face. Blaming the horse, he asserted he understood horses needed firm-handed discipline, as he had done. He spoke as if it was his birthright, not just being an authority on horses, but also educating me.

I stared at my book, belligerently not reading now, as the one-ride expert lectured on, insisting that horses needed to respect us. It was the old "show them who's boss" tripe, and it wasn't working with me either. When stoic horses get pushed too far, they react. It was probably why that horse dumped him. I made eye contact for the first time and told him domination training approaches had been scientifically debunked for decades. That fear-based training was ineffective and often damaging to horses, adding that I'd written books about it.

He didn't miss a beat and switched the would-be conversation to dogs. He claimed they all loved him as if to make up for the poor judgment of horses. His Golden Retriever was obedient, and everyone was so impressed, he said, that he bred her because so many people wanted her puppies. He seemed to relish calling her a "bitch" like a boy permitted to swear.

Did his dog hold her breath, roll over, and show her vulnerable belly, cowering in submission? I wondered how many of the dog's calming signals, meant to settle this man's jangling oblivious energy, were ignored as mine were. I wondered if he thought I was her human equivalent. Not on my best day am I as tolerant as a Golden Retriever and I had not consented to this intrusion.

"Enough," I said. "Just stop talking." I made my eyes hard, and he laughed at me, face to face. His breath was sour.

Without emotion, I said, "I need you to change seats."

It surprised him enough that he paused, but I held my glare until he turned to the passenger who was reading across the aisle and interrupted them.

I stared at my book, still cornered in the window seat. Did that bully think his know-it-all guise made pushing so far into my space more palatable? I didn't turn another page. Instead, I stewed. Does he deserve polite behavior from me when he shows me none? I could turn the other cheek and feign tolerance while holding a Christian superiority. That's been a respite for the women who think suffering is their lot in life and a ticket to heaven.

Buddhist adages usually speak of kindness as being more important than ego. The dictionary defines ego as self-importance, which sounds like narcissism. The second definition is self-esteem, a quality we should aspire to demonstrate. Opposite meanings of the same word don't help with clarity. I could practice non-attachment with a Buddhist lean. Would it kill me to let him drivel on? In our culture, women accept the overreach of strange men as a standard experience. And this guy was blindly obnoxious. Would some think he was worthy of my sympathy? Meaning my false sympathy.

Therapy is a kind of spirituality, and I've spent a serious amount of time there. I learned to speak in "I" statements. To tell the truth about personal feelings without blaming others. After a childhood of keeping family secrets, bearing that dark weight in my gut, I found my "I" voice. I learned to say no and let that bluntness hang in the air with no apology. But even now, it had to be a choice to speak, to leverage my voice against social expectations. Not that the face-talker noticed.

Like most girls of my generation, my parents taught me to defer to men, to revere priests, and to subdue my intelligence to teen boys to get a date. I was not a good learner. I was born with a notion of equality, although I rarely saw it. My earliest memories were that "men's" jobs were outside and interesting while the "women's" jobs all seemed to be involved with cleaning up. Did the accident of birth trap me like the window seat on this plane? I've been resisting the painfully ingrown idea of submission since I could speak. As an adult, I'd worked in traditionally male careers, still pushing for fairness, and asking myself the same teenage questions about where I belonged in the world.

The face-talker was going on about sports to the ex-reader across the aisle, as everyone in four rows could hear. I shut the tiresome man out and let my internal dialog ramp up. Why do we place the highest value on kindness? A better question might be why is autonomy seen as rudeness.

In my work, I take on the challenge of rehabilitating and retraining horses, many with mental damage caused by forced submission. Most of my clients are women searching for a kinder approach to training horses in a cowboy world. They face the same sort of tin horn tenderfoot that just lectured me. I call myself a horse advocate, with the ironic awareness that I've had to advocate for my own voice first. But now, was I asserting my voice by not talking? What a ball of twine.

Domination doesn't work with horses because they're large flight animals who are never quite tame; never truly predictable. Maybe horses aren't really domesticated at all. Maybe they only tolerate us because we have them trapped in their own kind of window seat.

Is that true of women as well? How many women stuff frustration and pain inside, stoic as an old mare, until the day there's nothing left to lose and then they let loose, bucking their way free? Have men emasculated women? Egad, the thought made my eyes go wide. My lips stifled a guilty grin like I swallowed a live mouse.

The plane descended into Colorado Springs at dusk. I was still mulling over how to balance the pressure of social courtesy with the personal price paid for chronic aching submission. Where is the demilitarized zone between bucking him off or rolling belly-up? Or perhaps I've just aged out on even pretending to be domesticated.

Becoming a Clinician

Clinician is a strange name for an occupation without a medical degree. And not all horse trainers want to become clinicians. We don't start training and giving riding lessons out in the sun and wind, and then get more ambitious. It's ambitious enough to think training could be a primary source of income.

I went to lots of clinics when I was an amateur. The clinician always had a slightly different approach, used unique examples, or described the old basics in a new way. I craved knowledge and the learning process was more inspiring in a group.

When I first started training professionally, I gave riding lessons and worked with horses at my home farm. We have a friendly sand arena out front, and weekends were busy.

Sometimes, I drove my truck to other farms, or I invited clients to my farm for a day of obstacles or riding to music. Randomly, a local club might invite me to give a small clinic. Doing rehab work for a rescue and working with clients filled my week. I was just happy to be working with horses and writing my blog.

Then my first book, *Stable Relation,* came out in 2015. I was tidying things up on my computer and it occurred to me I hadn't updated my website since I put it online years before. An idea came to me while I was mucking, which is when all my best thinking happened, and I started to sketch out ideas for a new format for clinics.

Rather than a day of individual unrelated lessons, I wanted to come up with an idea that would be a more holistic experience. We would talk about one big topic but in a group of individual scenarios. To start with an umbrella of an idea and then let it trickle down to each person's horse. I called them Concept Clinics. We might delve into Affirmative Training, or Calming Signals, an animal's body language. Some participants might do groundwork if they wanted, while others might work on advanced riding movements.

I ruminated, then scribbled out a few rough paragraphs. I did not use spell check or add photos. Some sentences were one word long, and there was a list of things I meant to write about soon. Then, I hit the save button and went to bed.

When I woke up in the morning, I had several emails inviting me to do clinics. I squinted, trying to make sense of it. How did I get popular all of a sudden? My incredulous smile froze.

Scurrying back to my draft, yup, I hit the wrong button. I'd published the list of ideas and rough notes. I frantically tidied the web page, turned the lists into paragraphs, and added photos. I tried to make it look like I meant to publish it, but I still didn't know why so many people were on my rusty old website that night.

I'd like to say I had a meticulous plot for fame and success, or that I dreamed of international travel, but it just isn't true. What

I had done was more of a tripping stumble than an inspired leap. Either way, I'd take it. Now I needed a plan, but it had to be simple.

My new clinic business plan was one word long: Yes. I accepted any invitation from any organizer. I said yes. The word served me well working with horses, so why not? Business plans aren't my strong suit, but this one felt right. I drew up information sheets and altered an online contract form and returned the emails.

Here's the job description: I board a plane headed to a place I probably haven't been before. Then, I get in cars with strangers who drive me into the country. Yes. My mother warned me, but I went anyway.

The clinic location could be a quiet, humble little farm like my home barn. Other times, the clinic hosts ushered me to an equestrian facility with elite horses and barns nicer than my house. It was like crowd surfing. I never knew what to expect.

Clinicians rely on organizers to set up clinics. There's simply no way we could know local facilities or groups of people interested, so we go where we're invited. I have those organizers to thank for what was simply the most mind-expanding experience; I got to learn from so many more horses than I could have ever met staying home.

As a local trainer, I might work with a couple dozen riders over a month, but now the numbers felt astronomical. I encountered horses in other climates that were managed differently. They had different health concerns and different training challenges. I had novel experiences with rare breeds. I could see behavioral tendencies with a wider view, and the horses taught me well.

My learning curve exploded, strengthening my perception and understanding. I saw what training approaches hadn't worked by recognizing a consistent pattern of anxiety or insecurity in the horses' demeanors. They were fearful around people.

But I had a larger number of horses showing me what had

worked, and my training methods improved. Best of all, the horses settled, and their owners gained a sweet confidence. It wasn't me with a single horse; we were a group who supported each other. The biggest sign we were on the right path was our results: the horses blossomed.

Clinic work required having the same unflagging focus and energy at five p.m. that was needed at eight a.m. It was like the rush a rider gets during competition, but it lasted longer. It was more exhausting and exhilarating than anything I'd ever done.

The exhaustion came not just from long days of doing work I loved, but also from the constant change in beds and food. Dragging a suitcase, re-packing it, and dragging it on again. I stayed with people I didn't know, trying to be a polite guest. Grateful for the stay, but also needing rest, I was no more able to behave than a cranky kid at the end of a birthday party. I wanted to whiny cry sometimes, but I had to be "on" for days with barely a break. I had become an itinerant insomniac.

The best situations had an apartment in the barn or a guest house with a kitchen. There was one stop where the apartment was so elite there were fluffy white bathrobes, and I couldn't figure out how to make my coffee. Other stops had breathtaking views that made it hard to discipline my eyes while I was teaching. At one Australian farm, kangaroos waited for their turn in the shady arena. They were the big, heavy-muscled ones as tall as me, looking bored and ready to rumble.

At one home, I stayed in the organizer's bedroom, the couple's clothes folded on chair backs. The adults then slept in the kids' room; the kids slept on the sofa. Their youngest child got over-tired and cried for most of the night. No one's fault, but I still feel uncomfortable remembering it. The organizer loved being a mom, and coping with chaos was her superpower, but she never gave me a towel.

Being a clinician is an intense job and horse owners are passionate people. I materialize at clinic sites to stir things up with ideas and insights for two or three days and then disappear as quickly as I came. It's the wild luck of getting to work with fascinating horses and committed riders in varied environments. All the while, watching the horse world changing for the better. From Scotland to New Zealand, Florida to Alaska, I've had opportunities I'd never dreamed of. People were unfailingly kind, and it was a relentless cycle of strange beds, swollen ankles, and chanting *no-thank-you*. Because people are deaf as a stone when I say *no-thank-you*. But more about that later.

Barely catching my breath before the next flight, I thrived on long, hot workdays, and sprints to the airport. Decades in the making, I had become an overnight sensation, all because of my memoir and an unplanned update to my website one night.

Non-essential Worker

By the time I had been home from that flight from Arizona for twenty-four hours, I felt weak with a headache that wouldn't go away. Sick enough to go to bed. Of course, I blamed the sour breath of the face-talker. The only air to breathe was what he exhaled.

Two weeks later, I was still in bed feeling miserable, so I did the nearly unthinkable thing of going to the doctor. The nurse ran some tests; not flu and not strep, she said. There were no COVID-19 tests then. I noticed she didn't start the appointment in a face mask, but when she came back to the exam room, she had one on. I got a shot, came home, and continued being sick, and then weak, for a while longer.

The news used the term "pandemic." I had been packing to leave for Australia, but now the borders were closed. Hospitals became overcrowded, they warned at-risk groups to stay home, and the death toll rose as the pandemic crisis hit its stride. Months of planning evaporated as I canceled three international trips and a full series of clinics here in the US. Just when I was on the brink of something big… splat.

Pandemic detention pulled me up short. I was like a mare pacing the fence line, separated from the herd. I would have been pacing more, but I was still bed-sick, so while I was only mentally pacing, it was no less frantic. COVID-19 didn't care and, like so many others, "non-essential worker" became my new job title. I was having a career crash; not ready to quit, but with no idea how to go on.

For horsewomen of a certain age (we prefer the title *gray mare)* the idea of change is more inevitable than shocking. I pulled up my chins and launched an online program called The Barn School. Training horses became a desk job with new computer programs to learn while translating clinics into courses and designing ways to teach them. But I could train complicated dressage movements, for crying out loud. The new software would not get the best of me.

Convincing horse people to try an online course was next. It would require a leap of faith for them as well. They had to figure out a way to video themselves working with their horse when we were all camera shy. Then they'd wrestle their videos through cyberspace and to The Barn School. If that all worked, there was the online classroom to negotiate. Some came with a hatred of Zoom meetings from work, and some had never heard of Zoom. It meant that horse people who took a certain pride in hating technology had to circle back and reconsider. It was for their horse, after all.

In class, we worked from weekly videos recorded at home and it was as if instant replay was brand new. Video doesn't lie, but most people said they looked better than they thought, and we had the chance to see and discuss instants in time. It slowed us down.

The classes were international, so there was a feeling of travel, seeing farms in other countries. Dogs and cats joined the meetings, which helped us get comfortable, and we made new friends. I found I could read faces better on a computer. Ironically, in online Zoom meetings, we are all face-talkers, but at a safe distance.

Here's a bit of hindsight-obvious information: It ends up that horses didn't miss clinics at all. They enjoyed working from home. No stressful trailer ride, all their friends were right there. The horses encouraged the initially reluctant riders to continue. Physical distancing was not the same as emotional distancing. The participants found the same sweet camaraderie that clinics offered, but the courses lasted longer. Zoom meetings ended up being an intimate and effective tool for horse training, and I bought a more comfortable desk chair.

Months passed. I walked in my pasture. It took the first year to realize how exhausted I'd been as I rested my way back to health. I edited my friend Elaine's book while I mourned her death, as well as four other friends, each gone too soon. I daydreamed about turning a shipping container into a tiny house to write in. A stray cat came to my barn, and I tried to catch her to be spayed. Too late, I ended up with a rowdy litter of vampire kittens under my desk for two months. Life slowed. The Dude Rancher (a title my husband gave himself) and I had more time together than we had in years, and I breathed.

As the pandemic months passed, my online client's horses made genuine affirmative changes. The courses also encouraged me to think there must be better ways to hold clinics. Ways that were more supportive of horses, while still providing learning opportunities for riders, and less stress for me.

International borders still weren't open by the end of 2021. I'd be foolish to trust the pandemic was over and wind up quarantined in a hotel somewhere. We all needed to find a "new normal" version of our lives, but still stay safe. As if anyone could figure out what safe meant.

I didn't know what my clients would be comfortable with post-pandemic, but I wasn't done working with horses. After two years at home, I missed the spontaneity of clinics. I wanted to train live again, but I didn't want to give up on the online school. Could both methods dovetail somehow? I could have quiet months at home teaching courses and travel during good weather months. Yes, it meant longer hours, but I was self-employed, so it wasn't like I'd lose any paid vacation time.

I set about reinventing how I worked one more time. The plan wasn't to work less; I wanted to take more time doing it. Going slow is a charm with horses and I wanted time to say *good girl* to myself in a more sustainable way. I wanted the flexibility of not being at the mercy of non-refundable plane tickets. Instead, I wanted to enjoy the ride while finding a way for a clinic to be less like an airborne assault and more, well, relaxed and forward.

The solution was to not fly. Sure, I'd miss the airport bars, but if I drove, I could lollygag and take side trips. I admit, it wasn't a revolutionary idea. I have friends who have taken the nomadic path for decades; insert their cackles and nodding laughter here.

This kind of travel would suit me because I perpetually look like a tourist anyway, squinting at road signs and doubting maps. My Cardigan Corgi, Mister, could come along to be my Self-Care Specialist. It would be my job to stand tall in the morning sun and call out, "Wagons, Ho!" and Mister's job to ask if it was time for a lunch stop. He'd walk me a few times a day, so my hips stayed limber and give me a place to be at dinner time. He'd keep me marginally tethered to reality. I can lose time around horses.

As 2022 began, I noodled on a variety of ways to teach clinics without flying. Finally, my idea took shape. I would start by taking an RV on a sort of victory lap to visit the clients who inspired me in the last two lockdown years. I needed to scratch their horses. Mister and I planned an easy start in the spring, with hopes for a year on the road.

What I was afraid to say out loud was that I wanted to see this country, to fall in love all over again before it was no longer recognizable. It didn't feel like a romantic challenge so much as a reasonable way to come out of hibernation.

I'd previously clocked thousands of miles between farms while giving lessons in Colorado. Often, I spent more time traveling than teaching, and I swore I wouldn't do it again. But this new plan was long-haul driving. Truck stops. Sunflower seeds to stay awake. I was no stranger to road trips when I was younger, but now it seemed I needed a nap every sixty miles. Would I be able to do it?

Mister and I would start out after the spring thaw. Slower but no less enthusiastic, we were nomads looking for horse training adventure and liver treats. It was part clinic tour, part travelogue, part squirrel hunt, but mostly an unapologetic celebration of sunsets, horses, RV parks, roadkill, diverse landscapes, and undomesticated women.

I would be sixty-eight years old by the end of the year. Maybe I needed to make peace with that, too.

Inevitable RV

My family had a tradition that was one more problem to overcome, and this one was all in my head where the best problems lurked. Most farmers of my parent's generation had little money. It was expected that dilapidated farmhouses would give way to mobile homes. They were depression-era kids, and their siblings and neighbors did the same. In their defense, it was about the only way they could afford something new.

Our family lost our farm in Minnesota when I was in the fourth grade. We auctioned everything and moved west to Washington State. President Kennedy was dead, and the flags were at half-staff as my father drove us west in our Ford station wagon. He bought a share in a co-op plywood plant where he would hate working until retirement. My mom worked at Sears and later moved to a job as a receptionist.

After we got to Washington and settled in our new home, my father decided it would be a good idea to go camping, and why not? After all, four silent, angry people are so well-suited to sleeping together in small spaces. At first, we had a canvas cabin tent bought with my mother's Sears discount. It was cold misery in the wind and rain at the Washington beaches. We went there because it was all the free clams you could dig.

The drives were silent. My sister and I didn't bicker. We followed our mother's lead and became sullen and passive-aggressive passengers. With our chins in our hands, we each stared out our respective windows as we sat pouting on opposite edges of the back seat.

My parents upgraded to a small travel trailer, and we eventually took our two-week family vacation to Yellowstone. We stopped at every scenic overlook. Old Faithful dutifully exhaled a puff of anticlimactic steam and hot water. My parents were both smokers then, and I remember a constant haze in the car and trailer. My head ached all the time. The geysers were a welcome sulfurous break.

Everything and everyone embarrassed me. An RV seemed to advertise all I wanted to escape. When I was old enough, I refused to go with them. By then my sister had left home, and when I was seventeen, I finally escaped. I meant to find a different life and part of it was swearing I'd never set foot in a camper again.

In the following years, my parents got a van with a box camper on the back. They sold our house and moved into a double-wide. Finally, my parents retired to a mobile home community in Arizona with a camper in the driveway.

I suppose even the most rebellious teenager has to make peace with their roots if only to appreciate the distance they have traveled away. I didn't know then how hard I would eventually fight to get myself back to a farm. Or that the thing we call the "past" was lurking up ahead all along, as I unwittingly reinvented and recycled myself.

Now I wear glasses and hearing aids. I can't remember the last time I recognized my face in a photo. My skin tears and my joints squeak. I take all the vitamins. It was time to buy an RV. I could make excuses to justify it, but why fight gravity? The circle is complete.

Our Year of Living Compactly

Our year of living compactly began with hours researching RVs. It had to be smaller than the horse trailers I'd been dragging along for decades. It had to have good light and not feel like a soda can. I landed on A-frame models that are all windows with a high ceiling. They fold down like origami and would be an easy pull, small and lightweight, but with all the conveniences.

When unfolded, the trailer formed an eight-by-twelve-foot space with the ceiling topping out at eight feet. There were six windows, including one enormous picture window and one skylight to watch the moon from the double bed. The stove had three burners, the sink drained well, and the fridge was totally usable. I thought I might dispense with the microwave at some point, and I got a small tee-pee tent for the outdoor shower. The entry had a Dutch door, just right for Mister to stand guard.

Folded down, it transformed into a sleek flat rectangle on wheels, nearly invisible in my truck's rear-view mirror. I found an end-of-model-year sale and put the money down.

There was a manual about the gas furnace, a manual for the forced-air heater, and the water heater had its own manual. That's just on heating. Onward to the water filters, refrigeration, hookups for fresh water, stored water, gray water, and black water. There were electrical things that I could run on a regular extension cord, but others that needed thirty amps. I quickly discovered the fuse box and breakers, which trip when you plugged too many things in. There were batteries to keep charged and propane to manage. Some things need to be plugged in and other things work when you're boondocking, but first I had to find out what boondocking meant. I turned on the stereo and it took three days to turn it off. My notebook of manuals was inches thick, and why was there an electrical cord sticking out of my mattress?

All my world-class overthinking skills, the ones so useless around horses, were marching in unison, planning for everything I'd need on the road. First, a way to make coffee with either gas or electricity. Lightweight dishes and cooking gear, and then an odd-sized container that would fit both the dishes and the cramped space under the sink. A traveling hotspot for my computer, the right bed linens, a new set of tools for small repairs. I tore out the larger table and bench seat cushions, replacing them with smaller ones, and fashioned more storage to suit me. Naturally, I added some dog amenities.

I planned backups for my backups. I'd spent years traveling by air, my luggage pared down to a small spinner bag for clothing and a carry-on for my tech equipment. Imagine the thrill of an entire room, with a kitchen and bath. I could bring trinkets from loved ones and muck boots for wet days! It would be a luxury beyond imagination.

I hated living out of a suitcase. Now I'd upgraded to living inside of one.

For the first sleepout, we parked ten feet from the house with an extension cord. It was also the first dog pack separation. Preacher Man, a Pembroke Corgi, and Jack, a terrier mix, stayed in the house. Mister, the only one of the three who is not reactive, came out with me.

Reactive is a term for a dog who has anxiety issues. Many end up in rescue. In Preacher and Jack's cases, they had each flunked out of other adoptions twice because of habits that annoyed their adopters. Coming here was a last chance, but don't feel bad for them. No one gets the boot here, not even Preacher who hasn't stopped barking since 2014.

Mister had only been with me a few months. He came to the rescue for different reasons, but I worried that he'd become reactive just to fit in with the other dogs.

The first separation went perfectly. Mister got along well with the other dogs, but he surely didn't mind leaving them for some quiet time alone. Since the trailer had wheels, Preacher Man and Jack seemed to worry that a "car ride" would be involved. A car trip to the mailbox was equal to a trip to the South Pole, so they weren't interested. There was no jealousy or separation problem. Silly me, they each wanted to be where they were.

Mister and I turned out the lights for the night. He is a profound sleeper, silent and still. Maybe his sleep was infectious, or maybe the camper bed was magic. I woke up at six a.m., which is about noon my time. I'm usually a fitful sleeper, getting up before dawn. It was disorienting to open my eyes to find sunlight filling the high ceiling. I made French press coffee, better than what I made in the house, and answered some emails. Mister rolled belly up and slept for an extra hour.

The next camping event was a trip to my south pasture to boondock, which I was now educated enough to know means no hookup of any kind. I used the gas heater, made coffee on the gas stove, and with my small generator, Mister and I watched a movie on my computer, hooked up to my hotspot. A second night of deep, dreamless sleep.

Not long after Mister came to live with us, his unique approach to herding duty became clear. If Mister heard something he was uncertain of during the night, he cautiously moved to plant his breastbone in the center of my stomach. Anchoring me to the bed gave me the opportunity for some isometric gut braces. Then he waited, motionless, with concern and foreboding. If something bad happened, he needed to know exactly where I was. I've had other herding dogs who had to follow every step I took. Mister simplified the technique by pinning me down. Energy efficient, no steps at all. I predict outlandish success for him. It's remarkable how hard it is to dislodge a thirty-seven-pound dog from your torso, so I don't try. Instead, we dozed off as we waited for the danger to pass.

With two successful camping nights under our belt, we officially welcomed our new addition, an extra room parked next to the house. When I travel, it will be a place to call mine at day's end. Movable roots.

Of course, the trailer needed a name, so it became my Rollin' Rancho, a bit of *Home, Home on the Range.*

Miles and Miles of Texas
March 15–April 4

Maiden Voyage

I'd planned and packed, then unpacked and repacked until this little Rancho was as efficient as ice cubes in an ice cube tray. The storage area under the bench seat had containers that filled the space without an inch to spare, each holding related groups of necessities. Yes, I am that person. Plastic drawers held my clothes, equine-themed tea towels, and a quick dry camp towel for me. Other drawers held my writing supplies, more pens than I could use in ten years, cords for every tech thing I'd ever purchased, and a small generator. I tucked tools, locks, and a power drill into the outside storage compartment. The bed had a weighted blanket, just like my bed in the house. I was fully stocked with coffee and dried cream. Trail mix and apples. Soap, cleaning supplies, a stash of dog chews, and water in a three-gallon jug.

The dogs hadn't stopped barking for the last thirty-six hours straight. Preacher Man looked a bit dehydrated, and Jack was only jumping waist high. Mister had broken out of the yard twice a day for the last week and ran to the Rancho to sit by the door and look nervous. The farm was levitating at a screaming hum.

The bed of the truck got a final once-over. I'd under-engineered a simple yet elegant system of plastic tubs with ropes of different lengths. I pushed the less-used ones farthest back against the cab and filled in the rest by priority. The ropes meant I could pull tubs out without climbing in. These tubs held all the training gear: a saddle, neck rings, bitless bridles, half a tack store, and a cooler with ice for the first day. There was a foldable wagon and an X-pen for Mister. Naturally, there were some extra buckets, halters, and rope, just in case. I pack them like other women pack those little tissue packages. I did the last check and felt like I had covered it all.

For decades, I had used a fool-proof method for hooking up my horse trailer. It was a highly developed technique of Sharpie marks on a stick held in place with part of a brick. It worked flawlessly with my old truck because it was missing a tailgate. I bought a new used truck last year, only six years old, and my traditional method was worthless. My new truck had so many varied headrests that my rearview mirror was useless, but the truck was not fancy enough to have a dashboard backup camera. Maybe the theory was folks would use the side mirrors, a definite upgrade over the old truck, but they didn't help with my hitch. Do they assume we want to ask for help to back up? That can't be it.

Like I said, I am that person. I bought a small backup camera to Velcro on my truck bumper and connected it to my phone. Now I could see everything. It was brilliant. My phone clamped into a dash attachment and the app gave a clear, colorful marking, so I knew exactly where the ball hitch was. That took a couple of extra hours to align and hook up. There was a bit of a learning curve, but I called it a win. Petty victories over technology can't be overrated.

Now it was almost dark. Ready to roll at last, I pulled the truck ahead a few feet. The Dude Rancher wandered out to see how it was going and told me my turning signals weren't working. I felt like a birdie whacked to the ground in a badminton game. Frail, minimal bounce, ready to get whacked and sent into play again.

The previous week, I had taken my truck into the repair shop to get my tow package checked out and ended up replacing it. My trailer wasn't there to check the wiring, a mistake that was obvious now that it was after sunset and too late to call. I was going to have to delay my launch with a stop at the shop in the morning.

I went inside for dinner and then early to bed. That way I'd have more time to lay awake overthinking about the trip like every night in the last few months.

I gave up on the mental marathon at about four a.m. and got up and showered. I double-checked everything again. Before it was light, I went out and threw hay one last time, and said so long to the horses. They were drowsy but greeted me with lounge singer nickers, soft and low. Even on brief trips, the hardest part was getting past my mailbox.

Finally, Mister got strapped in. I put a new travel cup of coffee into my console and started my engine. We said our goodbyes to the Dude Rancher and our little farm and headed over to the repair shop to wait for them to open.

The guys were kind and fixed the wiring in a blink. Mister and I drove back past the road to our farm, our first double-back of the trip, and headed for the freeway. Three hours later than planned, we were on I-25, driving south from Colorado Springs. It could have been like any other day, except for one thing. There was a little flat Rancho following us.

God's Horse

My farm is perched at 7,100 feet in elevation on the edge of a high desert prairie, so it was initially a downhill cruise. The landscape quickly changed to a scrub desert. The Sangre de Cristo mountains, the southernmost subrange of the Rockies and perhaps the sweetest peaks ever, shouldered us to the west.

GPS Woman is directing us as if we're deaf. We are, but

she enunciates and repeats herself, sounding confident and a bit entitled. Before leaving, I downloaded a map from a trip planner online to Google Maps, where I had a choice of voices. I never enjoy men telling me what to do, so I picked a woman's voice. With my phone mounted on my dashboard, all I needed to do was click, and she began the next set of directions. I never had to fumble with folding a map, but in the tiny snapshot of the map on my phone, I also never quite knew where I was. I just trusted GPS Woman would get me there.

We climbed over Raton Pass and two and a half hours after leaving home, we exited the freeway for our first rest stop and our first dilemma. There was a fork in the entry road and a sign with two arrows, one way for cars and one way for trucks. Did trucks mean semi-tractor-trailers, because I was way too tiny for that? Should I go where the cars go? If you've ever tried to park a three-quarter-ton pickup in a strip mall parking lot, you understand the need to weigh your choices carefully.

The memory of all the old trucker songs echoed. My father loved them. *Rubber Duck* and *East Bound and Down* howled in my memory and that wasn't me, so I guessed and took the arrow to the car parking. No, totally wrong. Nothing but diagonal parking. I circled around, found the entrance again, and pulled into a huge pull-thru spot between two semis. We are forty-four feet long, just over half the length of those big rigs, but I was one of them now. I had a bit of a swagger on the way to the restroom. It might have been from sitting for a couple of hours.

Walking back to our rig, I saw the silhouette of Mister's ears watching for my return. I was sure he had watched every step as I walked away, stared at the door I went in, and waited for me now. Yes, my boy, it's just you and me out here in the world.

Mister and I walked to the dog area, which was even less tidy than the restroom, with road trip trash littered around the sign to pick up after your dog. Did they need to mention picking up after themselves as well?

Back at the truck, we did the ritual that would come to color the trip. I asked Mister if he wanted to load up, and he stood up cheerfully on the running board of our truck. I steadied his chest with one hand and hoisted his backside onto the seat.

There's a dog car seat with an edge around it to steady him and straps to secure it to the seat in a couple of places. I clipped his travel harness to it. Then I clipped a second strap that attaches to the headrest, too. I know he should travel in a crate for safety. Have you ever noticed, especially with dogs, that we know what the best practice is, but we pick according to our habits and spoil our dogs as we choose? My dogs don't get table scraps, for example, but getting on furniture is just fine.

When Mister first arrived, he traveled in a crate. We have one in the jump seat now, but he doesn't want to be in it all day. I could make it pleasant, train it again, but I don't really want it either. So, I double-strap him in the passenger seat, knowing there will be concerned eyebrows scowling at us. I spoil us with each other's company.

After strapping Mister in, I walked around the back of the trailer, visually checking the hitch, the tires, and the latches. By the time I got to the other side, the trucker parked there was doing a walk-around on his big rig. We nod to each other as if I belong, and then I climb in and crank up my tiny rig. Mister had his head on the console and as I hit speed and glide into traffic, my right hand went to rest on his noggin. On driving days, Mister gets the all-day ear rub.

We skip across our first state lines, into New Mexico, almost Oklahoma, and then Texas, all in a few miles. Crossing state lines so quickly feels liberating. Look how much progress we've made.

Our first view of Texas was a holding pen for cattle just off the road. There are trucks like mine, with long stock trailers, cattle in the pens, and horses standing around. Men wear the obligatory hat, looking like a TV commercial. There's a horse standing off to the side in a pen alone. He was wearing a saddle, but his back had an unnatural arch. Even from a distance, I could see he was in pain. It's none of my business. Those cowboys aren't waiting for a white-haired tourist woman to tell them what to do.

I let him be God's horse. It's what I do when I see roadkill or animals not within my puny sphere of control. I can't let my heart hurt all the time, and if you are an animal welfare advocate, that is the major malady. It's called compassion fatigue. Isn't that an excruciating name?

Horse trainers are receptacles of horror stories told to us everywhere we go as if animal abuse or death is a mysterious, rare event. As if we don't see it all the time, as if those mental images ever leave us. No one can survive that constant ache. Focusing on self-care is a serious survival skill and having a mani-pedi spa day would not do the trick for a horsewoman.

I had to let go of the pain and helplessness of knowing I couldn't save them all. So, I taught myself to trust the Universe. I trust the Stars, or the Earth, or that Thing that holds us in balance. Use any name you want. I can see an order to life, and if gravity works on all of us, then all the rules do. I have to trust that those I can't help are being known and held, just as I am. I release them with a small prayer. God's horse.

The road pulls us forward like seconds on a clock. Miles tick past. The scenery morphs from volcanic rock and stone canyons to sparse prairie grass and eventually irrigated green fields. So much of this country is vast unused ground, inhospitable for growing and without water enough to sustain humans, so we huddle together in cities.

Here in Texas, the state highway traffic cruises at sixty-five miles an hour, the locals much faster. We pump the brakes at the city limit down to thirty-five for Main Street and blast back up again when we're past the city limit sign. These towns are too small for fast food, but some have off-brand gas stations. The people seem neighborly, some wave. Others look as if we're intruders. It's a strange balance of friendly and critical at the same time. They are right. I'm a stranger in a Texas town, just passing through their lives. Like a gunslinger in an old western, I try to keep my eyes straight ahead.

Flying has given me a sanitized view in recent years. There's roadkill galore, mainly domestic animals. God's dead cats. For all the billboards with bible quotes from community churches, I wish they would put up fences around their yards, but the lawns go right up to the highway. God's broken puppy.

The land is flat and brown, with a wide view of what's ahead. I haven't had to pull over for a nap. My audiobook, *The Story of Edgar Sawtelle* by David Wroblewski was progressing, and Mister is in dreamland because the dogs in the book weren't his kind of dogs. It's just the first day, but it's easier than I thought to stay awake. Maybe it's adrenaline from finally starting the trip after all the planning, but we are here now, rubber to the road.

When I was young, my VW Bug roared like a lawn mower from state to state, me popping whites, those tiny speed pills, and driving fifteen-hour days. Now my drug of choice is coffee. I limit driving to less than four hundred miles a day, but the call of the road is still there. We cruised into the first RV park of the trip. Hello, Dalhart, Texas. It's mid-afternoon and I feel marginally invincible.

They Call Me Mister Dog

Sidney Poitier died this year. I swooned over him in *To Sir with Love,* but my infatuation deepened to respect. My rural farm upbringing didn't prepare me for anyone like him. Not just that he was the first Black actor to win a Best Actor Academy Award, but it was the way he carried himself. I credit him with planting liberal seeds in my mind, but it would be years before I learned the part he played in the Civil Rights Movement.

It was his voice that I loved most. The performance that galvanized my opinion of him was *In the Heat of the Night,* with his famous line, "They call me Mister Tibbs!" He demanded respect. I was thirteen and watching it with my father, who voted for George Wallace, the segregationist governor of Alabama. Enough said? I held my breath, thinking my father's olive green Naugahyde recliner might burst into flames. Respect was a big word to my father, who felt no one gave him what he deserved.

Being a teenage girl, feeling respect was a totally unknown thing to me. I reflected on Mr. Poitier when I got in trouble with my father who told me that my horse didn't respect me. I wasn't sure why horses should respect me when people didn't.

Since then, I've learned that respect is an executive brain function that takes place in the frontal lobe. Since dogs and horses have only a cursory neo-cortex, they are not burdened with philosophical discussions. Nor are they capable of cheating, deceit, or any of the questions that make for good drama.

Now it's fifty-five years later and I'm a clinician whose job is to negotiate an understanding between horses and people. It's more than a little like being a therapist who specializes in couples who fight during car vacations. My father wouldn't have much respect for what I do, or what my dog does, but I'm sure he'd like my truck.

Mister looked at me through half-closed eyes with his snout floating in midair. I don't usually pick my dogs. I have friends who work in animal welfare and the dogs arrive like mail-order brides. They usually have personal habits that make them bad roommates. Some are insecure but not Mister, who had the snug confidence of knowing he had a job and it was certainly more important than mine.

Mister is a Cardigan Corgi, just like the sweater. The name comes from Cardiganshire, Wales, and they are an ancient breed, built low to the ground for moving livestock but also protecting the herd. They are not as common today as the smaller Pembroke Corgi breed, so naturally people ask me what kind of dog he is.

"Is he a Corgi mix?"

Not a bad guess. Mister looks like the result of a German Shepherd who had a few too many on a terribly blind date with a Pembroke.

Cardigans are a separate breed with a body that's longer and heavier. His tail extends like a fox's and makes big circles as he runs. Mister is a rusty sable color with a few too many waves and curls on his rump. He has demure white legs with feet as thick and wide as walrus flippers. White markings trail from his throat to his deep chest and belly. Black hair darkens his muzzle and tail and looks like kohl liner around his eyes. He has a precise line of white hair starting at his black nose, tapering narrower up to disappear at the crown of his head.

If he was standing at eye level, he'd give you pause. But he keeps a low-to-the-ground profile. He doesn't appreciate having to look up all the time, so he doesn't. It makes sense to me. I remember dating very tall men who seemed to lurk over me all the time. I'd tire of looking up, too.

Mister wouldn't want me to mention his belly. He doesn't show it often. Some dogs show theirs all the time, giving humans the wrong impression. The dog may be acting submissive, combined with an anxious wag and panting tensely, with white rimming their eyes. It's a full-body scream, hoping we will pass by. Not all dogs are asking for belly rubs.

Mister would never be submissive in that way, but when it's just us, he gives me a small peek. It was a tiny invitation, almost flirtatious, but only because we have a secret ritual. His belly has the softest hair, white with fragile pink skin visible. No rough scratching ever, I could easily tickle him into that frantic back foot air-itch movement. I understand he is offering so much more than his belly.

It's crucial to describe his ears well. They are his most visual feature, huge trophy ears that you might find on a hundred-and-twenty-pound German Shepherd stud dog. But handed down to a decidedly less intimidating thirty-seven-pound short-legged dog. The ears are monuments rising to the sky, defying gravity and common sense. He wears them level on his head but a little too wide. The ears stand at attention, never folding over. Even in sound sleep, they are directional indicators for intruders, be they rodents or devil cats. Sadly, they are also beacons for baby-talking humans who think he's cute.

Queen Elizabeth famously owned Corgis all her life, and they routinely bit the press. She must have seen it as an excellent trait and might have had them for the same reason I do. They are brave and independent working dogs. Mine can't be bothered with children or cooing adults when the world is so filled with rodent drama and stinky intrigue.

The dog world is divided into two groups of humans. Those who have dogs as a conversation starter, wanting a social life talking with other humans, and those who have dogs to avoid the same. Mister and I should be glad that most people who want to pet him ask first, but that ask also adds the pressure of feeling "no" isn't a polite answer. My first thought is always, do you have to? Why do we need to touch everything? Who's marking territory now?

"Can I pet your dog?"

See it from Mister's side. A strange human leaning over him in that dominating way and then they stick their fist in his face. Are dogs all in the window seat, pressured to be polite when the answer is no? I offend people often enough as it is, so I let Mister field this one.

"Ask him," I say.

Sometimes he walks off for a sniff of more interesting things, sometimes he condescends. Like most dogs, he doesn't like his head patted, but people are slow to learn. As they reach down, he drops his head and blinks his eyes with a mixture of tolerance and dread. I work with him to be less fearful because dogs are easier to train than people.

Every time I get a new dog, I make a point of trying to apply what I have learned from previous good dogs and listen better. We're supposed to progress as humans, aren't we? This time I've promised to never say the word "no." It made him nervous to be scolded, and by his response, he had heard it often, so I'll find a workaround. He's right. No is a word I've never enjoyed hearing either.

We signed up for an agility class. Obedience classes should come first, but they remind me of Western Pleasure classes, with horses moving like drug addicts on the rail. I'm the one who'd flunk out. Besides, agility is like paying a quarter and getting seventy-five cents back in change. It's all about affirmative communication and building confidence.

At our first agility class, Mister flew over tiny jumps and through tunnels, careful to keep his eye on me. He didn't attack other dogs, and he came when I called. The only problem was me. My tongue stumbled over his old name as often as my feet stumbled over each other. I praised and hooted and hollered for this good dog, but I had to change his name. Some think a name is sacred, but for Mister, it's the best way to start over. Besides, he knows exactly who he is, and he had a good line on me, too.

Just to complicate things more, there is a word I hate as much as any insult: "cute." I've been raging against that word long enough to make people nervous. The problem with the word "cute" is that it's subtle and socially acceptable, but it still creates a hierarchy. Cute is dismissive. We mean no bad intention. It's just a way we maintain our superiority, a sweet way to instigate domination. People said he was cute. Really? How was that an achievement?

Corgis are herding dogs, tough and loyal. Committed to their job. Mister is opinionated. He is the kind of "bad" dog that is a perfect fit for me. And now people tell me my new dog is cute. Swell.

I'm a little testy about Mister being underestimated, over-patted, and seen as a stuffed toy for strangers, but I did a baffling thing. I decided it would be a good idea to get Mister groomed for the trip. It was unknown territory for me. I've showered with dogs to clean them up but have never gotten one of them a paid salon treatment. The Corgi trait I haven't mentioned yet is Olympic-level shedding.

As soon as the front door of the grooming salon closed behind us, it felt wrong. A woman came out from behind the counter, baby-talking in a squeaking pitch, and leaned over to grab him. His ears drooped, his eyes showed white, and his belly slunk to the ground. He was bluntly eloquent.

Turid Rugaas, a dog trainer and behaviorist from Norway, coined the term "calming signals" to describe how dogs communicate, avoid conflicts, invite play, and share a wide range of information. But this woman didn't listen. To her, his signals were invisible.

I suggested my dog was nervous, which inspired the woman to prove me wrong. She got louder, bragging that she'd find his spot, ruffing his collar. Such a cute boy, she chirped. As she was groping his belly, he held his breath. He looked in my eye to let me know I'd betrayed him, and I took a deep inhale. He didn't nip her, but he should have. She was cute enough to deserve it. Instead, he tolerated her and came out an hour later, with an Easter bunny kerchief and a withering glare.

All animals give us calming signals, body language messages of anxiety or resistance or pain. But it's them asking us to calm down, telling us we don't need to be so loud or try so hard. This intelligent language is a huge part of the work I do with horses. Do we acknowledge an animal's autonomy or assume our human dominance and blow through their signals to have our way?

Mister is having his usual nap before bed as I write this. Soon, he'll take me for an evening walk. He sniffs and I look at the stars. We both sleep better. In the night, he'll hear something, position his breastbone in the soft center of my belly, and give a small boof of a bark. I wouldn't think of punishing him. All any of us want is acknowledgment. I tell him he's good because he's a dog, the very definition of good. He stops barking every time.

Dog stories all end too soon. Eventually, the day will come

when he takes his last breath. I will exhale with him, thanking him for his precious company. For all the mornings getting his breakfast before mine, for the days he waited for me to return. For the passive half-wag welcome I am guaranteed without fail and for the immense gift of feeling his eyes follow me. Dogs give us their lives without judgment, and I will respect him for that most of all. I promise he will know his value every day. I will ask the world of Mister Dog, but I will never call him cute.

Miles and Miles of Texas

We stopped for the night at the Corral RV Park on Liberal Street in Dalhart for a humble fee of thirty dollars. We got a pull-thru spot with electricity and water. Mister was in no hurry to get out of the truck, so I set the jacks and unfolded our rig. I pinched a finger because I did things in the wrong order, folded it back down partway and back up again. It was early in the year, but it was already hot. It was sweltering in my little metal Rancho. I cranked the roof vent fan open and slid a window, and like magic, there was a breeze.

I went back out for Mister, still reclining in his bed, the passenger door wide open. After I un-clicked him, I waited. The seat was too high for a long-backed dog to jump, and this had been one of our challenges. He didn't arrive with all the confidence in the world. Letting humans lift him was no different from those trust challenges where you fall backward into the arms of strangers. I focus each time, with no complacency.

I stood close, offered my forearm, and waited. He put one foot on to test it, the second foot when he eventually felt safe, and I cheered "Yes." Then my other arm curled around him. Sometimes he gets nervous halfway and twists his spine. We go slow.

Trust takes time, and I can gauge how we are doing each time we attempt this death-defying exercise. We've left home and won't be back for over three weeks. How will Mister cope on the road? I don't take chances. His trust is our bond.

It was still hot in the Rancho, even with the window breeze. Dinner is a bag of salad from the cooler and a glass of boxed wine. Mister is panting. Partway through, I open another window. Each day of our journey, I have computer work. Emails to answer, and classes continue at my online school. I'm not a fan of social media, but small businesses have little choice, so I post. The last ball to be juggled is clinic planning. While on this trip, I'm working with organizers for the next trip.

Dang, I guess a hot breeze is better than no breeze, but this is only March. Is it going to be like this all summer? Mister had rolled belly-up on the bed, slowly simmering. How do people live in this kind of heat?

Wait. Do I have an air conditioner? It wasn't my first thought. I've always lived in older homes without air conditioning, but strangely, this little Rancho had luxuries I didn't expect. After getting out my twenty-pound notebook of manuals and reading the instructions, I got it started on the third try.

I stared at the gas heater vent. Nothing. Then the electric heater/AC motor at the other corner of the floor hummed, and poof, there was a fresh breeze. Like I say, a high learning curve to the RV reality. Within seconds, I can feel it. Call it a cold front, a change in the weather. I knew just enough to close the windows. Mister rolled to his side and dragged himself a few inches to put his head on my bed pillow and I went back to my emails. It was a little chilly.

We woke up in the morning a bit disoriented. It was seven, not late for normal people, but I usually think half the day is over by then. No wonder people enjoy sleeping so much. I never made friends with sleep and wouldn't nap when I was a kid. Now, I can see an entire universe between these sheets and under this weighted blanket, with a dog who snores like waves breaking on the beach.

Mister likes the taste of my skin in the morning. I tell him, as I do every day, there is no lickin'. There is scratchin' and belly rubbin'. I am firm on the no lickin' rule. We quietly debate this issue until he dozes off, and I roll over the edge of the bed and stand up.

I started the water heating, mixed some dried cream into a bit of water, and then dumped a huge scoop of ground coffee into a filter and let it drip. Back in bed, I opened my laptop and began writing. I still have a few hours before checkout time.

Eventually, Mister rolled over and dropped his head on my keyboard. Then we read the news and continued the debate. No lickin', I mean it now. He watched me wash my face and make our breakfasts. After eating, he returned to bed for a post-breakfast nap, and I wrote at the table for a while longer. Then we sauntered out for a morning stroll.

At home, the dogs hail breakfast with hysterical glee and relief, lots of scurrying and barking as I get the bowls ready. Each dog goes to a separate room, and I put the bowls down, serenaded by much yipping and wagging. It isn't food aggression so much as a frantic celebration. The incredible luck of yet another meal. Oh, the joy!

While Mister and I languished for a few hours, the rest of the world was awake, and it was time to move on. We began the fold-down process with my checklist. I still got it wrong the first time, but I'm learning. I do the walk-around check and then we're off across the middle of Texas. But we need gas, so it's a stop first thing. Note to self: Let's fill up at the end of the driving day if we can.

Mile by mile, the land changes; there is more grass, and the grass looks greener. There are more people in the towns. The land is more usable now and watching land changing slowly is the minutia that fascinates me. It starts a tiny detail at a time until, sometimes so gradually and other times so quickly, we aren't quite sure how it happened. Cities can distract you from the environment with man-made landscapes, but that becomes the game. Can I see through one to locate the other?

By afternoon, I give the audiobook a rest and crank up *Miles and Miles of Texas,* by Asleep at the Wheel. It feels perfect, but I can't stop there. Saints preserve Mister's ears, I howl along with Bob Wills' *Yellow Rose of Texas* and totally torch sing *She's Got You* with Patsy Cline.

The state borders are far away now. The highway had split wider to become a freeway with more traffic. We tucked in between our brother truckers and covered over three hundred miles in about five hours, counting rest stops so Mister could stretch my legs.

The Birth of Affirmative Training

On the Road Again… twang, twang. There's something about Willie Nelson's voice that always feels nostalgic. Not so much for how long he's been singing, but as a sense of nostalgia for my own times past. Driving forward over miles of pavement seemed tied to traveling back in time, too.

I was remembering how the roots of Affirmative Training, my method for working with horses, came to be. It wasn't through brilliance and forethought. Like usual, I fell into it backward. I've always known that I have to be the change I want to see in my horse, but that's a platitude. Reciting clever words isn't the same as recognizing I was the problem and then wrestling to make a change.

It was the mid '90s and things had been going badly for me. There were a series of losses. Both my parents died, other friends died, and even one teenager I knew. I floundered through a hard divorce and lost a couple of riding friends who I thought were family. I was beyond lonely. The grind of life had me so exhausted I lost all perception.

One day, a friend in California called and told me I should consider antidepressants. It felt like an intervention, and I was the addict. And the idea made me incredibly sad.

I asked her why and she said it had been so long since she had heard me laugh or say anything positive. I took stock. She was right. It was even flattering that someone noticed. I'd been dull and filled with dread for so long that it felt normal to be in a perpetual state of dusk. Not to mention the things I was sad about were life events that were normal. Should I have to medicate myself to deal with ordinary life? It was sad that life was so sad.

I did a small survey of my friends, asking if they knew anything about antidepressants. My oldest friend said she'd been on them for years as casually as one might admit they shower in the morning. How did I not know? As I continued asking my small circle, almost everybody said they were on antidepressants. Except for the ones who were on anxiety medications instead, while others needed help sleeping. How sad that we were all sad.

My sadness became more noticeable to me than my problems. It was the only response I seemed to have for any situation. Sure, I loved my work, and my horses were wonderful. I had fought for success as a self-employed artist and done well enough to board two horses and learn to train them. Success didn't matter. I would never be happy, and that was awfully sad.

All the color had drained from my days, now that I noticed. Every breath I took was thick with unreleased tears, but I was terrified if I let myself cry, I would never stop. I'd been in therapy for over a decade by then. Why hadn't the question of medication come up? Because when I started therapy, anti-depressants weren't widely on the market yet, but I had no health insurance either. Oh. And of course, that made me terribly sad, too.

There was a teaching college nearby doing a research study, and I signed up. There was a maze of interviews. During one visit, a nurse asked a series of questions about my overall health, but in ways that made little sense to me. I assumed it had to do with their research and answered truthfully.

As we ended, I told her I didn't know if I was bad off enough to need medication, because really, I was probably being lazy.

The nurse paused and looked at me. Without a smile, she said if you had diabetes, we wouldn't tell you to snap out of it and create some insulin.

I turned that thought over for the entire week, but I wasn't the kind of person to take pills. I might be in therapy, but my body was strong. Aspirin seemed as bad as heroin. Vitamins seemed like the wimpy way out. I thought it was a fundamental weakness to take pills.

At the next appointment, I talked to a different nurse who asked me a series of questions about family history. She wanted deeper details about my parents and siblings. We created a family tree of dysfunction and when it was all listed unemotionally, the facts were undeniable. None of us smiled. My lens of recognizing depression widened. I didn't feel like I wanted to go hug everyone, but I had a better understanding of why not. That alone led to a giant leap forward in therapy.

The nurse gave me a stack of xeroxed copies of seven or eight types of antidepressants, along with explanations of how they worked and their side effects. Prozac wasn't the only thing on the menu. Some decreased your sex drive, but I couldn't decide if that was a benefit or not. I wasn't sure if I had a diagnosis, but it looked like I would choose my medication. Naturally, I went back to my friends armed with brand names. Sure enough, they knew them all. Some of them had even compared different brands.

My last visit in the series of interviews was with a doctor. He paged through the previous paperwork. I was feeling more confident about my depression. No longer being in denial was almost blissful. My depression sat next to me in broad daylight, like an evil twin with poor hygiene.

The doctor's questions droned on for an hour. Some were repeats and some were new. While reading from his page, the doctor asked me if I was pleased with my body image.

The question was so foolish that I couldn't answer. I asked him a question back. Had he ever met a woman who was happy with how she looked? He chuckled, perhaps at the ludicrous notion that women would ever find peace inside their bodies. My back talk was a sure sign I was waking up, and we went on for another twenty minutes.

Finally, he said the words Clinical Depression. It was a strange relief to know my affliction had a name. He asked if I'd gone over the paperwork, and I told him I thought maybe Wellbutrin seemed the least bad to me. Again, he chuckled and now I wondered what he took.

Antidepressants weren't what I expected. It ends up that they don't solve any of your problems. But what antidepressants do is give you a little space to breathe. One morning the next week, as I was walking between two barns leading a horse, I noticed I was humming in rhythm with my horse's stride. I'd been doing that since I was a kid, but I hadn't noticed I'd stopped. In that moment, the dew was sparkling, my fingers were cold, and the light on my horse's face looked like a halo. The antidepressants had begun to work.

In the process of interviews for the antidepressants, I understood that depression was our family culture. It was the air in our home. Each family member had their personal issues and probably their own depression, but we had created a culture of depression as well. Depression was our worldview. We were people with little hope.

How had I not noticed the dark haze over everything? The first thing that became clear to me was my comfort with my current corral of negativity. How could it not feel like home? My negative friends supported my habitual gloom. We had a pact to suffer together. But now, as I tried to lift myself out, they didn't all cheer me on. And I was so fragile that I could lose ground if people around me merely complained. If I indulged myself, I fell back into that familiar dark hole, and climbing out was difficult.

Depression was partly an addiction, both comfortable and debilitating. I had to fight for every breath of clean air.

Sometimes the darkness overtook me. I had to learn to be vigilant. It was smarter to steer my way clear of triggering situations I could recognize up ahead. Going cold turkey until I got stronger, I had to walk away from some of my friends. The meds gave me just enough awareness to watch myself lean toward relapse. There was too much to lose. I wasn't scared straight; I was scared affirmative. Oh, the irony.

I welcomed my evil twin to an internal family dinner. We weren't pretty, but we were pulling ourselves together after years of self-loathing. Therapy was working better now, and I didn't always feel I needed to apologize for myself.

The door to my studio/gallery was an entry to an emotion-free zone. I left my depression outside. As a self-employed artist, I couldn't allow myself to be disconnected from my creativity. It seemed like common sense. I had bills to pay, so when I stepped into those rooms, I left the darkness outside with my muddy boots. The fancy word is "compartmentalize," and I kept work apart. It had taken effort; I disciplined myself to be positive at work, and work became an oasis. Now I expanded that space to include my horses.

Not that my barn mates were nasty; I was hypersensitive, so I groomed and tacked up away from others at horse shows. As they lightly complained about their horses or the judging, I was saying affirmations getting ready for our rides, my horses breathing the same clean air I was. I could see my horse's emotions level out and the idea of punishing them, even the idea, left me. I stopped fighting myself and animals in the same instant. Not a victim of the whims of my horse, I was in honest conversations about resolving their anxiety.

Some of us call horses our therapists as a joke. It never seemed funny to me, but now that I knew them free from the heavy load of emotions I'd put on them, the desire to change was overwhelming. That was when I began two years of couple's therapy. You read that right. It was the therapist, me, and my significant other, my horse. He wasn't physically there, of course, but the work was about who I wanted to be in that relationship. Less selfish, more consistent. It was heavy lifting; the changes weren't easy. One of my horses was proud and dynamic and I wanted to be good enough to stand at his side, whole and reliable. I had to heal myself so my horses could be free of my burdens, and I took the work seriously. No surprise, sitting on that couch improved my riding.

No, we did not reenact *National Velvet*. We got some pretty ribbons, but the competition rewarded me with an undeniable knowledge of the seeds of what became Affirmative Training. It brought me closer to my horses in ways they acknowledged, undeniably visible in their calming signals. When I stopped making their behavior all about me, a dark fog of emotion lifted. Instead of trying to fix my horses, I set them free to find their own balance, as I found mine. Confidence became who we were, a new normal, and I had some of the best conversations in my life.

The more autonomy and emotional steadiness I gave the horses, the more they spoke up. I recognized their behaviors, their calming signals, had profound meaning. It was a language I could share by offering calming signals back. I stopped making up stories I wanted to be true and really listened. I began training professionally, getting good results with other horses, and then I wrote about it.

We love to rave about dogs knowing when we're down or how horses read our fear, but those two myopic beliefs are just a tiny start. Animals read everything and if you don't believe it, go on antidepressants. The response from them when I was lighter made me feel guilty for the darkness that I'd heaped upon them. Once it became visible to me, I saw the same in other horses. It took some soul searching, asking myself, just because horses can carry the weight of our shortcomings, do we have the right to ask them? Or do we have a serious responsibility to improve ourselves to partner with them?

We might think if we don't discipline horses to obey or bait them with food, we would have no control and horses would quit us. It only seems that way because we have no faith in them. We see them with human shortcomings like laziness and meanness. We create horses in our worst human image. Instead of letting horses be horses and having the humility to learn from them. Horses were never about domination; herd life was always about cooperation. We must rise to be their equals instead of behaving like whiny, squabbling children.

This is when Sting's song *Set Them Free* seeps up through the earth and the sway of the invisible dance of listening to a horse begins. Can we trust their heart? Their intelligence? Horses consistently volunteer. They shouldn't do it, considering how we behave, but they do. When I gave horses their autonomy, their willingness to partner astonished me. If I took a breath and asked politely, they always gave more than I expected and then asked an even better question back. What if they are leading us in a better direction?

Mister says it's a question of perspective.

Between Two Dog Owners

On our second night, there was a near-altercation between two dog owners. I was one of them. When we finally got the Rollin' Rancho to our Wichita Falls RV Park for the night, both of us were a little bottom-sore and hangry. A-frame trailers aren't common, so there are usually eyes on me, fumbling with the order of unfolding. It made me hurry; I got more practice pinching my finger without yelling.

Mister travels in a harness, and as soon as we're in the trailer, that itchy thing must come off, along with my itchy things. Mister had some kibble with a digestive pumpkin sauce on it and I had another bag of salad. When you travel with a dog, you both get way too involved in each other's bowel movements and today it was Mister's turn. I keep a mental record and it's been a while.

We headed over to the clearly marked area for dogs to relieve themselves. Clearly marked meant the twenty multi-colored statuary fire hydrants. Mister was okay with those, but the giant ice cream cone was not all that enticing. The human-sized foot-less flamingos in top hats and bow ties made him a bit nervous, so we took another lap. Trying to evade them landed us right in front of a seven-foot-tall chicken head with a self-satisfied smirk on his beak. I wouldn't have been able to go in front of that bird, either. We took another lap to the farthest corner this time, close to the highway. Finally, success. It ends up that strange bathrooms make both of us uncomfortable and this one was more like an amusement park.

Then we wandered along the edge of a pond filled with ducks and geese. These were live ones, so we scoured the shoreline for poop and dead things to roll in. It was more than a fair trade for what he does for me. I need to be walked like this after a day of driving. Even more so after a clinic day. I need regular meals and he isn't about to let me miss one of his or mine. I wear hearing aids, but only when I want to hear what people say. If it wasn't for him yipping and yodeling, I'd have no idea what was happening outside the Rollin' Rancho. These and other tasks buy him the right to roll in anything he wants. It's a democracy.

Mister didn't come with a police record. He's just a guy, stoic and good-intentioned. Not overtly affectionate, but he follows me with his eyes. Randomly, he'll press his back close to me. He likes to make the first move, but I don't mind. It's sweeter that way.

Mister is a good dog, but I've been around enough reactive dogs and rescue horses to know they all started out good. My goal with Mister is to protect his goodness in this human world. Do I sound cynical?

We sniffed along the shore until Mister's belly hair was muddy and the socks in my Crocs were wet. Crocs are foam shoes that are not remotely fashionable, but pretty much all I wear. Then we found a bench. Mister prefers to sit on chairs and benches. He leaned in and I held one of his thick flippers in my hand. Rainbow clouds formed layers above the horizon and I'm a total sap for sunsets. I felt mushy about Earth and my wild luck at being with this wonderful dog. I marveled at the endlessly fascinating intersection of the animal world and the human world. It's what I teach most often when working with horses. I love this life.

Mister turned his head away from the view and that's when I heard a man's voice. There was an older couple with a dog standing behind us. RV parks seem to be filled with older people, I notice, and it was a testament to how rarely I look in the mirror that I don't notice I'm one, too.

"Would your dog like to meet our dog?" the man repeated. His wife had white poodle hair, unlike me. I'm more of a wire hair.

"*No-thank-you.*" I smiled, had no hard feelings, and returned to the sunset. Mister did the same.

Then the man repeated his question again, louder because clearly, I had misunderstood him, or I would have leaped to my feet and dragged Mister off the bench. So, I repeated my answer, enunciating it slower this time. Maybe he doesn't wear his hearing aids either.

What is it about our persistent deafness to the word no, even said in a polite voice? I think about this a lot. I seem to have to say *no-thank-you* at least three times to be heard. Could they possibly think I don't know my mind or that I want to be cajoled? No, I'm being honest, but the kinder people are, the more hard-of-hearing they seem. It feels like an oxymoron: aggressive kindness.

Some people struggle with saying no, fearing it will offend the other person. Give up if you are trying to learn because saying it and being heard are two different things. No one takes no for an answer unless it's the eighth or tenth time and you're screeching. No wonder animals give us calming signals.

"Is your dog bad with other dogs?" the man finally says,

thinking he's solved the puzzle of my rudeness. "Because our dog is a good one to learn on, and I know all about how to do this. Come on, bring him over."

Oh, good. Now I've got someone ready to teach me about dogs. Why isn't my polite answer audible to this man? I understand people are just trying to be nice and I'm the jerk. I'm even fine with being the jerk because of that sunset.

But is this man really being nice? Maybe I was overthinking it, but since the window seat incident on the plane, I wonder if anyone can hear me. Why is this man so pushy when I'm a stranger? He didn't ask if my dog was aggressive or fearful or reactive. The man didn't know Mister's sex or if he was intact. He just had a point to prove and by now it doesn't even feel like it's about dogs. Do I have a warning label on my forehead that says "fool" with an arrow pointing toward my nose?

"*No-thank-you,*" I say, more insistent this time. The woman finally registered and touched her husband's arm. I frustrated him and his voice became louder, but I turned away. They will probably tell people about the rude corgi woman. He surely glared a sour face at my back, but they moved on.

Mister and I have an agreement. He doesn't need to be petted by everyone or need to meet every strange dog every strange day of this unpredictable travel life. He doesn't need to perform for anyone, least of all for me. And neither of us had to listen to the high-pitched baby-talk politely. Okay, that last one's more for me.

Mister had been with me for barely six months. This was our first extended trip, and although he behaved perfectly, I can see the stress. People say stoic calming signals are harder to read, but his minimal language is as blunt as mine if you care to listen.

He is more reserved and stays closer than usual. Mister is less snuffly on our walks. His eyes become still and dark around strangers, his ears softened, and leaned farther off the side of his head. Sometimes, he won't chase his stuffed trout toy tied to a lunge line. He loves that fish. He cowered almost imperceptibly when more than one person was close, but he took a full-body ear-flapping shake as soon as they left and the pressure eased, his go-to release of anxiety.

Sometimes he was a little growly, too, protecting me. Corgis to herd cattle. They're tough dogs who abhor chaos and I'm a little that way myself. Spending so much time together, we're both a little clingy. Conversely, if people weren't pushing him and he had time to think, he'd likely climb onto their lap and drop off to sleep with unbidden sweetness.

The older couple's dog? She was a rheumy little black dog with cloudy eyes. Her ears folded back from her face and her name was Millie. She might have weighed twelve pounds, standing there nervously or painfully, I wasn't sure which, holding one foot in the air. I'd seen her earlier with her back arched, taking mincing steps. The little dog jigged behind the couple, barely able to keep up and a little worse for wear. I wanted to ask the man, "Is she your sacrificial lamb?"

But then, my dog is better than I deserve, too.

Thursday Nights are Sacred

Our third night on the road was in Bryan, Texas, and only an hour from the first clinic location. I would have been welcome early, but it was Thursday, and I wanted the night to myself. I pulled into the Primrose Lane RV Park and unfolded. Thursday nights are blog nights. Just for the last thirteen hundred and some odd Thursdays without fail.

At first, the blog was a way to learn to write better. I'd always written, but it was time to get serious. I had a book stuck in my throat, but I knew I didn't have the skill to write it.

Each week, I gave myself a writing assignment. Write something hard to describe, or something intentionally funny, or something poignant. Blogs were an exercise in staying on topic because, by definition, they are a shorter form. I can't wander off into the vast innards of my mind. I needed to describe what I was writing about and make a point. If the articles that I started didn't ignite my interest in the first few sentences, I didn't finish them.

Then it was time to edit for a few hours, my least favorite part. In the beginning, I used a spell check and called it good. Occasionally, I'd have a typo happen that dramatically improved the idea. Serendipity mistakes introduced me to a deeper idea of editing. Now I touch each word, pick it up and look from all sides, and ask if another word would like to take its place. It's tinkering or maybe playing with paper dolls, trying on different outfits. That's where our stories get interesting, but for me, editing was the place where I started enjoying reading my writing and wanting to spend time with it.

Writing is an art that requires practice. I had been homeschooling myself and creating a habit through consistent affirmative behaviors. If that sounds like how I train horses, well, writing and riding have lots in common.

The best part of writing is that I write what I want to read, so I chuckle along, sometimes cry along. My words are good company, whether I'm traveling or mucking my pens. It isn't just that I like the sound of my own voice, which I do, but it's making sense of my conflicting thoughts. And finding words that translate a combination of humor, anger, and confusion into something I can understand, and maybe even change.

After all these years, the books I've authored have stacked up. I write like other women knit. It keeps my hands busy, thinking with my fingers. Now it seems what started as homeschooling, then progressed to airport-bar-schooling, had settled at mobile-homeschooling. Gosh, I'm funny.

Mister and I ate our dinners, I tidied the dishes, and I started writing. I don't wrestle with writer's block, but I'm also not judgmental of the first few words that volunteer. I just put words down and worry about a grand message later. In a couple of hours, the first draft was done.

It was dark by then, so Mister took me for our evening constitutional to look at the stars. He knows I sleep better after a stroll, so he wanders sniffing for stinky things because that is a crucial part of a walk. He goes for quality rather than distance. There may be enemies about, and he keeps a good eye. If he barks, it might be a serial killer, but more likely it's a cat staring at him. In ten or fifteen minutes, after we have clocked a distance of less than two city blocks, we are back at the Rollin' Rancho to tuck in for the night.

Long before dawn or my alarm, I'm awake and thinking of changes. I made my coffee and crawled back to bed to edit. This is the fun part. Mister, being a good literary dog, is very still because he knows I don't like to be disturbed when I'm writing. He thinks my writing is another reason to practice yoga, belly up meditating, with his lips parted a bit, emphasizing his exhale. And yes, it's a lot like snoring.

Another three or four hours of tinkering with words and rearranging paragraphs and the blog is ready to share. The thrill of clicking the publish button never gets old.

Then Mister was fully awake and it was breakfast at last. Then time for our morning stroll, which went slower but not farther. Mister's nose is busier in daylight. This stop had a small, fenced dog park, so I took off his leash and tried to get Mister to jump around and snort with me. He sat on a park bench and let me get it out of my system.

I had worried about whether I could look presentable traveling this way, but it seems camping hair is about the same as my professional look. On driving days, I wear my version of driving pajamas, leggings and a loose shirt. I'm comfortable and cool, and it matters since Mister gets three AC vents to my one vent. One of us has more hair.

If it's a workday, I tidy up with black riding pants and a sun-protective shirt topped with a vest with pockets. Since my dermatologist doesn't give a bulk rate for freezing pre-cancerous growths, I keep covered. People tell me I look hot, but they're the ones sweating.

Folding down is getting easier. I remember the list of things to do, usually out of order, but even with that, it takes less time now. Less finger pinching means fewer muffled screams. I'm getting the hang of this slower nomadic life.

Who Will the Horses Be Today?

We're at my first work stop just northeast of Houston, near Brenham, Texas, and it's a one-day clinic with real live horses and real live participants. I'm as giddy as the first day of school. This is my first live clinic after hunkering down for two years because of COVID-19.

The land here is like living history. Huge ancient trees and grassy meadows sprinkled over rolling hills. It's a large ranch that was originally purchased by the organizer's mother and grandmother. The driveway passed the house, a two-acre pond, and ended at an old hay barn perfect for square dancing or clinic meetings.

The organizer pointed us to a beautiful grove of trees to park the Rancho. I want to know these trees. They are a species of oak, but the branches hung low and almost covered us. It felt like a tree house on the ground, with a ceiling of branches and leaves. She showed me where to plug in and then Mister and I had the place to ourselves.

I can't thank her enough. It sounds like a simple thing, but it was so peaceful here. And I am finding out that driving for three days isn't a vacation.

In the morning, the leaves diffused the light, and the sun rose extra slowly. There was little noise, and the trees had a way of making us feel safe in their low branches. Both Mister and I slept well, the birds woke us in the morning, and I felt washed with relief. My Rollin' Rancho was the best idea ever.

I know people have changed since the pandemic, but how? The sense I've gotten from organizers is that smaller is better, so I've offered options for that, knowing there is a financial tightrope. My expenses don't change but with smaller groups, the margins are thin. Then, should we require masks? I plan to keep my distance and be outside for the day, but masks are still a charged topic. How have I changed from being home for two years and out of clinic rhythm? Best of all, who will the horses be today?

This is a one-day event with auditors, but using the farm's herd so there will be no hauled-in horses. A half-hour before starting time, I gave Mister a big bone and set out for the day. I saw the organizer haltering out in a field with another woman, so I headed over. The organizer introduced me to her sister and explained that the sister's horse was hard to catch.

I practically exploded with excitement. "May I please halter the horse?" Haltering reluctant horses is one of my favorite things and it's been so long.

The women agreed, and I kept talking with them, as I took the halter and began my body language conversation with the horse. It's a chess game for a few moments. The horse and I reposition ourselves, steps that communicate my peaceful intention, until he knows I will not rush or intimidate him. That's always what it boils down to with horses. Are they safe with us? With all the harsh fear-based training methods out there, they are right to ask.

When the horse tells me it's okay, the halter goes on, without stress. The horse's reputation had been longstanding. They love him, he's a great horse, they tell me, but for this difficult haltering problem. But now what? The horse was standing beside me with soft eyes.

It was not magic. All I did was quietly ask, breathe, and give the horse time to process. He knew what I wanted. I didn't chase him and soon he volunteered. My exterior was calm, but inside, it was a fist-pumping happy dance. This is my job and I love it. It was a beautiful morning. I got to halter a new horse, to converse in a language I had worked hard to learn, and all was well with the world.

The day officially started a few minutes later with a group of enthusiastic horse lovers. There was laughter and learning, the best combination for horses. Laughter is a human calming signal; it helps us breathe and relax.

I am a dressage trainer, but most often at clinics, we talk about calming signals and then spend time haltering horses. It seems simple until the horses chime in. We often get complacent, rushing our horses for a quick halter and groom, so we can get in the saddle and ride. We underestimate the importance of how we first greet the horse; it sets the tone for the day. So, we halter the horses with their consent. For us, it's a language lesson. We take notice of their breathing. It gets shallower every step closer we come. The horse might look away or graze quickly or walk a small arc, all signs of stress, but in the act of telling us, they also let it go. The conversation is seen in the physical tension and release in their body. It isn't a refusal. Like the gelding in the pasture, they just need a moment.

By midday, we were outside. A little pickle of a donkey had become curious, watching us, and began inching her way toward me while I talked to the group. We were told she doesn't like to be touched by anyone, so I did what I do. I ignored her and she couldn't stay away. I let her think about that and kept my eyes to myself.

Processing time is crucial to equine learning, but for a clinician to actually demonstrate patience is dull to watch. My superpower is making stillness interesting, and I do it by narrating her calming signals. The challenge now was neutralizing the stress that a herd of coyote people staring at the demo horse or donkey caused. The equine will choose to communicate when they feel safe.

We all enjoyed the little pickle's predicament. She was very expressive and now, instead of bolting away at the sight of us, she inched closer. Soon she was within arm's reach, and her curiosity was sizzling. Sometimes her muzzle touched me while sniffing my leg. An equine might give an involuntary nip just about then, so I prepared to not flinch or correct if it happened. It isn't bad behavior. It's a message, not my favorite. But she was telling us about herself. My response must be consistent; I let her know I was no threat. When she knows that, no more nipping.

I'd seen this pattern often, and given time, her anxiety seeped away. The little pickle just sniffed and spared me her teeth. I didn't betray her trust and try to touch her. She especially needed to think about that, so she was all ears. Nothing beats curiosity to bring about changes in behavior. It works better than correction ever could.

Equines are like cats. It's faster to go slowly. Humans will always be predators and horses prey. We have to prove they can trust us before anything else. But we can't force trust to happen. We have to present ourselves and let them decide.

Other attendees did some thoughtful haltering, and two participants got a shared riding lesson. The horses licked and chewed, shook their polls, rubbed their noses on their legs. All messages of stress and relief. I wish people communicated so clearly and honestly.

The day went well, but much too quickly. As I was finishing up, I thanked the organizer who was gushing about the hard-to-halter gelding who started the day. She'd haltered him easily during the afternoon and her sister had the same result moments before. I was glad the clinic had gone so well for them, but even happier for the horse. He must have been ready for a change. Old habits continue, usually from a previous owner, and were taken for granted because it had always been that way. But change was waiting to happen, we just needed to ask. What a sweet end to the day. And just like that, I'm back. I have that happy, tired, end-of-day-and-I-love-everybody feeling.

It's been Mister's first clinic day, too. He had a walk at lunch but stayed quietly in the trailer all the other time. Now as I return, everything is just where it was before I left him and he's belly-up on the bed.

"Honey, I'm home."

He bobbled his snout toward me while not a hair on his belly moved. It's funny how rituals begin, sometimes without noticing. I knew there were emails to answer, and I was hungry. But I slipped my boots off and laid down, consciously letting the bed hold my body. Then I quietly rested a hand on Mister's chest. He wasn't in a hurry about dinner as he would be at home, and he wasn't affectionate in the way other dogs might be. With less than a full wag, he welcomed me back and closed his eyes. We spent a few quiet moments while the bones in my feet let go of their ache. I don't need a voice to talk with Mister. Calming signals have become my first language.

I didn't know how much this ritual would mean to me as time passed. The two of us in this little room together without the need for more. Mister ate first, then I had a freeze-dried camp meal that was near restaurant-quality Pad Thai. After answering some emails, it was early to bed, partly wanting the feeling of the trees holding us again. And partly because we had an early three-hour drive before the clinic tomorrow morning in Boerne.

Austin City Limits

Most clinicians offer a day of lessons for a set rate of pay, with auditors allowed to watch for a small fee. Clinics are usually two to five days long, with participants hauling their horses to the facility. But not all horses haul well in trailers. Not all riders like to be watched. Some of us have more than one horse. And then the new unknown elephant in the room was how COVID-19 impacted us. Would the same numbers turn out for a clinic, or would people want something else?

I came up with the idea of Barn Visits. They were shorter days, four people or fewer, and no auditors. More intimate, with less planning, and the horses could be more comfortable at home.

The online clients kept me going during the pandemic by taking a leap of faith and thinking that horse training could work through cyberspace. Maybe we had more time together because the meetings ran long. Or maybe it was the feeling of meeting in their homes, as their computer brought us inside. Now coming to their home barns felt like a strange situation of knowing them for quite a while, but meeting for the first time.

This Sunday stop was a Barn Visit at a therapeutic center in Boerne, with a roomy pasture of horses and a small group of people I'd worked with online. I got to see a client's young horse whom I'd met before, a spirited young Arabian who I loved. And she had a Grandfather Horse who was a legend like mine had been.

After some time doing groundwork with those wonderful geldings, we went out to meet the horses in the field. It was a large pasture with lots of trees. The horses didn't race over to us. Confident, calm horses went about their business grazing, and being ignored was a good sign. I could tell they managed this herd well. There were few calming signals, and the horses weren't mugging us, but living their lives as naturally as possible. It's not as common as I'd like. Horses might have been the real pandemic winners with some extra quiet time.

We did some haltering in this big open space, and the horses were honest and clear. Each individual, each conversation was unique. It was like a cocktail party we wanted to attend. Just casual conversation, but we all felt good about ourselves. It was a friendly day and people shared a heartfelt affirmation that we had survived COVID-19 and the months of isolation.

A tall black mare particularly touched me. I was told she had survived breast cancer, something I had never heard of in horses. At first, I wasn't sure if it was the area of her mammary glands in her udder region, or if it was a figure of speech. When I got closer, I could see scars on her shoulder area and muscle loss. The mare was a draft horse with a long neck, beautiful and wary. She'd had enough vet care that she'd become reticent around humans. She was slow to want our company, didn't need our sympathy, and I didn't blame her a bit.

Internal cancer is hard to diagnose and treat in horses. I lost a mare to cancer, only diagnosed by my online search and a process of elimination. Her name was Grace. She was also a beautiful mare, and her last months were miserable. By that point, I just wanted her suffering to stop. Seeing this mare grazing was a balm to my loss. If you can keep your heart open and squint just the right way, one horse can be all horses. I kept glancing back at this black mare for the rest of the afternoon and showed her respect by holding my distance.

Horse people would be the last ones to admit they missed people during the pandemic, but in our quiet way, we did. We'd put it this way: it thrilled us to be with horses again and the hours of the Barn Visit passed too quickly. But we'd been with horses through the pandemic. It was the human company that was renewed.

We went to the parking lot to say a happy and reluctant goodbye. Mister got a short walk, and we headed out, just an hour's drive to our next stop.

***

Horse Dreamer Ranch, owned by Sarah, a longtime client and friend, was our next stop just outside of Austin. There were several Barn Visits in the area over the next week. We planned to stay here, unhook the trailer, and commute in the truck, returning each night.

GPS Woman got us close but then seemed to lose her way and wander. We drove around, left-turning our way back to the entrance to the neighborhood, and asked again. She changed her mind and gave us different directions. Half-heartedly, we headed down a dead-end lane, hoping that was the right dead-end. Once we saw the Horse Dreamer sign, I heaved a sigh. It was past dinnertime and our drive had started at dawn. We were happy to be done. We unfolded and made ourselves at home.

The next morning, GPS Woman dropped us off for a Barn Visit at the front gate of a client an hour away. I met my client's husband and dogs, and then we strolled out to the barn and talked *with* the horses, not just about them. I gained new insights and asked better questions. Time flew by. Horse time always does.

The horses each told me about themselves in a way that was so palpable. Not that the video doesn't, but there is a nuance in calming signals, small and slight, like different accents in a language. I learned more about her horses, her property, and the general environment. Undeniably, the most precious thing was all of us standing together, horses and humans in their barn. It felt like a reunion, and I wondered if clients knew how often I thought of them and their horses outside of our work time.

When I meet horses, sometimes they exhibit behavior that the owner says is unusual for the horse. It's happened enough that I understand it isn't a coincidence. There is something the horse is saying, and the owner is missing, but not for lack of trying. It could be anything from pain to environmental anxiety.

When a horse makes a point of showing such a behavior, I don't take it personally. It isn't that the horse recognizes me from Facebook. My theory is that I have a "stink" on me they sense and understand. I think they know I speak horse and will listen to them differently.

Until we understand the information, the horse will persist in sending it, and when we resolve the question, the behavior will end. Behavior is communication, and it's never about us. Humbling, isn't it?

The day was gone in a blink. It occurred to me how easy it could be for a Barn Visit to veer off to visiting more than working. It was important for me to hold focus, do my job, and give the client value for their money. As friendly as the day had been, I wanted to hold to my intention. Barn Visits were never meant to be a social call or even a practical way to work. It was gratitude for being able to work through the pandemic. And I meant it.

Driving back to Horse Dreamer, I received news that Scott, a friend in San Diego had died. I knew his time was close, but it was still hard to hear. He was the husband of my lifelong friend. My friendship with him always held her in the middle, but I loved him for himself. I loved his banter and his ability to make being with them easy for me. And now my high school friend, who stuck with me over some hard times of my own, was about to face a big life change. I hoped I could be a good friend to her now.

So much loss since the beginning of COVID-19. None of my friends died from that illness. They died of the usual things, cancer mostly. But dying during a pandemic had special significance. It was a painful reminder that normal life might have changed, but normal death didn't come to a halt for that virus. The road ahead got a little blurry, and I took a deep grateful breath.

Sarah: She Wants to Ride

I'm uncertain when Sarah and I met online. She is a Clinical Psychologist by profession and a lover of horses. We worked together with one of her horses for years as we gradually fell into a friendship.

Sarah grew up on a farm in the Blue Ridge Mountains of southwest Virginia. Glory's Top Man was her first horse. He and Sarah were both nine years old when her maternal grandfather gave him to Sarah. Her grandfather was a horse trader and had earned respect and knowledge enough to judge local shows. Sarah and her grandfather rode together. He gave her tips on horses and riding and shared precious hours. Sometimes he hauled Sarah and Top Man to compete in local horse shows.

In time, Top Man had a good retirement, grazing in the pasture with other horses and cattle, and he lived a long life. Everyone has a horse who is special above the others, one that haunts us forever. Sarah never forgot Top Man.

Sarah moved to North Carolina, eventually went to college, and earned her Ph.D. After moving to Texas at sixty, she came back to horses. Sarah wanted to ride.

She bought Lightfoot, a twelve-year-old Tennessee Walking horse who came to her in December 2010 from a ranch north of Dallas. He was an "upside down" high-headed horse, but energetic without being flighty. Being upside down is a little like being swayback, a way of movement that might include back pain or anxiety. Biomechanics teaches us it isn't a sound position, but we can help that, and she gave him a chance. They tried to get along but ended up not being a good match. Sarah gave the horse to a friend who was better suited to him.

But Sarah wanted to ride. She kept looking for the right partner. Her next horse was Jackson, a twelve-year-old Spotted Saddle Horse, in April 2012. He passed the vet check sound and healthy, with a sweet temperament. They were good riding partners. Sarah had an apartment at the barn where Jackson was boarded, and things were finally working out.

But there was a flash flood when she'd had Jackson less than a year and a half. The floodwaters drowned most of the horses on the farm and destroyed the barn. It was sudden, tragic, and heartbreaking. Gone in a flash and no way to bring them back. A devastating loss.

Still, Sarah wanted to ride, and she picked herself up. It took courage; it felt like the world was against her. Sarah had a type she was looking for. Horse lovers usually do. It's a beloved breed or a horse suited to a kind of preferred riding. It can even be a color preference.

Sarah moved to a small farm and found Johnny Cash in January 2014. He came from a sales barn in Sherman, Texas. Another Tennessee Walking Horse, on video Cash looked perfect, like a been-there-done-that ranch horse. Very set in his gait, with a nice collected canter, but Sarah was told he could be "barn sour." No horse is perfect, so again, she took a chance.

When she got him home, he started to unravel mentally. It isn't unusual that a change of homes can release anxiety in a shut-down horse. It happens in the gap of time between when the horse leaves his herd and when he lands with a new owner. Many horses change in ways that make new owners wonder if the seller drugged the horse before. Change is a greater challenge for horses than we understand.

Cash became very fractious, even uncontrollable at times. He intimidated her, but more than that, he was dangerous on the ground, spooking erratically and sometimes running over her. Sarah, an educated horsewoman, had worked with some of the best people in the field. She sought help far and wide and consulted extensively with a California trainer who came with an excellent recommendation.

In that trainer's estimation, he could work with Cash for a couple of years, and maybe he'd improve, but there was no guarantee. I thought it was an honest evaluation. Cash's early training had traumatized him. I've met horses I felt just that same way about. This kind of challenge is never a quick fix.

Sarah couldn't sell him in good conscience, so she let Johnny Cash rest at her farm. It was years later now and Cash had found some peace. He had moments still, but Cash was safe from failing other homes and safe from a trip to slaughter. Maybe that had to be good enough.

But Sarah wanted to ride. Not to compete, not to do anything extraordinary. She just wanted to ride. How many tries should it take? Was she cursed somehow?

The next horse she found was another Tennessee Walking Horse, this time in a horse sanctuary in Knoxville, Tennessee. Sarah went there to see a different horse. A previous adopter had returned Zen Bear just before Sarah arrived. It was love at first sight, and Bear came to Texas to live with Cash.

Things went well at first. He was a calm horse. Sometimes, he didn't want to go forward. Picking up his feet for the farrier could be a challenge. These were minor issues at first. There were good periods of time but then resistance. Was it pain or a training issue? He kicked at his belly; he nipped anxiously.

This is where I came in. Bear was showing calming signals, and Sarah sent me videos. We started working online, and the videos made me think the challenges moving forward were pain issues rather than training problems. It was good news initially but soon changed to hard news.

Sarah's vet diagnosed serious ulcers, and after that, Inflammatory Bowel Disease (managed on steroids). After three visits to Texas A & M., Zen Bear still wasn't as strong as he should be. It's a daunting thing to delve into these questions with only nebulous answers. In the end, it's never just one thing. We continued, sometimes working with her patient farrier and doing riding lessons during the good times, but it was always with the understanding that we needed to listen to him better somehow.

Sarah's veterinary education took her places no one would want to go. There was a diagnosis of lameness; etiology unknown. Maybe a residual effect of EPM (equine protozoal myeloencephalitis), possibly DSLD (degenerative suspensory ligament desmitis), or another muscular degenerative disease. Next, he lost an eye to an infection; the vet thought it was because of his compromised immune system caused by ongoing steroid medication.

Sarah tried every option. The decision to retire Bear came with great reluctance, mixed with constant hope it wasn't true. It would mean Sarah had two retired horses, the limit for her land and finances. The best part was that Bear and Cash lived like brothers, peaceful herd mates. Sarah took impeccable care of them. There's just this one aching chronic problem. Sarah wants to ride.

How many horses do we have to own to have one to ride? What had seemed a simple request was elusive. Many barns are the same, filled with retired horses for various health reasons. There's no room for more. We aren't willing to ship them off to uncertain futures, and they aren't in so much discomfort that euthanizing is an option anyone could live with. My home barn falls in with this crowd.

Of course, we have their company. We live with their beauty daily and they are much loved. No one had to tell us how fragile horses are. These immense creatures who gallop and play, who share breath and warm our hearts every moment, also have frail gastric systems and hidden pains. They have chronic lameness issues, even if not ridden. And we would never give them up.

There is a thing riders know that's different from those who love horses from the ground. It's a different perspective. We have surrendered our bodies into their holding. We have come off and gotten hurt. But we still find the courage to allow ourselves to give over to their movement; to feel lifted and carried on the back of a powerful sentient creature who will always be a mystery. Knowing that we have no literal control, we dance through space together. There is a spine-to-spine intimacy that exists nowhere else in the animal world. It is unique and powerful beyond all reason, and we never want to stop.

Riders know this special connection. If we never rode again, and that was the price we paid for our memories in the saddle, we'd have zero regrets. We are grateful for the experiences we shared with quicksilver horses and have no right to ask for more. Except for one undeniable truth. We want to ride. Sarah and I share that desire.

A few months after my visit, Bear seemed to lose control of his body one afternoon and could not balance or walk. Sarah kept me in the loop, but I was as helpless as she was. By morning, it was clearly neurological, and the vet didn't hesitate to euthanize Zen Bear.

When a horse dies, they leave a hollow place in the middle of every moment. Cash was coping; he and Sarah mourned their loss. There was less work to do, less money needed for care, and more time now that there was one horse, but it felt horrible.

Sarah has over seventy undomesticated summers to her credit, and she isn't a quitter. She might be stronger in her heart than her body, but that's a plus for a rider. Horses appreciate that her patience and her negotiation skills have never been better. She is looking for her next horse, wishing her grandpa could help her find one. She wants a Tennessee Walking Horse. Her love for Top Man abides deep in her heart, the good horses since will always be with her, but she cannot refuse the call.

Sarah wants to ride.

Beating Hearts

The next morning, Mister and I loaded up and drove an hour to the appointed farm. We arrived a half-hour early and parked in the shade. The organizer came to greet us. At least, I thought that was her walking toward us underneath two boxes with the recognizable Chewy label, an online pet supply. Presents for Mister was my guess.

Mister sat at my feet, looking innocent and charming. So, this is how it was going to be. I've become a traveling scam for dog treats. Not only would his fame proceed us, but our bed would look like it belonged to a little girl who collected stuffed toys. I thanked the organizer and Mister softened his ears, so they were a bit wider on his head.

Since we left the Rancho back at Sarah's and I don't leave him in the trailer if I'm not on the property, I had a plan to make the truck pleasant for him. Parked in the shade, I roll the windows down a few inches and put sunshades up on all sides. There's a large fan plugged into a generator. It should stay in the 70s today, but I'll check back. I have a heat sensor inside and if I need to, I can start the truck and turn on the air conditioner. Mister and I have an agreement that I don't leave him with strangers.

We were at an equine therapy program. The organizer contacted them and set the day up. She wanted to do a heart monitor experiment after a Calming Signals presentation. I'm often hired by therapeutic programs of different sorts. Sometimes I do an in-service day for their volunteers or give input on challenging horses. Listening to body language in real-time is an important tool for assessing the horse's mental state, and crucial information for a program if they're concerned for their horse's welfare, as well as their client's. Working in a therapy program can be the hardest job we ask a horse to do.

I began setting up my presentation and tried to figure out who did what in the program. Since the organizer wasn't a staff member, I was unsure of the group dynamic. Usually, you can tell the hierarchy of the group because the ones doing the most schlepping are at the top of the staff roster.

When we were in a circle, I began by asking everyone a question. "Tell us your name and job title. Then tell us three things you love about horses and one question you have."

The first person gave a perceptive response, and I acknowledged it with an inclusive comment and the same with the second person. Our interchanges were light and welcoming on both sides.

The third person introduced himself as the founder of the program, and he immediately said he strongly disagreed with three things I'd said already. He was my age or older, tall with gray hair, and had the general attitude of someone used to being listened to.

And we're off! I made my shoulders soft, cocked a hip, and smiled. "Only three?" I ask, not willing to get defensive. I know better than to take the bait offered by those who disagree with me. My Affirmative Training methods work on me, too. I stay positive when things go off the rails.

He told me about his history, what he knows, and what he does. I tried to pull us back on track by finding some small place of commonality, even just a word we could agree on. But that feels like a challenge to him, and he digs in deeper. Careful to keep my voice casual, not wanting to escalate the debate, I did ask for the studies he had that supported his viewpoint. He will get them to me, he said, even as I knew they wouldn't come. I wonder if the other six people will get to introduce themselves.

What to do when the disrupter is the founder of the program? It's common to get questioned a bit during speaking engagements, but this was more like heckling. I smile because it's the last response hecklers want from me. Women who smile under pressure might be crazy. I try to go to the next person, but he continues with his story, and I keep smiling. It feels like an unwanted competition. Then he stops and waits for me to say the next thing, and then he disagrees with that.

When working with horses, I refuse to show frustration or aggression because it doesn't work to pressure horses. Fighting makes things worse. It was horses who taught me how to ride through a "heckling" environment. Instead, I find ways to say yes. I strive to find commonality, things that we can agree upon. The remaining people eventually introduced themselves but shared little else.

The founder had a big personality. He said he'd learned that domination didn't work with horses or kids in his program, but respect was necessary. But wasn't demanding respect similar? Is it necessary to earn respect or can we acknowledge everyone deserves it, whether they are horses or humans? I let that idea rest right there between my ears.

I continued my talk on Calming Signals, but we spent the rest of the morning wrestling with terminology. Searching the group for an ally, there were a few attending who seemed interested in what I was describing but were very reluctant to comment. I knew my words were being heard and I stayed the course.

The founder said it was profoundly necessary to anthropomorphize everything horses do to connect with them. It was important, he said, to make horses more human, so we can understand and relate to them. How horrible, I thought, to make horses over in our image and call it understanding, but he's right that my belief is the polar opposite. I believe horses are better as horses, and changing who they are to suit our needs isn't knowing them. Horses live for their own reasons, and if we learn from them, it's our luck and not their job.

But then, I'm a trainer who has seen too much trauma in horses, brought about by misunderstanding. Horses do have emotions, but they are not identical to ours. I stayed in the conversation, taking nothing personally, remembering I'm an advocate for horses, not my own ego.

By lunch, my abbreviated presentation was over, and I was done with my clinician work for the day. I didn't know the group's perception, but as they set up our meals, I went to walk Mister so I could shake off the morning. He was happy to remind me I was nothing special, and that I was his person just the same. As always, I was grateful for his insight and gave him a copious number of snacks and toys from his fresh supply.

Statistically, women own 92% of the horses in the country. Here's another fun fact. My social media followers are 97% women. Men rarely come to my clinics, and for a while, I tried to engage them in different ways. But this is how bad I am at math. Look at those numbers. Men are a tiny minority in the horse world. I couldn't stand around holding the door for those few stragglers when I had clients really interested in what I was training.

When I got back, the conversation over lunch was quieter than I would have expected but friendly enough. The preparations for the heart monitor tests began. I won't pretend I understood the experiment at the beginning or the science behind it. The organizer worked in this field, taking these readings on people with heart issues. She was curious about this kind of comparison between horses and humans. I'm a happy lab rat, grateful I won't be doing the math.

There was a monitor on a strap that went around the horse's chest to measure their heartbeat. There is a slightly smaller one that went around the human and the video recorded them working together. Eventually, we would see a video of the session with a readout comparing the heartbeat rhythm of both the human and the horse. There would be three of us measured that day, two trainers from the program and me.

In a few moments, the founder came over to say goodbye. He gave me a doff of the hat before leaving for more important things. I gave him a firm handshake.

After the strap was attached, the first trainer began working with a horse in the round pen. He used swinging arm cues and when the horse retreated, the trainer followed. The pressure continued without release. Sometimes the horse stood still and seemed to question the cue. At one point, both of them became quite agitated, and the horse nipped the trainer. A few moments later, things were quieter, and the session ended.

I'd been standing by the organizer, and she showed me the first trainer's heart rate. She looked at me meaningfully, but I didn't know what kind of number we were looking for, low or high.

Then it was my turn to get strapped up. I wasn't sure what I should do when I entered the pen, but I decided on an exercise in giving the horse autonomy called leading from behind. The horse waited, watching to see who I was. I stood by the horse's flank and exhaled. The horse dropped his head and blew out a huge breath. Dread rolled off in calming signals. This sometimes happens when I greet a horse this way. I let the horse know I was not a threat to him. He'd been holding his breath.

I asked for a step with an inhale. The horse shifted weight in response. I paused and praised him with another exhale. Then I asked for another step. This time he took a whole step and got another exhale-reward. On the third ask, he walked several steps, confident that was the right answer. No need to be greedy. I wanted him to learn he was right, and I knew the best way to do that was to praise him and stop asking the same question. I said, "Good boy," as I stepped away. We did a few other things, small and quiet. I finished after being in the pen with the horse a fraction of the time the first trainer had been. I shrugged; it's how I work. Small sessions with think-time between.

When I was out, the organizer rushed over to tell me my number. She repeated it, but I didn't know what it meant. She said, "Zen Master!" My heart rate was impressively low and steady. I can't take credit; that comes from learning to ride in competition. Horses taught me to stay steady. It was how I rode up the levels in dressage and it was how I survived the morning with the founder during my presentation.

The third trainer got her horse ready, and the test began. This was a different horse who was a bit anxious about his monitor strap. Things didn't start as the trainer had hoped and she got coaching help from the side. I could see the trainer was as confused as the horse. After a few moments, she did a miraculous thing. She asked to be let alone to think with her horse. I loved her for that, and her horse soothed himself quickly.

It's never easy to work with railbirds watching and that was probably an aspect of this test, I thought in hindsight. I'm used to it. Being a clinician means everyone is a railbird, scrutinizing everything I say and do. Again, credit to my horses for teaching me to give up my emotions because they get in the way. Credit to them for teaching me they are the only thing that matters. Horses crave safety, and I make myself an oasis of yes.

When we finished, Mister got out of the truck, peed on some grass, and then sat by my feet, as disinterested as ever. The two other trainers saw me off, along with the organizer. We parted with smiles and best wishes all around.

Driving back to Horse Dreamer Ranch, I thought about the horses. Just because animals can help soothe our emotions, is it fair to ask them when they are already coping with their own emotions? Is it fair to ask them to do it with strangers every day? It is always the question I come back to. I'm concerned, not with whether they calm our heart rate, but with what our presence does to theirs.

We misunderstand calming signals from stoic horses.

Sometimes when a prey animal can't escape, they remain still and slow their heart rate and metabolism, hoping danger will pass. It's like a possum playing dead. This freeze response is most common in stoic horses who can't escape easily. If we assume that a horse with a lower heart rate is a good thing, we may have that wrong if we don't consider other signs. The heart rate doesn't tell the complete story.

A few weeks later, the final readouts came, along with some more explanation. My horse's heart rate came down quickly as I breathed by his flank, not facing him. Then our heart rates nearly mirrored each other the rest of the time, going up a tick when I asked for something and returning down again with the answer. Perhaps it would have been better science if I'd gotten a different horse, but this one was upset and that made him easier for me. He was already looking for what I had to offer. Horses and humans share similar autonomic nervous systems. Breathing is a literal cue to relax and return to our parasympathetic side. The results seem to confirm that when there is no fighting, we all breathe better. No surprise there.

I appreciated that the study showed the horse's calming signals aligned with their heart rate. Not the goal of the testing, perhaps. But we could see their heart rates going up and down as their bodies showed increasing and decreasing anxiety in their body language. The tests confirmed my understanding of calming signals, illustrating a visual map of the horse's anxiety ranges.

We know horses feel our emotions and respond to them. While training, I want to keep my emotions quiet and let the horses express theirs. But why would we doubt them? This horse today told me he didn't like loud energy. He was happy to offer what I asked when he had time to think. He offered a small try, and when he knew his guess was right, he offered more. The answer is much sweeter when given freely. We need to trust the horse's intelligence and we should be awed by their willing nature.

But this is just me. Each of us probably read the results to suit our belief systems. We all think we're right.

Riding Out a Tornado

We got back to the ranch as the skies were getting dark. I parked next to the Rancho. Weather was coming, and it had been a tiring day. Before long, Mister and I tucked in for the night. The rain started quietly, and big slow drops rolled down our windows. Not our first rain, but welcomed for the gentle sound that reminded me of growing up in Washington State. The shower was sweet in the Rollin' Rancho, and it soon grew to a steady rain, a dull noise at voice level inside. Then it grew in intensity, screaming rain. Don't let the sound scare you, I thought.

Then a tornado watch was sounded. I have a weather app on my phone, which I use for alerts when I need to stop a lesson for lightning close by. This warning let me know severe thunderstorms could easily develop, including heavy rain, strong winds, and perhaps a tornado. A watch isn't a warning, I reminded myself. I checked that again online to make sure I had it right.

Warnings are the real thing, but I felt a wave motion that seemed to come from all directions at once. I knew I'd set the four jacks well. They brace the trailer, so it's steady when walking inside. We were on level ground. How is the wind making the movement? Ah, when I move, the pressure is toward the earth, so this must mean the wind is lifting from below. Figuring this out did nothing to calm me or make me feel smart.

Should I hook the Rancho up again? Then the wind would have to carry both truck and trailer off to the next county. Maybe my truck would work like an anchor. Damn, my love for movies. All I could see was that scene with a cow flying in the arc of a black tornado in *Twister*.

Doing the work to attach the truck would be miserable, but also nearly impossible. My velcroed backup camera would be blown out of the state. Besides, there was caution, and then there was anxiety. I was probably letting my mind run away with me. Drama and disaster are never as common in real life as they are in the movies, thinking that flying Holstein milk cow didn't look all that authentically bovine.

I checked the weather app again, now we were in the middle of the storm. If the watch became a warning, I would hear about it.

Of course, I was welcome in my friend's house. Mister would have fainted dead away from the coven of cats, but he would have been welcome, too. But we were in a relatively sheltered spot, and I wanted to know how much weather was too much. I wanted to explore the give-up line in a place where surrender would be easy if it came to that.

I wasn't sure what to do next, but Mister was well into his nap before bed, so I joined him with my phone handy next to us. He planted his big warm head on my belly and that was anchor enough. The trailer rocked mightily, and the wind was a steady roar. But I didn't hear any obvious destruction outside and the tornado watch didn't jump to a warning level. The trailer didn't fight the wind, and I didn't fight the trailer. I let the storm rock us to sleep.

Of all the things I could worry about on the road, the weather was my first concern. Any attempt at control is futile, but this trip can't be about fear, and that's the last thought I remember.

Mister and I slept soundly and woke up a little late. The news reported that a tornado had touched down close by. So now I know what both things are like, fear and trust. We rode out the storm, as they say. Rode the trailer like a quick trot on a green horse. If you don't pick a fight and keep breathing, they will find their balance. To beat the analogy with a whip, we rode out the first stumble; we landed the first jump.

Writing with Donkeys

The next morning was fresh and moist. The storm cleaned the air, and the land felt brand new on our morning walk. This ranch had a stand of trees with lots of rodent dwellings, or so Mister said.

It's been good to not be pulling the Rancho every day; good to return at night and not need to set up. Most of all, it's good to have a home along with me. Today was going to be a change of pace and I'd looked forward to it. We packed a lunch and some dog chews. Mister would wait in the truck again, but it was a short day.

Sarah joined us and we drove to a farm outside of Blanco for a writing workshop. I had never considered giving them, but a few years ago, a group in Scotland asked me if I'd do a workshop at the end of a clinic. I had three published books then, but it surprised me. Do riding clinics and writing even go together?

I said yes, because it was my business plan, short and sweet. Then I set about finding out what happened in these workshops. After some research, I knew there would need to be writing prompts and thought I'd talk about practical things like helpful software. So much changed after my first book that I had written a series of essays about the journey, and I'd share those. I'd never been to a writing workshop, but I didn't bring that up.

This is what I know about writing workshops now. They start awkwardly. It's always a weird mix of people from different backgrounds and economic realities. There is a full range of age, education, and experience. Some want to write about their horse, some write for work, and some dream of a book. It isn't unknown for a woman to write about lifelong secrets, like sexual assault, and the first people to know about it are a group of strangers who embrace her courage.

Anything can happen. I focus on the parts that work best, but there is never any criticism of the writing. It's a wildly vulnerable thing the participants are doing. I practice my best listening and am careful with my words. I know whatever I say will be remembered, so I want to get it right.

When it comes time to read, someone reluctantly volunteers to go first to get it over with. Her first draft essay is breathtaking and perceptive. Her talent impresses the group. No one wants to go second and read after that, but someone does. Her piece is entirely different but equally illuminating and we want to hear more. The entire day goes reliably this way. Each reading is well-written, imaginative, funny, heartfelt, and totally inspiring.

Somehow, this happens at every event. So yes, I'll happily give a writing workshop every time I'm asked because I get the same inspiration that everyone else does.

I encourage the writers to continue writing, for their own sake, even if it's a journal never meant for another's eyes. We devalue our own voices and so does our culture. The world needs us, even if they don't particularly invite us. Our words matter, but if we don't take them seriously, why should anyone else?

Here we are at a small farm in south Texas, a ragtag group of women with folding chairs, water bottles, and notebooks or laptops. We made our way downhill from the barn along a path to a small opening in a grove of trees. This group was slightly different because some of us had been writing in my online group and it was the first face-to-face meeting of friends. We pulled into a circle and began.

The donkeys and the horse got curious about us once we sat down and got quiet. One woman was wearing a straw hat against the sun and a donkey wandered up and tried to steal it, but that was totally understandable. Who wears food that way?

We talked for a while and then people separated to write, going off a distance in the trees. I pulled out my laptop and continued where I left off that morning. The birdsong distracted me in the best way. So many songbirds up in the canopy of branches, heard more than seen, and in the silence of writing, even more eloquent. Donkeys wandered in and out of the group. There was a quiet bay mustang who watched us, and when she chose, came to stand with us awhile.

When the writing time was up, we came back to the circle. People took turns reading their work with some balance of pride and anxiousness. Most of all, courage. Adults rarely read aloud, other than children's books to their kids, but this is much more personal. The conversation that followed was thoughtful and kind. I was, as usual, gobsmacked by their talent and moved by their perception.

Writers always benefit from reading the work of other writers, and most of us are avid readers, too. Days like today break down the arbitrary line between the published and the unpublished. It can feel like writing is futile chatter in a world where [insert your favorite author's name here] exists, like it is audacious to even try. But no one owns words. Art is free for the making. Pens and paper are the price of admission to a world of our own design. Some were shy about their writing, but we all knew our words mattered a little more than before. Our lives were a bit more understandable in ways we didn't expect. Words are everyday magic.

The sun crossed the sky, and we stood up, folded our chairs, and started on the trail back up to the barn. The trees held a high ceiling above and our voices got quiet as we climbed. So much like a recessional at the end of a church service, we were leaving a sacred space and grateful for the community we had shared.

The donkeys followed us back and got some hay for their trouble. We said our goodbyes and got into our cars. A little richer for the day, but most of all, in love with words.

I appreciate women's ability to come together and support each other this way. I've found this camaraderie to be dependably present on these days and at clinics as well. Women can be quick to judge and be critical of each other, and I have garnered my share of put-downs. But this type of positive experience happens so much more often that I know this is the bigger truth. We acknowledge our commonality through our voices and words with an honesty and compassion that always leaves me awestruck. It never fails.

**

The rest of the week was busy. I had a single lesson one day, with just three of us: me, my client, and her golden horse. I might have gotten more out of it than the grateful rider.

On another day, I had a full clinic with lots of auditors. One lesson after another, lots of good questions between lessons, but the day ran like a race, and it left me feeling hurried and unfinished. That meant the horses were as rushed as I was. One-day stops aren't long enough. It's hard to sleep after days like that, as I hashed out what I could have done better.

One afternoon, I gave a talk to a small group about Affirmative Training. They all sat in chairs on a screened porch. Mister could be there with us, and he chose a central chair. As I talked, I made eye contact with the group and tried to be interesting. Mister dozed with his body draped over the arm of his chair like a wet towel. Profoundly asleep, not hanging on my every word. Horse talk always does that to him.

There have been a few of the new Barn Visits now. They still feel awkward to me. I'm surprised to admit that larger groups are easier. I intended these Barn Visits to be a mini clinic, but it can seem more like a social call and those are harder to keep on track. It would feel horrible to be paid just for my company and not for horse training. These are workdays for me, and I don't want to feel like I'm selling false friendship. Just like horses, a relationship had to be a choice on both sides.

Other times, I can feel I'm a disappointment to them, but I don't know why. There is a rhythm here somewhere and I'll find it. By now, I know how much every day on the road costs me and it's more than I thought.

Mister seemed to cope with all the chaos and change, but I wondered what he thought about traveling. Did he miss bit-ey-face games with Preacher Man? I try to keep to a routine for him, because it keeps me on a routine, too. He'd been alone all day and I had not. We both needed each other.

Doing clinics at first-time locations is as stressful as a blind date. The organizer takes the risk of hiring me and hoping I'll be someone her friends will gain insight from in our time together. If I don't manage that, her name will be tied to a bad day. I take a risk going into the unknown, and my kind of horsemanship isn't all that common. Horse people are tribal and proud of their traditions. Some want new information, but some are defensive of the old methods.

It works out most of the time, but I'm not always a good match. This week had moments of every emotion, and my return to work hit a couple of bumps right away. One organizer didn't pay me the full amount owed. It wasn't obvious until later and I could have complained, but she tried to bargain for a cheaper fee from the beginning. If I loved my job so much, she seemed to think, I should do it for free. I wanted nothing more to do with her.

I was still trying to make sense of the heart rate test day. Just because I dealt with the heckling well doesn't mean it didn't leave a mark. I don't get used to it. Like most of us, I am not as Teflon as I act. So, I overthink how I might improve while chiding myself to let go of the day.

Most of the time, I knew I was connecting with people. Horses answered and stuck up for me when people doubted me. Some participants saw immediate changes in their horses because what I said gave them a better understanding. And that was enough for their horse to soften.

Part of my job is being responsible for the experience of others. I can't control them, but I hope our lesson will open a door for growth beyond the clinic. Most of all, I hope they find a new appreciation for their horses. Then, piecing those individual lessons into a bigger overall message for the group, I want to tie the entire event up with a bow. It's a thrill when that magic happens.

This job also means that I focus my hardest when others are having time off and engaged in their passion with friends. I'm not part of the group, just that person with the flags at the airport. Add travel time. It's a marathon.

I'd had no days off all week in Austin, no time for me to rewind and unwind. It was the party that never ended. Obviously, I got tired, but couldn't show it, and that is a different sort of challenge to my acting skills. I'm just famous enough to be afraid of a rant on social media if I'm short with someone or if I say something they don't like. Working with people is so much more complicated than working with animals who don't text.

At least I wasn't in a strange bed. It was peaceful on our friend's farm and that counted for much. I'm more certain than ever that I want this Rancho to follow me, so I have an end-of-day hideout. When I'm inside is the only time that I'm truly off stage and not actively listening to others, judging my words before I talk.

Then there is another problem. I'm not a naturally social person. For all my spontaneity with horses, I think too much around people. I want to express my gratitude so much that sometimes I forget. Other times, especially if there had been a big breakthrough with a horse, my emotions swelled. My voice choked with awe for the horse and wavered with teary emotion. For crying out loud. (For me, it's not a figure of speech.)

But if participants hurry toward me with their arms up for a hug, I get nervous. They feel they know me, so it seems natural to them, but getting grabbed by a stranger will always alarm me. I'm a dork, not comfortable with attention. It's redundant to say, but no kidding, I am an introvert acting the part of an extrovert.

There is a thing horses have taught me about stress. It doesn't matter if it's the result of something we like or something that goes wrong. Anticipation and anxiety are two sides of the same coin, and both cause stress. It isn't about good or bad, it's about coping skills. After long clinic days, mine were down around my ankles like stretched-out gym socks.

One positive of this busy week was that Mister got a reprieve from small fluffy white dogs, the National Dog of RV Parks. That said, he'd like you to know there was no less drama for him staying at our friend's place. He faced a very curious ranch cat named Gusto, who sat on the truck and looked right in our windows. Mister is very brave with cats that run away but is always cautious of the ones who stare at him when he barks. Gusto didn't blink. Mister barked some more. Dogs and cats love soap operas and we are adventurers, just passing through. They did not need to meet each other, Mister on a leash and the cat free. That attempt at safety and control would have spoiled the fun.

One afternoon, the top of the Rancho's Dutch door was open for airflow and Mister had stared with his nose pressed against the bottom of the door for a few moments. He was silent and unmoving. I peered outside to see what he was listening to. Gusto was standing on the trailer step with his paws flat on the door, using his mystical mind control. They were an inch apart but couldn't see each other through the door. I returned to what I was doing. Mister didn't breathe, frozen on the spot. Danger was near. He defiantly held his position.

Brigades of Peace Eagles

We hooked up the Rancho again, and with Mister in co-pilot position, we pulled out after a grateful goodbye to Sarah. Gusto sat on the seat of a lawn tractor with no regrets. We drove north to our next stop.

Texas is in the top three states for the most roadkill, not something they mention on the tourist sites. The farther we drive, the more variety we see. Coyotes and dogs, raccoons and cats. Wild and domestic animals sleep together at the edge of the road as they never would in life.

I can't look away. Noticing detail is my superpower. I've always been the one to see something out of place first. Visual focus is a tremendous asset in watching horses move and helping with the minor, yet crucial, details involved in riding well. But it definitely made road trips more grisly.

Maybe because so much of my travel has been by air in recent years, I've lost my tolerance for roadkill. Now everywhere I look, it's God's raccoon, God's skunk, and God's kitty. It would be enough to burn my eyes if it weren't for the vultures. It seemed every few hundred feet, a few of them huddled around something dead at the side of the road, almost like a satin dressing curtain.

I've always hated the sight of vultures, but I appreciate them differently now, if for no other reason than they block the view of roadkill. The Turkey Vultures here are Texas-huge and shiny, with full black feathers and small bald heads. Why am I such a grouch? It isn't like they killed anyone.

I did some research. Once I saw photos of them flying, I realized at least half of the birds I thought were hawks were actually Turkey Vultures. They have white under their wings visible while flying, but I hadn't seen it on the ground. And it was difficult to see their bald heads from a distance. They soared and circled, like a hawk but with such striking colors and a lovely shape to their wings.

It grossed me out if vultures were eating something bigger than they were, like a deer, but the game department doesn't pick up most roadkill. I had confused not wanting to see roadkill with not liking the ones cleaning it up. In this light, vultures are like first responders.

Sometimes groups of them loitered on a fence or downed tree, with their wings spread, back to the sun. They use UV rays to clean up the nasty bits of bacteria and decay from their bodies, I read. They are ironically fastidious birds. Their bald heads seemed more practical now, considering where they put them, and the ease of cleaning needed afterward. Vultures have a keen sense of smell, able to sense carrion up to eight miles away when they are a thousand feet in the air. Not to mention how strong their immune system must be to live on rotten meat. I like them a little more, as every mile there are more of God's skunks and God's rabbits. I hoped I wouldn't see any armadillos.

A little more research: Indigenous people saw the Turkey Vulture as a holy protector and cleaner of the land, calling them Peace Eagles. Pueblo Indians used their feathers in purification rituals for people and objects. Tibetans saw the vultures as Dakinis, spirits who take souls to the heavens to await reincarnation.

Driving across this country had only deepened my environmental concerns. There was so much land taken for housing developments and strip malls. Urban sprawl was a predator and wild animals must move to land with less food or find ways of urban survival. Some wild species were going extinct. Horse owners struggled to find pasture boarding for horses within a reasonable driving distance from town. It was all changing so fast.

But right here, right now, on a back road in Texas, Turkey Vultures were doing their part. These beautiful black birds were looking more sacred to me by the mile. How had I never seen vultures as recyclers? More than that, full-blown environmentalists. I might be late to understand Turkey Vultures, but I respect them now. When passing, I gave the birds a peace sign from the cab of the truck along with a quiet, "Thank you for your service."

Sandy: Different Freedom for DejaVu

The next stop was for Mister as much as me. We drove north to Mansfield and stayed at a friend's B&B for a couple of weekdays. It's called the Corgi Farm, and it was a beautifully homey, comfortable place; a small farm on the edge of town, with lots of long and low dogs, some barn cats, a herd of sheep, and a couple of horses.

I met Sandy years before when she'd gotten my name from a Corgi rescue in Wyoming as someone who could take challenging dogs. She sent me Preacher Man, a small Corgi who over-yapped his welcome. It's how you'd get that name. By then, my farm had already become a location for the Corgi witness protection program.

Both Sandy and I write blogs and laugh at the same jokes. We came from similar backgrounds, and we're outraged at the same insensitivity toward animals. We both juggle burnout and self-care. I'm honored to know her. She'd turn and walk away to hear me say it. She's ridiculously humble and generous.

It was Sandy who suggested that Mister might come live with me. Mister had even fostered with their pack of dogs for a while. Then she and our friend, Peggy, drove over seven hundred miles to deliver him to me. Mister didn't exactly run into my arms at first, but Sandy recognized me in this dog, or the dog in me. Either way, she was right about us.

This was before I'd hatched the travel plan, but Mister quickly let me know he was the missing link. He and I are so alike that it's hard to tell whose idea we're following. I'm sure it's him that has me on a leash, attached to things that make me sane. A literal touchstone.

So, we stopped for a family reunion of unrelated people and animals. We're not related by blood, but by something that runs *in* our blood. Mister and I met new friends, and other animal welfare folks came, all of us on our particular slightly anti-social spectrum.

We ate well and swore freely. Our sort loves private profanity. It comes from biting our tongues in public. We swore and laughed and swore and howled into the evening. Mister was happy to romp with the dogs, and even happier when it was time to go back to the Rancho to talk about his belly in private.

There are a couple of horses in the pasture behind Sandy's barn. One is an elder gray pony, every little girl's dream. The other is a mustang named DejaVu that Sandy and I had spoken about often. I was looking forward to meeting him. I'll let Sandy tell this part of the story.

Around May 2011, he was one of three mustangs chosen by a trainer for competition in that year's $250,000 Extreme Mustang Makeover. At the time, it was the largest purse ever offered by the organization, held in partnership with the BLM (Bureau of Land Management.)

At the event, I worked the in/out gate to the arena for the freestyle element. I watched DejaVu's go-round; bridle-less, he tracked a large heifer around the arena while the trainer shook out a loop. When the cow was caught, the horse slid obediently to a magnificent sliding stop right in front of the gate where I stood; the trainer bailed off. As he ran up the rope to flip the cow and tie her legs together, I watched the horse's eye as he paused a second, correctly holding the rope taut and the cow to the ground. Then the horse stepped up, just one step. The cow leaped to her feet just as the trainer was reaching over her to grab her flank and flip. He was knocked off his feet, his glasses flew off his head about 20 feet, and the cow and horse stood there, tied together by the rope on the saddle horn. I've always felt the horse's footwork that day was absolutely deliberate. I could be wrong.

At the end of the event, the top 20 mustangs in the competition were offered for adoption to the highest bidder. No one bid on the 17th place horse called DejaVu. Rumor was the horse was "crazy." The trainer had planned to haul the horse back to the Oklahoma BLM holding pens. The foundation denied the trainer's request, instead telling the trainer to re-home it as best he could. I offered to adopt, and filled out the BLM application, paid the $25 adopt fee, and accepted the trainer's offer to haul the horse to our farm.

He arrived in early October 2011. The trainer insisted on observing my ability to remove the halter, then catch and re-halter the horse before he left. And so we did. He gave me suggestions on what type of saddle to use. I replied I would likely not ever ride him. The trainer just looked at me. I gave the horse a pile of good hay, a trough of clean water, and space. He was still wearing aluminum "slider" shoes on his rear feet. It took weeks for the shoes to fall off. I was grateful they did so without complications.

This May he will have been here for twelve years. According to his original BLM Coggins, he was estimated to be four years old at the time of the 2011 event. I've had a halter on him once or twice, mainly for the benefit of my young niece who fell in love with the romantic idea of taming a wild horse, and so we worked together to establish a quiet trust between them and she haltered him, then brushed him, then led him around the farm. She was profoundly impacted by what the horse taught her.

As am I. I've made many mistakes with this boy, mistakes that were illustrated to me more clearly than any video, any book, or any horse I've ever worked with has been able to do. He has taught me to recognize my mistakes and live with them, just as he lives with us now. We have no choice, he in his five acre pasture with his pony mate, me with the memories of the many horses I've pushed, bullied, hurried, and turned a blind eye to as they struggled to understand my traditional training efforts.

I've only touched him a half-dozen times. But he has touched me every single time I am in his presence.

Sandy brought him home because he had no other place to be. DejaVu wasn't good advertising for the Mustang organizers. Rushed training for the competition was stressful and often the horses were pushed too hard, too fast. More than that, an animal trained with fear would never be truly reliable. It was a foundation made of broken pieces.

The mustang lives on her farm as in a sanctuary, meaning she gives everything and asks nothing back. She took him at his word and let him rest, accepted him just as he was. She offered the mustang a different freedom.

It took years of quiet barn chores for the simple achievement of him continuing to eat while Sandy worked nearby. It was a huge offer from this horse who knew humans were predators by experience. His intelligence was undeniably intact, bent but not broken. Eventually, after years of quiet and positive work, Sandy and the mustang came to something like an armed truce. He didn't always bolt away and some days, she could touch him. But DejaVu's memory was as clear as if the competition was yesterday. The scar will never go away.

Recently, Sandy was gone for a few days, and hired a kind person to care for the barn animals. The helper mentioned she might work with the mustang, offered with the best of intentions.

We like to think we have a special skill, that animals like us. There's hope that the animal isn't really that way. We want to pet dogs whose owners ask us not to; we think we can touch the cat no one can get close to. The result is the animal having to prove again and again that their fear is real and not a whim. Sandy's years of good, consistent presence had already proven DejaVu was honest.

When Sandy got back from her trip, she saw the old fear had returned in the mustang. He had regressed, no other word for the look she recognized. It doesn't matter what happened, and her helper would never be knowingly cruel. The mustang might have felt pressure that reminded him of his past. Horses remember everything. But the break in routine when Sandy was gone may have been enough to soften the trust he'd allowed. Horses don't like change any more than humans.

It was no one's fault, but Sandy blamed herself. Why is it that the people who have the least to apologize for make the most heartfelt and committed apologies?

After a couple of weeks of the old slow approach, in a moment of frustration about the progress lost, Sandy raised her voice and swore, more at herself or up to the sky. Sandy barked out the F-Word in the middle of her rant, and the mustang took a step toward her. She rewarded it with a laugh. He likes her just the way she is, too.

That horse and I might appreciate the same qualities in Sandy: Natural intelligence. Acceptance without judgment. An undomesticated appreciation of wildness.

Passive-Aggressive Heckling

The story of Sandy's mustang isn't uncommon. Competitions with horses have always been part of the relationship, whether rodeo or horse races or neighbors just looking over fences.

Rehabbing horses is a large part of what I do as a trainer, more so than starting youngsters. But meeting DejaVu also reminded me of another side of the story. It was the everyday version, always happening on a smaller scale.

We were still wrapping up at a Barn Visit. It was an hour past quitting time. We were in overtime, so I brought Mister out. He needed water and a bathroom break. As we walked back to the group, Mister was on a leash ahead of me. Not pulling, not done with his snuffling, and minding his own business. A man who had been disruptive all day while I was working said under his breath, "Who's walking who?"

He meant this to be a sharp little barb; passive-aggressive heckling. Maybe he thinks Mister should relieve himself in the heeling position. Or the man just wants to poke me one more time because he thinks we both need discipline. He is looking for faults and is ready to correct them.

I bit my tongue. Who's leading who, he asked? The one who's been quiet and well-behaved is leading me. The one who waited in the truck all day is leading me. I'm happy to follow. Sometimes one of us leads and sometimes the other. It's what partnership means.

The man set about telling me how he started colts. He wanted me to know he was cowboy-tough and strict. He'd watched me all day, working quietly and getting good results, but it seemed to challenge him more than impress him.

I thought of DejaVu and those competitions, where the art of horse training looked like a reality show spin-off, with horses doing the stunts. The training challenges, using colts, rescue horses, or mustangs, started not long after TV reality shows were springing up. The idea was for trainers to compete against each other to show what they could do with a horse in thirty days. At first, it seemed like an okay idea; trainers won money, and they got some horses into new adoptive homes.

For some trainers, the competitions immediately became about showboating and ego. The horses were props more than partners. They suffered under the brutal push for the most dramatic tricks, dominated into submission for the enjoyment of the audience.

Some trainers did kind, patient work. I have a friend who competed. Her horse did well in training but needed more time. She didn't push her mare. They did less; they didn't win. She swore she wouldn't do another event like that.

They asked me to take part in one of these competitions, too. At first, I thought it was a practical joke from someone who knew me, and it cracked me up. But it was serious, and I declined the invitation. As much as I enjoy showing horses, this kind of event felt like a gladiator spectacle to me. Besides, by then I'd worked with several clients who purchased these horses, only to get home to find the horse wasn't safe or easy to ride. Once the pressure stopped, the horses unraveled.

Not all horses in these competitions come out damaged, but it happens often enough that many well-known trainers in the industry started asking hard questions and taking a stand against these competitions. Times are changing. The public complains more about cruelty, and attendance at events like rodeo is down. The beloved image of the American cowboy has taken on a sad double meaning; to "cowboy" a horse means rough handling.

Fear-based (domination) training is a common approach,

but a horse trained this way won't trust the rider and will always look for his own survival. Speeding up the training process puts even more pressure on the horse. Eventually, the competitions stretched to ninety days of training. It was more time, but for some trainers, the pressure to put on a show was still too much and the tricks only got more dangerous.

Training sensitive animals takes nuance and patience. It was painful to see my occupation cheapened this way, but there is a bigger harm for the horse-owning public. When we see domination training normalized and cruelty as common, we become callus. Horses remain as sensitive as ever, so more end up in rescue, some after hurting riders.

Domination training is based on a false narrative about herd dynamics. Horses live cooperatively in herds in the wild, knowing there is safety in numbers. It was never about fighting between horses for dominance, the excuse for humans acting harshly.

As kids, they taught us to show the horse who was boss and to demand respect. But there were always quiet horse people around who did not use force, legends told of horse whisperers. A bit of history is helpful. These two training approaches have always existed. The Greeks thought everything was art and trained with respect and compassion. Xenophon's philosophy of training has survived and is worth reading. The Romans were more warlike, with a plan to dominate their world. They used horses in battle. Those stories have survived, too.

Noticing different approaches is normal, but for some, competition means war. For others, cooperating peacefully to achieve the same end is an art.

The debate trickles down to passive-aggressive intimidation between horse owners. The most pervasive issue my clients tell me about is feeling shamed if they train affirmatively. Railbirds are critical, heckling them to be more aggressive with their training. Clients tell me they end up as anxious as their horses.

So, back to my heckler, who, after a day of challenging me to one verbal pissing contest after another, needed to correct the way I let my dog pee. Really? Maybe it was no big deal. Mister ignored him. Why don't I let it go?

Because this is how it happens that the horse world is darker than need be. He passively disrespected me all day long, sometimes under his breath, sometimes with body language, and sometimes by diversion. But he didn't have the words to contradict me honestly. He was like a kid shooting spitballs. It was a kind of gaslighting, trying to make me doubt myself.

Gaslighting is so interwoven into daily interchanges that we can misplace our self-esteem. After that, it's easy to become numb to the constant belittling. At work or at home, by family, co-workers, or other horse people, it wears us down in small ways until we don't know how we lost our confidence. Eventually, the loudest railbird is in our own heads. We only know others have doubted us so often that now we doubt ourselves.

Over the years, I've had a group of experiences that are consistent enough to see a pattern. It's an unstated, idiotic muscle-flexing that happens without my consent. It goes like this: Two horses are being moved on the same day. Great idea, less stressful for the horses that way. I arrived with my trailer to pick up my client's horse, and another trainer arrived with a trailer to pick up the other horse. We said a brief hello all around and set to it.

I gave my client's horse a scratch as I picked up the lead rope and the horse walked peacefully into my trailer. We closed the door. Questions asked and answered.

The other trainer was a little more aggressive, actively waving a flag on a stick. That horse was nervous and beginning to shut down. Blame the horse's calming signals, but anyone could see the horse's fear. We had to wait. The reason to have us both come at the same time was so neither horse was left there alone.

The other trainer got more frustrated, and now he was using the whip to intimidate the horse, and maybe the horse's owner, too. The other woman nervously looked over at us. Her horse was dancing now, the whites of his eyes showing. Finally, as the result of a loud pop on the horse's rump, the horse threw himself into the trailer, hitting a wall. His hooves skidded as he fought for balance, rattling the trailer. The trainer slammed the trailer door and shot me a look that made me think he'd like to give me a pop, too. Then we all left the property at the same time.

It's happened in too many situations and much too often to be a coincidence. It was an impromptu training challenge with an audience of two spectators. Did that horse get beat up because of me, or does that trainer's method normally rely on childish temper tantrums?

This chronic competition doesn't happen the same way between women in the same situations. I experience more ease and collaboration between women trainers. It was similar to when I was showing my horses. We got emotional, we tried hard, but we competed against our last scores, competed to improve our transitions, and then celebrated as a group later.

Clients tell me they don't like competition, but is it this competition-is-war behavior outside the show ring that they see between trainers? As I watched the horse get frightened into the trailer, both clients cringed. Both clients felt they'd lost.

Maybe I should have ducked my head and played stupid for the sake of the other horse. I could have waited for the other trainer to finish before I started if I'd known this would happen. But it only delays the inevitable. Nothing changes because the problem is that fear-based training works on people, too. Intimidating horses can intimidate owners as well.

If we bow to that kind of gaslighting, we agree to the assumption of our inferiority. Ignoring the bully doesn't make them go away, and heckling back doesn't work. It's uncomfortable, but better to speak up for ourselves and our horses than to choke down our emotions and anxieties. If we want the horse world to change, we must be the ones to make the change, finally understanding that self-worth isn't the same as arrogance. For DejaVu and other horses who bear scars of domination, I will talk back to bullies eye-to-eye, because silence equals consent.

Then my ghost herd, never far away, lifted their heads from grazing. One by one, they exhaled a "good girl" snort in my direction.

I Work for the Horse

The next morning, as I was folding down the Rancho and packing up to leave, I watched DejaVu grazing in a green pasture with that sweet old gray pony. It was a cloudless morning, with birds singing in the trees. The sheep were grazing off to one side of the field. A quirky barn cat oversaw the antics of the pack of long, low dogs bounding around the yard, sometimes jumping down the steps into the pool for a drink. It was a real-life diorama of a Walt Disney cartoon, but this wasn't a fairy tale. I climbed into the truck with a satisfied smile. Sometimes I still hear a tiny cynical voice that sounds like my mother warning me I can't save them all. So silly. It was never up to me alone.

We headed off for our next stop, sad to leave our Corgi family. The GPS Woman got us to the freeway. Mister dropped his head to the console, and I cranked up my current book, *Perestroika in Paris* by Jane Smiley.

The drive north through Dallas is the worst stretch of construction I've ever seen in my life. I expect road work in the summer. It isn't a road trip without construction, but this is baffling. They tore this freeway to shreds. Off-ramps stop in midair. They painted lane lines over others until the road looked like a game of pick-up sticks. Narrow lanes stop and go, with concrete barriers on either side, made narrower by the big boxy hood of my truck. We fit between the lines, but there is no room for sway. With semi-trucks in front and back, I have zero visibility except for a clear blue sky above.

It's both hands on the wheel, ten and two, and I must consciously ask my shoulders to let go of my ears, my white knuckles to soften on the wheel. My side mirrors are almost touching cement girders. I'm in a raft of semis crawling along the narrow lanes, each mile more treacherous than the last. Just as I thought my lungs might collapse from lack of oxygen, with traffic tight as ever, somehow, we all sped up to the posted limit. No width to spare, no place to pull over, and for once, no roadkill.

GPS Woman called out random turns, but the signs didn't match, and the exit wasn't always open. Traffic is tight and slow, then tight and fast. The brake lights flared hot again. I'm glad for the advanced riding I've done and grateful for the complicated horses I've rehabbed. They've taught me an in-the-moment focus that holds me steady with the iron horses in a road race.

The construction area was miles long and the tightness of the traffic had plenty of time to force its way into my body. I ached from clenching muscles and my mouth was dry from throat breathing for so long. Asking myself to feel my toes in my shoes, I tried to settle. I told Mister he was a good boy for sleeping so soundly, which he does with a slight gap in his lips, showing just a glimpse of his teeth. He sleeps like a little old man, a dry snore with no drool.

I'm not one of those people who is a nervous driver, riding the brake for fear of trouble. But I might start. The semi just in front of me still blocked the view and another right on my trailer bumper pushing closer and closer. My Ford F-250 feels tiny. I have no choice but to keep my foot on the gas and keep talking to myself, says this woman who feels like tuna fish in a semi sandwich.

Eventually, the barriers got farther away, the lanes opened, and the suburbs sprawled out. Finally, GPS Woman announced my exit. I was off the freeway and driving toward the next farm. There was a small town, and I pulled in to look for some lunch. There were no places open, so I drove on to the next small town, and still no lunch. It was already too remote for fast food and the small businesses all seemed to be closed. The town felt like a movie set; I circled blocks looking, but the only sign of life was a mom and her kids coming out of a doctor's office. I kept driving and ate some nuts and wondered how many businesses have failed over the last pandemic years. The cities have been bustling with growth, but the small towns in Texas look just plain worn out.

Naturally, the last clinic stop was a facility near the end of a road. The owner/trainer/organizer had almost single-handedly built it all in the last few months. It's brand new and as lively as can be. I can't imagine how she has managed it. I should count her as my second tornado watch.

The barn design is perfect, a tall roof over an arena and beautiful, bright airy stalls. There are no walls. It gets hot here in the summer, but there is so much airflow that it must be an oasis in the shade. Lots of room for turnout on the property and the place is bustling. I'm flattered to be the first clinician she's invited. We hadn't met before, so I got a quick greeting and a place to park before she went back to work.

It was late afternoon. After unfolding the Rancho and hooking up, Mister and I headed up to the arena for a look around. The trainer was riding a young horse who was helium-light, athletic, and fancy. He also had anxiety that she was working to direct in a positive way. She wants his energy, and she'd like to steer it toward more confidence. Too often, amateur riders see energy as a fault instead of a way for a horse to find balance. It was refreshing to see a rider not just allow her horse to go forward but encourage the energy calmly. Horses gotta move.

The barn owner is a pro, an expert rider, pushing her hands forward frequently, asking the horse to stretch his neck forward and find the bit. The youngster tends to over-bend and tuck his nose behind the vertical, not through any fault so much as youth and conformation. They are working it out, and I know she is a kindred spirit.

Some organizers are courageous first-timers, trying to find the line between throwing a party and being a school crossing guard with math skills. I applaud their audacity to take on the challenge of pulling all the parts together. Horse people are notoriously helpful but also hard to herd. I depend on organizers for their optimism and grit.

This stop felt easier, more familiar. We both know our jobs and we share the same riding discipline and approach toward training, more or less. This is what I've missed these last two years, this format of sharing and learning together. I let the horses teach all of us, doing little more than translating for the horse and helping the rider find a better question. Each rider gets individual help, but often it's seeing ourselves in other riders that is the most affirming.

Clinics follow a pattern, and this one is no different. At the beginning, the participants all looked at each other cautiously. Most are strangers with something in common. I usually meet longtime readers, auditors who have flown in, and local riders. Some horses live there on the property, and others are hauled in, but the activity makes all the horses unsettled. The riders don't all know each other; we share our usual reluctance to ride in front of a group. Everyone wants to have their best ride, and like every other day, the horses react to their environment.

This is the adrenaline sport part of my job. It's like speed dating. I have an intense focus on one horse and rider combination, meeting them in what is a stressful time, and finding a thing that can help them both progress. It's a puzzle that requires an intense visual focus to recognize small behaviors and trace them back to the fundamentals of training horses. Then, with affirmative negotiation, without blaming either partner, we resolve a path forward. I always remember no one likes to be corrected in public, horses or humans, even if that's what they've paid me to do.

Clinic days start early, usually around eight a.m. I walk around the facility to see if everyone's horses are okay. I check with the organizer to make sure she has no questions, and we start the morning with a group meeting to give everyone a launch to the day. We cruised through four lessons in the morning. At lunch, I answer more questions and then give four more lessons in the afternoon. We have a wrap-up meeting after the last lesson to give people one more chance to ask questions and share their thoughts about the day. It was a sprint.

Best of all, no two horses have the same history, identical calming signals, or training. The same is true of people. No two lessons can go the same by definition. This is where it gets fun.

One rider might be timid, perhaps coming back from a fall. It isn't unusual for a rider to develop a fear of their horse. It's a special moment to share when someone trusts me to help them back into the saddle. I might ask if I could give them a pony ride. Some might be embarrassed, but I describe it affirmatively and most riders are relieved to hear the idea. Emotions are fluid and contagious between a horse and rider, and I can smooth those initial strides out, so it's a gentle re-start for both.

We have a patient time with the horse at the mounting block, breathing and talking. When the rider and horse are ready, I brace the offside stirrup, so the saddle doesn't slip, and the rider mounts. Then we breathe some more.

For the first few minutes, I lead the horse and begin the lesson with a foundational warm-up. The rider supples the horse's body. This begins with the rider asking for long strides and shorter strides with her sit bones. I keep my voice relaxed and rhythmic to match the horse's stride, and I cue the rider's movement in simple words. The horse responds immediately and both horse and rider know the other is listening. Then we do some arcs, the rider using her inside calf to pulse in rhythm with the horse's barrel as it swings to the outside. It encourages the horse to relax but also gives the rider something affirmative to think about.

This start isn't special; the walking massage warm-up is how every lesson starts, but it's easier to learn with someone leading so the rider doesn't have to steer at the same time. By now, the watchers are considering asking for the same ride, so they can feel what this rider is feeling, so deep into her horse's stride. Fear visibly melts on both sides. It was an addictive slow dance, even to watch.

Then, I'll ask if I can unclip the lead but walk next to the horse. And soon, they'll be riding in a circle around me, focusing on relaxation. About 10 minutes before the end of her lesson, I'll ask her to dismount, usually before she wants, and give the last word to the horse. We step away and let the horse lick and chew or shake out their poll. Sometimes the horse gives a huge yawn, but it isn't about being sleepy. It's been emotional for the horse; he needs to express those feelings, even as I am asking the rider how she feels.

Sometimes at the start of the lesson, the rider will explain her horse's training issue, but the horse will tell me they're in pain. Maybe the horse tosses his head or doesn't want to go forward. This is a different challenge. We frequently mistake the horse signaling pain for disobedience, but not everyone wants to believe it. I have to negotiate that carefully. It might mean no riding. It might be a poor saddle fit or an ulcer flare-up. Usually, the rider follows the logic and understands. But if the horse is lame, we don't ride. It was not great news after paying for the lesson, so I engaged the rider as best I could in ways to help her horse. The best owners understand immediately, and we have the same goal. The horse comes first.

Sometimes the lesson is with an experienced rider on an advanced horse. I'm probably not going to find a huge issue to correct. My eyes will tell me where the weak link is. Maybe the horse's confidence or the rider's position is holding them back. Making a small shift in balance, the method of cueing, or a change in how the rider holds the reins will make all the difference. My favorite kind of lesson is where this kind of minuscule change has a tremendous improvement for the horse. This is how competent riders become expert riders.

When a sound horse has anxiety, that's a different question. It's like a mystery and we have to return to the scene of the crime, so that we can help the horse. In dressage, we always know returning to the fundamentals is the first step. So, we do the same massage warm-up just like every other lesson. And then begin simple transitions to see where the horse loses confidence. The rider might have thought the problem was with the canter depart when it was about an imbalance in the trot instead. Horses know how to canter; they know everything. Constant correction, back as youngsters or in daily exchanges, damages their trust in us and that might show up in their gait. Our only gift to horses should be to give them enough confidence that, when faced with challenges, they will continue to try without fear.

In the old method, trainers taught us when there's an issue, to tough it out and ride through it. It doesn't work because horses hold the memory of that stress, and it damages their confidence. They don't get through it, they get exhausted. Some riders value their bravado and ability to ride through difficult situations and spur the horse forward. Other riders don't want to fight their horse but fear being called quitters. Both sides are wrong; it's never okay for the horse to be pushed into their flight response. These lessons turn into negotiations, advocating for the horse, without insulting the rider.

During the day, I work to find a thread of commonality in the lessons. Pointing out different rides that share fundamental similarities, we feel less isolated and accept our horses in their unique ways. If there is a choice between siding with the horse or the rider, I remind the rider that they write the check, but I work for their horse.

My part is simple. The horses point me in the right direction, and I follow, trusting my eyes and the horses. I process what I see with what I know from a lifetime of study. Then I translate that experience into an understandable answer for the rider. Every clinic is different, but thanks to the horses reminding me, I talk about everything they need their owners to hear by the end. And of course, this is the closest thing some of us have to a vacation, so on top of the rest, it should be fun.

Day one has finished. It's been over eight hours. I had a quirky combination of exhaustion and elation, and it would take hours to settle enough to sleep. I was beyond ready to go back to the Rancho, where I'd think more about each horse and plan tomorrow. My smile hurt from loving my job so much, my mind crackled and ran like wildfire.

But Mister was waiting for me. This is the most important thing he does. He reminded me it wasn't all about horses. Some might meditate concentrating on a candle. For me, it was Mister's belly.

Bird Bath

After dinner, my brain isn't all that crisp, so no writing at night. Answering emails is an endless, time-consuming job. I field questions from followers in the online school or social media. I'm asked to respond to news of some horrific abuse case or a question about equine health concerns. Always, I continue making travel plans for future clinics, sending paperwork to potential organizers, and paying bills. Often, I respond to questions about euthanasia from heartbroken horse owners. They just want a personal nod of confirmation and understanding.

I was learning the bliss of enviro-frugality. Never a fan of suffering after a long day, it wasn't about doing without. Many of the habits I adopted on the road were better. I had purchased some lavender-scented foaming bath wipes, no-rinse, and self-drying. I thought I'd use them for emergency foot wipes, but they were too good to keep just for that. They were soothing after a day in the sun and cleaned really well. The process felt so much softer and kinder than a shower, and my skin wasn't as dry afterward. These synthetic towelettes felt like the tiny RV version of a spa, without using too much water. Call it a bird bath. Did I just share a beauty tip that was designed for invalid care?

Then I climbed into bed, sinking into the foam topper, and pulled the weighted blanket up. Nothing but luxury. Mister curled in beside me and the two of us fell into dreamless sleep. No matter where we parked in this trailer, I could sleep long undisturbed hours. Never in my life, but so normal here. The Rollin' Rancho altered reality.

When morning came, I washed my face with extra-hot water from the teakettle and wiped my short hair at the same time. Recently I'd read reports we use an unhealthy amount of soap. Growing up, I always had a hair-washing compulsion. I was a victim of my hair, a reality I fought from both sides at once.

As a teenager, I had oily hair, which was the same thing as having food in my teeth. The exact same thing as never having a date as long as I lived. Hovering on the brink of teenage angst and despair, I knew eternal solitary confinement would be my life sentence. Condemned if I wore the wrong outfit or looked fat, but most of all, if my hair was oily. Pimples were not as embarrassing to me as my bangs sticking together. Sometimes I washed them in the girls' bathroom partway through a school day. I noticed boys didn't bother.

Meanwhile, my mother had coarse white hair and didn't wash it often. She'd get it wet and put rollers in before bed. In the morning, it never looked different, washed or not. It was one more reason to be critical. I thought she had poor hygiene. Compared to me, who didn't? But white hair has a different texture. It's thicker, I like to think it's more like horsehair. By the time I got to that same state of gray, I understood.

I started gaining those white horse hairs in high school when my hair was still oily. The cool girls parted their hair in the middle and wore it long. They would pull it around from the back and drape it over one shoulder as if it were important for everyone to see it. As if it defined them as women during this time when our generation of men had long hair, too. We were daughters of the sexual revolution and feminists, but long hair was about as traditional for women as wearing ridiculous shoes and cooking. I kept my hair short, partly as a mark of rebellion. Partly for practicality.

Once, I let my hair grow to my shoulder but still missed the mark of being cool. After I started my metalsmithing career, I caught my hair on fire once or twice. Some got jerked out after catching up on my drill. If I was driving, it tangled in the wind or got in my teeth. If I had to keep it in a bad ponytail, what was the point? I looked bald from the front. If it was down, I looked like a mop from behind.

I gave up and cut it short again, probably too short, but I never went back. On hot days after a ride, I cooled my horse off with a garden hose and put my head under it, too.

Now I am a woman of a certain age, traveling in a trailer but not retired. I wash my hair using the same biodegradable Castile camping soap, also with lavender, that I use for the dishes. I spiked it up with some hair product, but it's been standing on end for long enough to not need it. With more important things on my mind, I've given up chronic self-loathing. I've outgrown my cosmetic death spiral. Horses and dogs taught me acceptance that I never found with my own species.

Some women stare at my hair and tell me they wish they could cut theirs as if it were illegal. When I asked why they didn't, it was always to please someone else. They kept looking at my head, making me self-conscious, and I wondered at this age who it was that they would have to ask for permission. How did hair get so sacred?

Collecting my hearing aids, tech essentials, and a hat, I'm ready for work. I kneel on the bench seat and tilt my head to look in the mirror before leaving. It was mainly to check for residual toothpaste. Stepping out of the Rollin' Rancho looking professional, or as close as I can pull off, I smile. I look like I would if I'd stayed at a hotel. The horses and humans will judge me all day at the clinic. I just hope it's for something more important than my hair.

***

Day two of the clinic is my favorite day. The first day had anxieties and most of them were anticipatory. It was something people had looked forward to, but the horses behave exactly like horses, and that means anything goes. If the clinician is too much of a hero, that adds a whole other layer of emotion for the rider. It's exciting, but my novelty wears off quickly.

The second day is easier. People know what to expect and that makes their horses calmer. If things come apart on the first day of a clinic, the second day is when things come back together in a better way. It was making progress. We have to let go of one thing to get another. Change is necessary because nothing stays static, especially horses. But even positive change is hard.

Sometimes horses are wildly talented and seem to be in a hurry to get someplace. Sometimes horses seem stuck in a place that shouldn't be a big deal but can't go on. But the answer both times is to find the spot where the anxiety started. It's a tiny place where they begin to feel reluctant or anxious. When we find it, we can breathe until the horse can process that moment.

Sound like therapy? Well, it is because it was never a training problem. It's always about relationship. I know I harp on this, but we need to learn their language and stop battering them with ours.

By the end of the clinic, participants connected with each other in ways that were unexpected. Each of the horses had something to share and we're better for it. We talked about the nature of horses, what it means to be a flight animal, and how they think. Once we listen on that level, the messages horses share have more clarity and people have better listening skills in the future.

I think change is possible because horses make us vulnerable and, at that moment, we fall in love with them all over again for the first time. I've seen horses do this again and again, and it feels like magic every time. Horses are reliable miracles.

By the end, there are hugs all around, and we have moved from a group of awkward strangers to newfound friends who share a passion. Some clinics felt like the horses were old friends and other stops felt awkward without enough time to get comfortable. Sometimes I felt I'd helped and other times nothing I could do would be enough. All normal in this line of work.

The sarcastic side of me wants a t-shirt that says "There will be no faith healing today." Who doesn't want a quick fix for the problems that have developed over the years? We want the best for our horse and hope it's no more involved than rearranging books on a shelf, but a horse has memory and emotions. If old training habits helped create the problem, more of the same technique won't solve it.

Instead, we need to build new habits. It isn't different from other areas of our lives. Genuine change is always deceptive. It might seem to happen as quickly as a fall, as abruptly as a car accident. It's the next days and months when growth truly happens, and in ways that are deeper than expected. I can be that spark, but change comes with a choice to make new habits. Consistency fuels genuine change.

Road Rage

The next morning, we were back to fast rural highways that slow down between city limit signs. I'd pulled off for a snuffling walk with Mister, a cool drink, and another tank of gas. It's a town with a handful of traffic lights. I looked both ways. There was a truck coming in the distance, but I was at the opposite city limit. With the slow speeds in town, I had more than plenty of time.

I rolled around the corner and then sped up. Checking my mirror, the truck was coming up fast, but I wasn't dawdling. I made it to the speed limit quickly, long before he would have to pump his brakes. Driving in Texas had been a very polite affair, with many folks waving me into traffic, holding a spot for me to fit. I did the polite thing, sped up to match the traffic, and gave a wave back.

Checking my mirror again, the truck was still coming at me fast. There's a man in a ball cap behind the wheel, his brim curled into an arc and pulled down low. He had a dark beard and sunglasses. No worries, big open roads bring out the speeder in most of us. I'm at the limit and there is almost no traffic. Still, I stayed close to the outer edge of the wide two-lane road, so he had room to pass.

Mr. Ball Cap drove a Ford F-150, a smaller truck than mine. He flew up to the Rancho's bumper, swerved to pass me with a furious roar, and then cut in front of my truck, with only a few feet between us. Close enough that I couldn't see his license plate. I floated my foot off the gas but didn't brake. He'd leave me in his wake soon.

But he waited. Looking at me in his rearview, he pumped his brakes, not that he had to on my account. Horses have bubbles and so do humans. It's the surrounding space that we claim as ours and Mr. Ball Cap must have an enormous bubble, easier to be offended that way. He wanted to be very clear that he meant to punish me for driving at the speed limit and make me suffer as profoundly as he had.

But I don't. It's always a choice. I can ricochet between emotions. I can accept the blame, suffer with guilt, or throw a tantrum back, but if horses have taught me anything, it's that nothing is personal. So, I breathe.

We drove like this for a half mile or so, in close formation like the Blue Angels of the Highway. I'm not being aggressive. I keep thinking he will pull away. Still, I don't pump my brakes and bow to the obvious superiority of his rage. When horse training, I call it Peaceful Persistence. Women of a certain age can get this kind of attitude about holding their space. I'm donkey-stubborn at owning mine.

I was breathing and driving with the calm I use when working rank stallions. They don't want to behave that way. Stallions are usually the sweet ones once they catch their breath and find a human not out for blood. But like I say, Mr. Ball Cap doesn't have that grace about him. Meanness is usually a sign of pain in horses. Probably true of this guy, so determined to punish me.

In a mile, he slowed down to take a ramp. Purposefully looking over at me, he mouthed a few words that weren't hard to imagine while flipping me off, jerking his middle finger up and down vigorously. Will his crass gesture pound home some truth, or intimidate me when his truck didn't? I doubt he'd see himself as someone who tormented gray-haired women, but here he is. Do I count as a woman, or do we both lose our identity behind a steering wheel? I expect by lunchtime Mr. Ball Cap's anger will level out and he'll look for a dog to kick.

The road opened up to the horizon; I gave Mister a lifting scratch just where the bottom edge of his ear meets his neck. Gravity is a constant enemy if you have big ears. He likes a little scratch to lighten that weight. It lightens my weight too.

***

My last stop in Texas is a half-day barn visit, and GPS Woman takes me to a narrow driveway. Of course, she does. She says to turn left and I do, the driveway barely wider than my truck. We roll forward into an otherwise beautiful wood, the road winding toward a blind curve and into a big dip. What if this isn't the right place? What if it's a dead-end with no room to turn? It feels nearly primeval, but eventually, we pull around a corner to see a barn and a beautiful home and a massive pond. I hope it was the right place. After my start today, the anticipation of a possible dead-end drama about did me in.

I wonder if my friendly GPS Woman is capable of practical jokes. Sometimes she sends me on alternate routes or down roads next to the right road. She does a good enough job most of the time. I don't want to be folding and unfolding maps, but my confidence in her judgment had just enough anxiety mixed in to keep it interesting. It's like bingeing *Twilight Zone* episodes.

When I haul horses, I always like to know where I'm going to land, so I might do a planning visit before the haul if the location is close enough. But we aren't local and with trees, it's impossible to see ahead. This trip had been just one narrow driveway after another, and I had better get used to it. What is it with horse people living on small dead-end roads?

I can't see a place to turn around. I think we're trapped, so when my client asks if I'd like her husband to park my truck, I say yes just to see if it's possible. Their horse trailer is parked three inches from their barn. He levitates the Rancho into position.

My client and I have had lessons online and we go to the barn straightaway. Her gelding is a kind horse who doesn't want to move forward. Others might pull out a whip and intimidate him, but I think there's something physical going on with her gelding. Something the vets haven't been able to find, a reluctance to try for good reasons.

The gelding's confidence had suffered in this process. It's the equivalent of a rider who gets fearful after a fall. Now the questions are both mental and physical for him. He is a stoic horse and not willing to show weakness, which is a frustrating but common trait in horses. The vet says he's fine, but the horse continues his kind refusal to work. Who to believe, the vet or the horse?

After meeting him, I'm even more inclined to take his word for it, even if we can't find the source of his pain. His calming signals are subtle but clear. Horses don't have the mental faculties to consciously lie to us. Pushing him through his polite refusal would be dangerous for both horse and rider. Now that I work online, meetings like this help me further develop and trust my eye. We spend time with her herd, and I meet a recent addition whose temperament is the complete opposite, a brassy and sassy pony.

Later in the Rancho with Mister, I relaxed just enough to

notice how exhausted I was. I was drifting with Ernest Tubb serenading us with *Waltz Across Texas,* when another tornado watch lit up my phone. Texts came from the house to ask if I wanted to come inside. I told them as long as it's a watch, we'll stay where we are. After all, this wasn't our first tornado.

Homeward Bound

Living in a central state means home is the hub of the wheel. I had broken my year of travel into four areas of the country, with pit stops in Colorado between the trips. This maiden voyage to Texas had proved we were road worthy. Mister seemed to like the lifestyle, and I'd gotten a delicious amount of reading done.

The next morning was sunny, and I was wearing traveling pajamas. No more clinics this trip, and it's a relief to be me again. I was excited to be heading home. Mister doesn't care. He takes his days as they come, and a driving day is a good day. It's our twenty-first day on the road and it's a seven-hundred-mile drive home. I knew better than to drive it in one day, so we headed northwest across the middle of Texas and took our time.

We drove across the land of enormous ranches, legendary for their acreage, cattle, and Quarter Horses. For a while, I was just dazed by the fencing. It was miles and miles of white vinyl boards and posts, beautiful to the eye, and I know it cost at least ten dollars a foot, before installation. It was a quiet affirmation of undeniable wealth. We drove through rolling grassy hills, herds of shiny black Angus cows, and a few Longhorns mixed in. Five hours later, we landed outside of Amarillo at the Big Texan RV Park. You could take a shuttle to the Big Texan Steak House. It was practically a theme park.

We had no place to be in the morning other than back on the road. Mister and I could relax for an extra hour. There were still emails to answer, but we could squander time. We could take a long walk, meaning not that long because Mister is like a

Thoroughbred. More of a sprinter, if you catch his drift. Not into the endurance thing.

Mister got some treats broken up and stuffed in a Kong with peanut butter. No matter how long he barked at the Kong, none of the treats came out, so when the time was right, he went in after them. Mister has a rich inner life.

RV parks welcome dogs, as long as they are well-behaved and of approved breeds. Looking around, you might think that meant dogs under fifteen pounds. They looked at Mister like he was a weighty reptile dressed in a dog suit.

Most RV parks have pet areas and are naturally strict about cleaning up after your pet. The most interesting rule is that we may not leave dogs alone in RVs. I had no intention of leaving Mister, but they don't allow dogs in the laundry room or bathrooms. I'm not quite sure where they think the dog's going to be during a shower or when the wash goes into the dryer. They don't allow dogs to be tied outside either.

We keep a fifteen-foot leash attached to the handle by the door of the Rollin' Rancho, so Mister can sploot out if there's grass and cool his belly. Sploot is the official term for laying on the belly with feet splayed out behind like a flying superhero. I left the door open, a sure sign I didn't abandon him. If there's a picnic table, he'll climb up on top and stand guard. Well, he sat guard, but you get the idea. He's much more imposing from that height.

Sometimes dogs bark at each other, but I tell Mister he's a good boy and he stops. If he saw animals he wasn't sure of but thought they'd run, he certainly barked. Squirrels are always good to bark at because they jump fast, don't leave entirely, but grapple to the other side of the tree, just out of reach. If a cat was sitting there quietly under an RV staring at him, he was extremely cautious. She might leap forward and attack him, so he pretends to ignore her, but fools no one with his throat breathing. Cats can be treacherous and are often foreign spies.

Most people in the park had a studied lack of hurry. People

talked slower, walked slower, and took precise care of their RVs. Not quite enough to do to fill the time. Some folks unhooked their rigs, so the tow vehicle was free for day trips. At night, there were communal fires outside with folks talking, and wandering in and out of camps. I wasn't much for RV park society. Clinics gave me all the interaction I could take. We're reclusive, usually the smallest rig in the park, but I enjoyed having this slow-motion culture going on around us.

At this park, I felt like the only un-retired person in the world. I'm proud to still be working, and happy to be busy. But it's good to know there is a place where retirement isn't the same as settling down.

After an hour of email catch-up and a call with the Dude Rancher, Mister and I had a stretch of time before bed, so we loitered through a movie. Mister likes these nights the best. He got brushed, and we played more. Then we took the last walk of the night to look at the stars and be worried about where the squirrels were in the dark. We came back to tuck into our safe dog crate of a trailer. Our travel scheme would get a few tweaks, but it's a marvel all we have seen on this first trip.

Road Luck

We got up early and after packing up the Rancho, we were off for the last driving day. We'll be home tonight. I obediently made all the turns that GPS Woman told me to. I never have a view of a large map, but we're going vaguely in the right direction. And suddenly we're in the Panhandle of Oklahoma. We should be in New Mexico. It's okay. I started the day with a full tank of gas. It looks like she's taking us the back way home on county roads, but she didn't tell me upfront. That's the altered reality of GPS travel.

The landscape is rural and soon we're turning down remote two-lane roads. A small sign marked the Colorado border, our home state. I didn't see where the State Patrolman had parked, but I saw his lights flashing behind me now. If my truck has cruise control, I haven't found it, and I've looked. That lousy excuse won't help me. I pulled over and got my papers ready.

The officer walked up, making the obligatory duty belt adjustment, and asked, "Do you know how fast you were going?"

Mister sat up and looked at the officer, who greeted him with a "Hi, Fella." Mister let his ears go wider so the officer could enjoy them. I've had dogs who bark at people in uniforms, so this passed as a Ghandhi-like gesture.

His question struck me funny. "Apparently not." I chuckled out loud. "But I bet you know."

Pickups do this. My last speeding ticket was over twenty years ago, coming down a hill and coasting above the speed limit. Glancing in my rearview mirror, I can see it now. There's a long gradual hill and I've done it again.

Still smiling, because I'm getting a ticket for speeding with a trailer in tow. Feeling ridiculous, I gave him my license and registration. He went back to his car, and I reminisced about speeding while I waited for the bill. The first time I got pulled over, I was in high school. Another hill was involved, but I was going too fast on my bicycle. As the officer was lecturing me, my mother drove by and pretended she didn't recognize me. It was a small town and inevitably someone you knew went by. I'm still a little proud remembering.

Is a speeding ticket tax deductible, I wonder? The patrolman walked back and told me he was going to let me off with a warning. I smiled like the grateful and guilty minor criminal that I was and thanked him.

He asked what I was doing out on this road, and I told him I'd been working. He gave me the "Aren't you retired" look, and we chatted for a while about horse training. I told him we both give people tips about their driving and now we're friends. We had something in common. Like me, he tries to help by giving the bad news in a good way.

Whatever time advantage I'd gained by speeding has been lost by now. No other cars came into view during the time we stopped. In the end, I thanked him genuinely, not just for letting me off but for doing his job kindly. He wished me well, and I wholeheartedly wished him the same. The thing about Affirmative Training is it works on people too. He wasn't looking for a fight and I didn't start one.

Policing is a hard profession. When I was a young woman, I dressed like an artist, whatever that looked like. I meant to do my part to soften the antagonism. I smiled and waved when I saw an officer, hoping to be the exception to what felt like a rule against us. No one waved back. I'm still on the fringe of where I'm supposed to be, but maybe having white hair and being an irrelevant age makes me seem harmless, but don't take that bet.

I pulled back onto the road and rolled along below the speed limit. The officer passed me, and it took a while for him to go out of sight. A wave of relief that it was over, but it was more than not getting a ticket. Traveling this way, I'm profoundly aware of the luck of my birth. Being a white woman of a certain age, I don't have to panic at a traffic stop when it's a life-threatening event for so many. I can't look away from my privilege, my everyday reality that, although I don't fit in, I still benefit from. Sadly grateful, I say a prayer for those who didn't look like me and died just this way; a traffic stop one moment, and the next, God's human roadkill.

***

It was flat unfarmable land, and I was sticking to the speed limit now when GPS Woman told me to turn left a few miles before Springfield. I worried she might kid, but I did it and even used my blinker. I just want to get home. In a few miles, the pavement stopped, and a dirt road continued. There were fields now with farmhouses a distance from the road. The older ones had trees around them, planted by hopeful previous generations. I have about a quarter of a tank of gas left. It seemed like a bad idea to go back. Surely there was gas ahead that was closer.

The land slowly transitioned to usable farmland. If I ran out of gas, farmers usually have some. But I was so close to home and surely just ahead....

I hate this; I do not enjoy playing dare with a gas gauge. And now that I thought about it, I really had to go to the bathroom. Sometimes there were old buildings at the corners of intersecting county roads, but no gas stations. I valiantly stayed the course, but there weren't many options. Mister had been sleeping since our traffic stop.

My fuel light was on now. I bought this truck at the beginning of the pandemic and then didn't drive it much. I thought I had a few miles before we sputtered to a halt, but I don't know how many. Each time I saw a sign, I did the mileage math again. When the GPS Woman directed me to turn, I checked for close gas stations and then did the mileage math again. The fuel light taunted me and there was just enough traffic that pulling over to pee seemed like a bad idea. Mister was awake now, but he could hold it a lot longer than I could.

Then up ahead I saw a grove of trees larger than what farms usually have and miraculously the road went straight to them. It was an oasis with all we needed. While filling the tank, I used the facilities. I bought something to drink to pay the bathroom toll, and Mister and I took a quick walk. I explained we were almost home as we pulled onto a busier road than we'd seen all day. A couple of hours and we'd be there, I told him. He dropped his head to the console, and I rested my hand on it. He was pretty sure he was home already.

It's April 6th, 2022. The last miles are the slowest, over familiar roads with street names I knew. It might not have been a fully triumphant last day, but sometimes avoiding disaster counts as a win. As I crested the last hill before home, my farm was visible if you know just where to look. I could see my horses.

Home Stay
April 6–May 14

Flying to a Funeral

We are home. It's my dogs and horses who pay the biggest price for my travel, but it's the travel that pays the biggest price for their care. It buys hay. Mister and I headed for the backyard and Preacher Man and Jack jumped and howled. It was a joyous reunion, and Edgar Rice Burro brayed an opera of honks when he saw me.

Sliding back to my home routine, I was happily mucking up the used hay. I liked all the parts of having horses on my imperfect little farm. If I had been home more often in the last years, I would have taken care of the peeling paint on the trim a couple of summers ago. I don't let myself think too long about how I missed home. There's a big bag of laundry to do.

In a week, I fly to San Diego. It was my first flight since the beginning of the lockdown and I will wear a mask, but what else? What do people wear to funerals these days? I'm a little teary at leaving home again so soon, but I must go. I'd lost five friends in the last two years and never made it to one funeral. COVID-19 stopped me from the others, but I can go this time. So as soon as I was back, I packed again for a quick trip.

I got to the gate early to wait for my flight, plugged in my computer and started writing. Then I noticed a dead man sitting near me. I recognized him as a man I'd worked with over forty years ago. He hadn't aged a day, and I knew I was staring. The resemblance to my deceased friend was unnerving. He was a stranger, but I couldn't keep my eyes off him.

I was on my way to a different funeral, but seeing this look-alike was not even remotely surprising. Sometimes it feels like all funerals congeal together somewhere in the cosmos. As if funerals exist in a nebulous place and all the memories and sadness wait to converge and follow you to the next funeral. There is no boundary on grief.

This funeral in San Diego was for Scott, my longtime friend's husband, but I was always a little in love with him, too. I could listen to him tell a story, the details bright with humor. I didn't want the story to end. The joy was in his telling more than the plot. He would return the favor, asking questions to others that made that person feel interesting and acknowledged. I would have loved to hear his version of his own funeral.

It was a beautiful day in their church's garden, the seating in a wide half-circle. I found a seat off to the side and closed my eyes to breathe. This space felt sacred, but with so much fresh air to soak up our tears. I wanted to mourn him, this good man who loved my friend. The music began, and it was the best kind of memorial. Family spoke, we remembered him, and there was a video made by his younger family members that had us all laughing. Memories from others reminded us of what he meant in each of their lives, and we were all in tears. Our lives were unmistakably better for knowing him.

And I mourned the others, who also passed away during the pandemic.

JoAnn, the woman I met at eighteen when I got my first silversmithing job. I hadn't seen her in decades, but when she died, I got a call from the woman who hired us both. Calls like this rarely bring good news. She told me JoAnn had always followed news of me. I hadn't known that. She was so unfailingly kind, and I was a kid, just trying to hold my own, living in a strange place with no real friends. Or so I thought. I remembered her at the age I knew her. Life took us in different directions, but it lifted me to hear her name and to value her friendship again. Goodbye, JoAnn, I didn't forget you either.

I mourned the man I thought I saw at the airport. He was thirty when I was twenty. Richard shared his art studio and gave me a safe place to gain experience in doing art for pay, even though I was not quite housebroken. I roosted there until I found my footing. We shared an occupation of making one-of-a-kind wearable art and a habit of being socially awkward. Some thought he was a bit of a snob. Poor social skills are easy to mistake for rudeness. It's a line I struggle with, too. His work was groundbreaking. He left an enduring legacy of beauty, and he was kind to me at a time in my life when I needed it. Thanks for the workbench, Richard, where many things got hammered out.

I mourned Heidi. I had known her only a few years, but in many ways, I felt I'd always known; an author and a horsewoman who invited me to do a clinic and a friendship began. She had divorced and needed to sell her farm. It was tragic, and it was a new beginning. We brainstormed about our next chapters, and both of us shyly mentioned trailers. Then, the pandemic began. She traveled in a trailer smaller than mine to visit family on the East Coast, stopping at my farm for a sleepover, shower, and dinner. It was our last talk. She died not long after that trip. A sudden diagnosis of an advanced condition that she didn't want to kill herself fighting. Heidi, as wide as the view from your old porch, I miss you.

I mourned Elaine, who lived in England, maybe even more than the others. I was still raw for her. Not only had I known no one like her, I wasn't ready to say goodbye. We met online and fell in love with each other's words first. Her shared writing in our group resonated with me. Her dark humor was delicious. During a clinic tour, I invited myself for a visit, and Elaine was the only person who ever met me with a welcome sign. I got off the train and saw a bald woman holding a white rectangle of paper that read "Gray Mare." Her first words were that she was glad I bought the whole cancer scam so we could meet. Love at first sight and I felt the same warm feelings for her husband, Mark, who also became a friend. We spent time with her horse, Bruce. How that horse and she took turns caring for each other, different sides of the same coin. I mourn Bruce as a brother, who carried her over rough ground and died not long before her. I hoped he'd be there to meet her. Elaine was irreverent and very British, and we had so much life experience in common. Her voice rings in my ear, and I talk to her in phrases that I write and laugh at her jokes over the miles that I drive. Elaine, my forever friend, I will never let go.

Road trips are perfect for visiting dead friends. Aware of how selfish it is to love someone for how they make you feel, I still cry for all my losses. I cry for how I miss them, and because keeping them alive inside of me hurts.

And I mourned our shared pandemic scar over the last two years. For the distance added between each of us during lockdown. For the slow-motion, quiet loss of so many, we also seem to mourn our previous selves.

I know I stand closer to the line between them and me every day. It was contemporaries I lost, closer to my age than not. Or maybe I'm straddling the line, trying to make friends with death because it visits too often to snub while trying to honor those who have gone ahead by living fully each bittersweet day without them. "Make it good," Elaine said.

The Sunset Side
West Coast
May 13–June 30th

Westward, Ho.

I had almost a month at home this time before leaving again. I'd scheduled classes in the online school back before the Texas trip. It was good to be back in Zoom meetings where we talked about our horses while our indoor pets made cameo appearances, blocking out our heads on camera. We can't see enough cat butts and dog snouts.

I had precious hours working in the barn with my herd. Mucking was meditation; it was going to church. Sharing small body conversations that go on in the herd is a necessity, and there is no substitute for Edgar Rice Burro on any level. I even half-way liked the indoor chores and bookkeeping. Home was that exotic.

Being self-employed means you have the freedom to work unpaid overtime all you want. It's a benefit that ranks up there with all the unpaid vacations you can afford. So, I was grateful for the endless emails, planning, and consulting that continued. The hours planning online lessons. The passion that was my work by choice.

I had wonderful dinners with the Dude Rancher. That's

what he calls himself, you know. He's retired now and I'm sure it wasn't on his bucket list to do chores. We met in our fifties, and he might rather be in town. Living on a farm was never his dream, but he'd grown to love the prairie night sky. He'd read some of the heartfelt thank-you cards that come in the mail and he might see things about me online, not that he'd say so. My business isn't part of our marriage, and he isn't what you'd call an animal person, but he volunteered to spend this year mucking and feeding. It was a tremendous gift, not easy for him to offer. And like the adage, my absence brings us closer. Our daily conversations are a grounding link with home for me.

Too soon, I started the prep work for the next trip, which would be longer than the first shake-out drive to Texas. My clothes and sheets got washed and put back soon after I got home. I updated my dry food stash and repacked some wine. I did some upgrading on necessities. The bench cushions were too uncomfortable to relax on and I replaced them with some that turned out to be just as bad. It's always a mistake to buy things to sit on without trying them. I replaced a rug that was hard to clean with a rubber-backed one that was easier and didn't slip. Now that I had a bit of experience, I did better at repacking. Mister watched every step I took.

I slept in the trailer sometimes, because the bed was comfortable, the coffee was great, and it was a quiet place to write in the mornings. Mister insisted on joining me. Maybe he worried he'd be left behind, or maybe because Preacher Man and Jack wear on his nerves. I missed being alone with him now that the two of us were in the larger farm group. One half of our lives pushed and pulled against the other half for both of us.

On one of our last prep days, I emailed the host of our first clinic stop. They were near Taos, New Mexico, and I saw there were fires in that area, but I wasn't sure how close. Being kinder than I wanted to be, I offered to postpone the clinic. It's never fun to offer to give up income, but the organizer responded with a photo from her arena of clouds of smoke over the ridge and genuine regret. It was a sad and grateful exchange, with a plan to reschedule later in the year.

Like detention on the last day of school, I'd been ready to roll again, only to be grounded for two more days, tapping my feet and not sleeping well.

Finally, I headed south out of town on the same roads as my first trip. I made that same first rest stop in Raton and took the truck lane this time. Knowing where I belonged at a rest stop gave me a confident air. I was already long-haul cool. Still, just as small on the semi-truck side, I felt like a tiny impostor, so I swaggered in self-defense now.

We stopped the first night at a friend's farm, another dead-end driveway with a bit more turnaround space, but not much. It dawns on me that people who tell me their driveway is easy are familiar with their surroundings. It sounds obvious when I put it that way, but I was feeling a bit discounted. They have forgotten their parking stress because they have developed a method over time that works for them. My side is different. It's a brand-new dead-end every day for me, accumulated stress like dead bugs on the truck's grill.

There is the added stress of pulling a trailer for weeks at a time. Even grocery store parking lots can be a challenge, so driveways are a looming threat. We get in and out fine, but instead of making me confident, I whine more. I don't worry about breakdowns or wrecks or crime. I worry about driving into a tiny spot that I can't get out of. It isn't a fantasy; it's a near-daily event. I'd proved I was bad-assy enough to do it. But I feel the familiar afternoon dread, reverse, straighten, reverse, straighten, until we get parked eventually. Those RV Park pull-thru spaces were bliss.

My friend and I didn't hug, didn't get too close. It was still new being out after COVID-19 and she cares for elders. Call it modified social distancing, we don't want to take risks, either of us.

Getting sick while traveling is always a concern for me. I had a horrible cold on a clinic tour in Scotland and had to blow my nose and discretely hack phlegm for three headache-filled days. No sick leave is another advantage of self-employment. But I never thought it might kill me. Early in the lockdown, the pandemic death toll was staggering and the advice for folks over sixty-five seemed to be "stay home or die." I'd had every shot they could give me, but we all felt fragile and lonely and not sure how to behave socially. I kept a mask with me all the time, but in the conservative small town I lived near, they had become as much about politics as health.

My friend and I shared the same concerns. It was the perfect overnight stop. We had time to walk with her horses and talk. Her farm was in the mountains outside of Albuquerque and it had a stark beauty. Close to the desert but with hills and trees in the horse's turnout. We allowed each other to keep to our tasks. Rather than trying to inflate the event into something bigger than it was, we were grateful for the time we had. Mister and I slept so well that night.

Privilege and Poverty

Pulling out in the morning, I was nibbling on sunflower seeds and almost finished listening to *Klara and the Sun* by Kazuo Ishiguro. Driving through Albuquerque reminded me of the years I'd shown my artwork in Taos and Santa Fe galleries. The area had grown but remained an interesting place with distinctive architecture. Tourist trade had come back to life post-COVID-19. The art scene had always been a part of that world, and a special part of the economy. I began showing my work in this area in the 1980s. It was obvious that businesses had tried to maintain the ambiance of that era, but there was so much money there now. Expensive condos just off the Plaza that artists could never afford. There is a different upscale feel everywhere, except past the city limits. In most ways, it has to be seen as successful growth, but there is always something lost. After all this time, I was somebody else, too.

We headed southwest along I-40 toward the next stop in Nutrioso, Arizona, and on the way, we drove through the Acoma, Laguna, and Zuni pueblos. The changes in the landscape came gradually as I drove. There is no recent influx of growth here. This indigenous land had not changed since the beginning of time. The land was vast but not beautiful in ways we are used to recognizing. If you woke up and saw it out the window, it might frighten you at first. It was as if an enormous storm was coming but in rock formations instead of thunderheads. If there were predators on this land, they were not visible during the light hours. It felt abandoned or otherworldly.

The road was carved between long mesas of rust and black. This is near to the land where Geronimo and his warriors evaded the US Calvary for so long. I'd read about it, but seeing it brings the story to life. It's treacherous in broad daylight. The road got narrower and the cliffs of the mesas more extreme.

From the cab of the truck, it was safe enough, but what would it be like in the dark on the back of a horse? For the hundredth time, I wished I could ride the current landscape. Usually, I think this thought as I view a sweet meadow snaking up a hillside, but this is a skill ride and its history felt like a present danger. There would be no picnic at the end.

Signs mark the change from one pueblo to another, but I saw no one, almost no traffic. I can't imagine how anything, or anyone, can survive here, much less thrive. The answer was obvious, and it haunted me for the rest of the year. It wasn't new, it was older than Geronimo. We put the indigenous people on reservations and made treaty promises. We took the best land for ourselves. Even then, we didn't keep our word.

It is our history, or maybe human nature since it seems to cross cultures and come down through time. We have normalized our predatory inclination in every way possible. My father would totally agree with how the land was split. But all those years of making the family watch Westerns on TV didn't evoke the feelings in me that Dad wanted. Horse-crazy girls like me could tell the "Indians" were the best riders on the prettiest horses. That alone would have been enough for me to change sides, even if I hadn't seen their poverty first-hand.

Poverty was not so obvious living on good growing land. Reservations in Washington state are full of wildlife, and blackberry bushes are rampant in the woods. Even our two-acre home at the edge of town had an orchard. Driving here in the desert southwest, the land felt beautiful and cruel, more than any of the other reservations I knew. Living here looked desolate and painful. The line between privilege and poverty was never more extreme.

Ghost hooves still scrambled over rocks and leaped into the dark clouds that hung low over haunted canyons. The chase continued, both sides were still at odds, a low thundering in the distance.

By late afternoon, the land morphed into woods with ground cover between the low peaks of the White Mountains. We'd arrived in the right small town, but I got lost trying to find the farm, which was down dirt roads through a forest. The farm wasn't on a dead-end, but it also wasn't clear to GPS Woman. I still partly trusted her, which would become a rarer experience, but the year was young. After a few laps of a circular road, I gave up and called. My host was more than a little confused by my landmark descriptions. Apparently, all dirt roads through trees look similar. They sent out a search party and found us.

I finally understood that the big destinations, like states and cities with long miles between them, were easy targets for GPS Woman. But the last few miles were a crap shoot. I only got lost when I was less than five miles from my destination. Yet, five miles ended up feeling farther than five hundred at the end of a driving day.

I parked next to the barn, and my kitchen window view was an overnight pen for two horses and two long ears. My front porch opened onto a long meadow with tall mountains on the west side. It's the spot that makes you hold your breath as the sunset begins because you know it's going to be a whopper.

Mister and I strolled out. No dogs on this farm, so it was a challenge to find the dog bathroom. Mister doesn't want dog company, but he wants to know dogs have been there. He is very fastidious and would never want to pee in the wrong place. So, we walked and walked. He sniffed but continued. I kept my opinions to myself, but I had a hopeful poop bag in my hand.

Had those mesas really been those dark Halloween colors? I can't dismiss my mental images of that desolate gothic landscape.

On the third stroll by, Mister hesitated at the area where the manure got dumped out of the pens and away from the horses, to be hauled off-property later. So, there's no confusion, it's not a single pile of manure, it's the annual pile. Mister climbed toward the top and I followed because there was no way I wanted to distract him at this point. He crawled up the side, and I stepped, sometimes sinking up to my ankles in soft dry manure, right behind him. He still wasn't sure. This vegetarian poop smelled all wrong. More like food than waste. It was confusing.

I can relate to his dilemma. I hate navigating strange bathrooms, crowded public restrooms, and most of all, loos on airplanes. He will get no side-eye from me.

Wolf Alert

At this Barn Visit, I'm with a client that I've worked with online through the pandemic. It's just her and I, a private clinic that kind of redefines intensive. Training is so individual that meeting the horse and rider on their own land can be a real advantage for each of us.

The client's horse is Moonshine, a Haflinger, who doesn't like to be haltered, can be challenging to lead, and tends to counter-bend. He was good under saddle, and also kind, polite, incredibly smart, and, if anything, he tried too hard. A bit of a paradox, he was one of those horses better in the saddle than on the ground, which tells us a lot. Riding created less fear, before my client owned him, than his handling did. Too much repetitive harsh groundwork damages horses.

We talked about the anxiety he showed in his flank at the four o'clock position, diagonal from his withers, and in his muzzle area. We knew part of the puzzle was a history of gastric issues and she's working on that. My client had eliminated most of the counter-bending brilliantly. I'm impressed. We made a plan for the day: She had a new bitless bridle to fit to him and then try out. I do just what I always do. I wanted to return Moonshine's calming signals and prove that I was no threat to him, either.

Haltering is the heart of so much of what we do with horses; it's when horses surrender their autonomy to us. It's foundational but easy to get complacent about. My client wanted to help her horse in a kinder way, but he was still a prey animal. As loved as he was, he struggled with people close to his head. We talked about positions a bit farther from his face. We had a slow conversation about his anxiety and gave him time to soothe himself.

This is the moment I'll remember: The gelding was passively resistant, not bad but worried and reluctant. After conversing affirmatively, giving him time to think, he turned to me and offered to take the halter. His eye was steady and peaceful. He volunteered three times. Moments like that live with me forever.

We had two sessions on the first day, and both went well. Under saddle, Moonshine was a little confused by the lack of a bit and by me walking beside him, but we continued on, and he found his balance. Forward is the miracle cure. His calming signals were eloquent as he processed his day.

Mister and I had dinner in the Rollin' Rancho down by the barn. I sipped some wine while watching the sunset, and a herd of elk wandered up the meadow, grazing the pasture. I love my job.

The alarm went off at four a.m., but I was already awake, thinking about writing. Mister is a late riser, so he rolled belly-up and sighed. Sometimes relationships work that way. I made my coffee and got to it, writing until an online lesson at six.

My client was in Sweden, and she had a sweet young draft horse who was anxious. He had been pushed to think a little quicker than he wanted to, and my client had slowed it all down. She shared a series of videos, and I gave some input and ideas. In the last video, she tried leading him from behind in a neck ring with his head totally free. The horse's movement with no halter was stark and dramatic. So much freer now, the horse lifted his shoulder, and the first stride out was a huge soft step, with his neck long and his head naturally on the vertical. My client's done good work. He wears his new confidence with softness.

Most horses have similar anxiety. How we let horses know we are predators is by over-managing their heads on the ground and in the saddle. Our hands are weapons of correction, and we destroy their trust while giving ourselves a false sense of security. Calming signals fill that gap. Horses are absolutely intelligent enough to know that we can leverage them by pulling them out of balance. And when they submit to a halter or bridle, it's a pretty sacred moment.

My text notification dinged. "Anna, call me before you go outside." Huh?

Then, "Anna, the wolves killed an elk in our pasture, so stay close to the barn if you take Mister out for a walk. Game and Fish are coming to remove the carcass shortly. This may change our plans."

This was recent and the wolf had passed yards from my trailer. I didn't wake up Mister to tell him because, like I say, he sleeps in. I slipped outside and went up on the house deck to survey the scene. Wolves had pushed a small elk against the perimeter fence and brought her down.

As we were standing there, the wolf came back for a second

pass at the carcass. He was magnificent, black with a light-frosted silver sheen. His mask was bloody red. As massive as a German Shepherd, but he leaped the fence as light as a rabbit. You couldn't mistake him for anything else. Coyotes have a way of slithering and stalking, but this predator carries himself differently. You could see him push off from his haunches and launch himself across the ground, fit and strong. So handsome, this guy stood on all fours and watched us watch him. He didn't look away.

The Arizona Game and Fish Department had been actively involved tracking packs in the area, and they quickly arrived. Not everyone likes wolves, so it's touchy, but the officers were friendly and informative. They pulled their truck into the pasture. I got Mister out of the Rollin' Rancho and walked him a few steps down the road toward where they were picking up the carcass. We weren't at all close, but he jumped back and forth and lifted his nose high in the air. He didn't make a sound. Mister always focuses on his own survival and it was no time to bark.

They used a winch to load the small elk carcass on the back of the truck. The wolves brought the elk down from behind. Later I'd see white fur on the scene. But from this distance, I can see a huge red circle where the wolves had disemboweled the elk, at the four o'clock position on its flank. Moonshine had protected that same spot.

We looked up the meadow and noticed the first wolf was headed back again with two wolves following. The Game and Fish officers shot a couple of rounds into the air, frightening the wolves back toward their usual less-populated territory. Turkey vultures were floating in arcs over the site, as if tracing the circle of life. Earth is beautiful even now.

And there's still a hole in the fence, one broken post thrown into the road. It feels good to drive in a T-post, just to fix something. My client and I worked together quickly; she said it was now more of a "psychological" fence. We'd done a temporary fix, tied with twine, as one does. It's an unusual use of my skills, but our day was off the rails, and we didn't know how the horses would be.

It was a visceral lesson in the predator/prey dynamic. We couldn't be complacent today even if we wanted to. We considered canceling the session but went on step-by-step slowly. The horse would tell us as we listened to his calming signals.

It was late to turn out the horses and donkeys, but they had been spectating all morning. It surprised us when her horse let us know it was a good day to work. He was bright and interested in us. It was as if the events of yesterday were bigger than those of the morning. It was just us humans who were reeling at the blood and carnage.

We spent our last lesson together talking about how deep Moonshine's fear of controlling his head was, how restricted he felt in halters and bridles. He seemed different after a night of processing yesterday's lesson in patience. Perhaps he'd gained some confidence. Not entirely solid, but he was leading us from behind on this one. My client trusted the bridle, and so did her good gelding. They had a brief but breathtakingly beautiful ride.

It was a Barn Visit we didn't expect, and all the lessons were valuable. Predator and prey are always part of the unstated conversation between horses and humans.

I met Mister for supper and then he leaned into a nap before bed, and I reflected on my day. The elk didn't return that night, but I'm full of awe for horses who find ways to trust us, fear always in their minds as their nature demands. Horsewomen have a special understanding of both sides. We are born predators yet vulnerable as horses. We work for the place where we can be partners by choice.

Donkey Speed Traps

We folded down and pulled out early the next morning because we had a long drive across Arizona and two days to get to California. It was a four-hundred-mile drive today. We found our way back to the highway, a little proud to do it all on our own, then continued through Nutrioso and headed north. We left the mountains and forest as the land stretched flat to a massive plain with sparse vegetation. It was a state highway, which meant you never knew what it would be like. Maybe a well-maintained four-lane freeway or barely two lanes with the potholes right where you least expect them. We were on the latter, but there was no traffic and we were making good time. It's the kind of landscape where you can see the road disappear over the horizon and no cars in sight. It happens more often than you'd think.

Off to the right, I couldn't believe my eyes. There is precious little wildlife this morning, but there was a herd of bighorn sheep. They are the color of the ground and at first hard to see, much less categorize. They appeared to be grazing on isolated weeds and those weren't green. There must be water somewhere, but it doesn't seem possible. I've seen them in the mountains but never on flat land before, so I made a note to Google them later, just to believe my eyes now. (Their numbers have fallen, Google informed me. But there are desert breeds and mountain breeds.) As I drove past, they didn't lift their heads. They were home, and we were passing through on these straight roads with monochrome horizons in all directions.

In a couple of hours, Mister reminded me I needed a walk-about before getting on I-40, and there had been signs about the Petrified Forest National Park. This was something I should look up. I always think it's a bad 1960s sci-fi movie. I also might have paid better attention to this in school, but if it wasn't English or Art, I was daydreaming. Did everyone just stop action and turn to stone? News flash: it didn't happen to people.

Just to be safe, we drove past any risk of turning to stone, all the way to the freeway interchange. Then we took a stroll and got a cold drink. Mister was back to sleep before we made the on-ramp. He doesn't bother to look out the window while we drive. Most dogs sleep twelve to fourteen hours a day, but I am certain he is an overachiever on this, at home and on the road. But he also spends long hours watching me, whether I'm driving or in the Rancho. It's the kind of companionable relationship we both like. No kisses or cuddles, but we co-habit in the sweetest of ways. We hold each other with our eyes.

Just after Kingman, Arizona, GPS Woman gave me a last-minute direction to take the Old Route 66 exit. This doesn't raise alarm. She will re-route us sometimes if there are traffic delays and I don't have a handy way to double-check. I usually think I'll just wait and check it on my computer later, while Googling the lizard we just saw. Besides, what do I know?

In the beginning, there was normal enough traffic but soon much less. Many times, we weren't on major thoroughfares, so I wasn't concerned. In a couple of miles, I saw a sign that said no trucks. Again, I asked myself the existential question: What kind of truck do they mean? Probably no big rig semis. Could they mean no trucks like mine? Surely not pickups.

We continued farther, and the land became more desert-like and less populated, and the road was in worse repair. It was a weekday, or maybe it's always quiet here. Or is this GPS Woman playing another practical joke on me?

The road started to climb and curve to the top of a mountain. Depending on your vehicle, it was a not-quite-spacious one-lane or a very cramped two-lane road. Loose rocks covered the cracked concrete, and the total lack of side rails made the view over the edge of the mountain unobstructed as if that could be a good thing. I inched along slower and slower, aware of my trailer, so aware of my tires close to the edge. There wasn't much traffic, but that was little comfort. I still had to cling to the outside of the road, especially on corners. If someone or something came around a curve quickly, I would never see it until it was too late, even if both of us were inching along.

It was the exact opposite of the terrifying construction traffic in Dallas, crowded lanes with no visibility and full speed. It was the opposite except for the gripped steering wheel, the cramp in my lower back, and the anxiety I felt. Did I have a faint memory that Route 66 was how people used to get to California? But it couldn't have been on this road.

Motorcycles loved this road for its thrill. There were several on my tail pushing and swerving to pass me on blind curves the whole way up.

Then we came around a corner to find something even scarier than the cliff. It was a donkey standing well into the middle of the road. We swerved wider and my three-quarter ton, heavy-duty truck with a trailer rolled to a quick stop with half of our tires in gravel inches from the drop-off.

The donkey wandered up to my window like an old man taking tolls. He was thin and had some scars. Domestic animals, "returned to the wild," I wondered. They are tame enough to beg for treats and wild enough to be dangerous in traffic. Was this their job now? It was sad. These intelligent animals were in a precarious place. I didn't give him anything. I didn't want to contribute to teaching them to make roadblocks. Mister was awake. It was not a napping stretch of road, and the donkey and he sized each other up. They took stock of each other's eyes and ears. Mister would never bark with this kind of size disadvantage. He was pragmatic that way.

I forced a deep inhale and pulled out, watching in my rearview as the trailer lightly grazed the donkey's jaw just enough to pass. His stubborn hooves didn't move. How many get hit on the road? But I just wanted to get to the next campground. I just wanted to stop driving. The stress was making everything a bit too surreal.

Exhaling, we got to the top. There have been tiny pull-offs along the way, the size of a compact car, but usually, I couldn't see them until I was already half past them. Slamming on the brakes with a trailer behind you is always a bad idea. I kept rolling along because I thought going downhill would be easier. It only goes to show how little I know about one-lane mountain roads.

The truck was heavy enough that it pulled our coasting to a quicker speed than I wanted to go on these turns, so I ended up riding the brake. Everybody behind me wanted to go faster. I tried to pull over if I had enough space, but it just wasn't there. I had to pump on my brakes even more and I worried I'd get hit from behind. Tailgating was a contact sport on this mountain pass. The hood of my truck was still high and boxy. In ordinary traffic, it's hard to see upfront. My view behind was even worse.

Finally, I saw a sign for Oatman. A town, relief, almost back to roads my rig might fit on. It ended up this was an old mining town, turned tourist trap, and I had met the first greeter donkey. It's a one-lane town filled with tourist stores with goods out on the sidewalks and rainbow whirligigs with streamers flying from every awning. The rustic buildings were tricked out for a party, not that I could take my eyes off the road to look. Donkeys were everywhere, on sidewalks and in the middle of the road, adults and babies, not tame and not wild. It would be a tight squeeze to pull through the busy town in a tiny car. There's little hope for the tandem barge I was driving. We rolled along the speed of a walk with lots of stop-and-go. I needed a drink of anything cold, but I couldn't have found parking if I wanted to.

I was that special hard-boiled-tired, but this complicated drive wasn't over. We inched along, stopping every few feet for a tourist to pet a donkey. The donkeys were smart enough to know who to stop, but humans were so obvious. They plant themselves and wait. People are easy marks for a treat. I'm not sure what people love so much about feeding treats. If people thought they were connecting or forming some bond with these wild donkeys, they're wrong. Feeding donkeys fed the storekeepers more likely. I didn't want to be the one to tell them they were doing more damage to these than good. The donkeys were just as pragmatic as Mister, holding their line.

Miners left the donkeys after the gold rush played out, I read later. And I know donkeys are easy keepers, living on much less than other equines. Still, this number was hard on such fragile land. I'm hoping the treats they are all being fed are healthy, but this isn't a clinic, and they didn't ask for my input.

As I was leaving Oatman, the road to the west was wider. This was the well-traveled road all those tourists took, not the secret outlaw mountain entrance I had used. We came up behind a hot red sports car with a middle-aged man in a suit behind the wheel, stopped in the right lane of a perfectly fine two-lane road. Donkeys filled the left lane. It was a small herd of five, including a young foal.

The man's arm came out the driver's side window offering the donkeys a treat, a literal tourist trap laid by long ears. But they didn't want the treat, whatever it was. It was a standoff. I couldn't get around and so I settled for a front-row seat to watch the donkeys ignore this guy. I've trained donkeys and had several of these life-altering personalities on my farm. They are contrarians who forever hold their own best council. The more you hurry them, the slower they go.

I knew how it would end. Donkeys are smarter than people. This group seemed to tease the man. It was good donkey fun, but they don't know about the number of terrible possibilities ahead for donkeys who block traffic. This wasn't like throwing bird seed in the yard. How could this ever be a good idea? The donkeys are all thin. There's no real vegetation here for grazing and the population is clearly exploding. I saw youngsters every-where. Was this herd being managed in any way? How many of them get hit on the road every year and killed, and what could this adult man gain by baiting donkeys with food? He was still waiting for them to come to his window.

I assume the businesses in town who depend on these don-keys to keep tourists coming, feed them a little and there was probably water there. But it was obvious the numbers were too high. I was afraid for the donkeys, but I had to let them be God's donkeys. I hope they have some human advocates, too, looking out for their welfare rather than the town's bottom line. Mister let me know he's done sitting in a parked truck, but no way can he get out. Donkeys are territorial and don't like dogs.

Eventually, the man threw something at the donkeys and sped away.

I wanted this day to be done. My muscles ached and the bones in my feet were cramped. This day's drive was a monster, and I wanted to have a word with GPS Woman about how we ended up there at all. An hour later, we pulled into the Cross-roads RV Park in the Mojave Valley on the west side of Arizona.

Over dinner, I asked Google and sure enough, in 1952, they moved the route from Oatman to eliminate a "twisty, hazardous section of highway." Better yet, they counted the curves at a hundred-ninety-one in eight miles. The number seemed low to me.

Steinbeck called Route 66 "The Mother Road" in *The Grapes of Wrath*. More like "Mommie Dearest" Road, I thought, a great place to scare children. And I wondered how those Dust Bowl refugees coming west for work managed it. Then I stopped whining.

I found there are advocates working on the problem of feral donkeys, with all the complications you would expect. Tourists and donkeys get involved in accidents, some fatal. The donkeys are thin and clearly breeding. Starvation was coming soon with over-population, along with erosion of the fragile ecosystem. They know the donkey problem needs to be handled, but the answers aren't easy. There will be a price to pay for all of them, but especially the donkeys.

One idea was to shoot the donkeys, like deer season, the proponents said. I stopped reading and closed my eyes. Well, I imagine that would attract tourist-sportsmen who wouldn't buy rainbow whirligigs or creations from local artists. On the high side, they wouldn't have to get out of their cars, and it would be hard to miss at that range. Easier than passengers shooting buffalo from moving trains in the mid-1800s and that took care of a large animal population. The article said they debated it, but the idea was "shot down." Arf.

Truly, well beyond enough for today. When Mister suggested we go out on a squirrel reconnaissance mission, I followed him.

Bilingual Dogs

We headed off early to miss the worst of the heat as we crossed the Mojave Desert to Bakersfield, California. The land was immense, with flat horizons on four sides and all open to the sky. The ground faded to a mirage of air. This khaki-colored landscape only defined the edge of the sky; the only conversation to be had here. The land was dry, but not wild. There's no feeling of possibility, only a long history. I wonder if it's a reservation, but I haven't seen any signs. I was just learning to recognize the general land type.

Hours passed. At midday, we took a small off-ramp, going nowhere as far as I could tell. I lifted Mister down from the truck for a break, but his feet didn't move. He looked at the ground, no steps at all. I touched the sand, and then I picked him up and buckled him back in his seat. He's always right about these things. The sand was scorching.

During our driving days, I've been teaching Mister to tilt his head when I ask a question. He needs another gesture other than his go-to, letting his ears go wide on his head, which he does in a range of situations. It's like the elastic on his skull lets loose.

Training odd tricks isn't an original idea. When I had my Doberman, Fritz, I read that Hunter S. Thompson taught his Doberman to attack with the word "Nixon." Years later, I accidentally taught Fritz to do a similar thing, only I kind of cheated.

Fritz was already bilingual. He knew the word breakfast, asked with a question mark lift to my voice at the end. And the phrase *petit dejeuner*, French for breakfast, but also with a question mark intonation at the end. One day I was having a conversation, and I responded to the other person with the question, "Republican?" Fritz was wild for anything that ended in a question mark by then, so he bolted out of the living room and into the kitchen. And a star was born.

It's not quite the same, but you can't tell when we might need it. There I was, asking Mister all sorts of questions. Then I tilted my head, chirping praise when his answer was to tilt his head back at me. It doesn't matter what the question was. Mister isn't a slave for treats; praise is a reward he totally understands. If we were staring at each other, he seemed to want words, so I searched for questions to ask him. After the question mark, he tilted his head so far to the side that one ear stood up like the Statue of Liberty reaching for the sky.

Sometimes he started it by tilting his head at me, and I thought perhaps I hadn't heard Mister's question. Then we each tilted our heads from one side to the other, listening. Now that I think about it, I'm not sure it wasn't him who taught me. But we both look irresistible, n'est-ce pas?

This desert drive went quicker than expected, or maybe anything that wasn't twenty-five miles an hour over a one-lane rocky pass felt fast. We landed mid-afternoon at the River Run RV Park. When I opened Mister's door, he looked dubious. We had green again, and there were shady trees and dogs in other sites. I lifted him down on the damp, cool grass, but I could tell he didn't trust it after that midday sand. From that time on, every time I opened his door, he checked the temperature of the surroundings. We were always in a strange place that wasn't home. Burning desert sometimes, but it was cooler now. As soon as he was done with his peeing business, he wanted to go into the Rancho.

We spent the rest of the afternoon answering emails, chewing on toys, and eternally cleaning up dog hair. As much as people want me to do my laundry when I arrive, it's one of those things I see as unprofessional. Not to mention that after a week, my bedclothes have as much hair as a horse blanket, even though I vacuum daily. So, I did some wash, and unpacked and charged up my microphones for the next clinic.

In the morning, as I was folding down and getting ready to leave, an older couple in a truck rolled to a stop to say hello. I remind you I don't look in the mirror often and they are probably closer to my age than I want to admit.

She was wearing a mask, and I pulled mine up and took a few steps toward them. Her eyes smiled, and she asked if I was traveling solo and I said no, I have a dog. She asked, but are you alone on the road? I look over at Mister. No, I say again, not alone. But finally, I understood what she was asking and said, just one driver.

She says she could never travel alone, and she thinks I'm brave. I don't have an answer; I feel safer in my body than when I was younger. As far as I know, there have been no mass shootings in RV parks. I was as safe as anywhere.

She said again that I was brave. I followed her eyes to my rig and wondered how we looked to them. If they saw something I was missing. Mister was sitting in the middle of the picnic table watching us. I told them I traveled for work.

The man had seen the logo on my jacket by then and asked if I worked with horses. I told them I was on the way to a series of clinics up the coast. I couldn't tell if his surprise was because of the unusual job or that I was working at all. He asked if I was online, and I told him yes. He probably does the end-of-day Google searches like I do.

They were proud retirees with two small dogs in the back seat and they stayed at RV parks for weeks at a time, enjoying the surroundings. Her health wasn't good, she said with her eyes still smiling, but travel this way was easy. They're best friend spouses who don't interrupt each other, a noticeable politeness.

And they are the first RV people to say more than hello since I started traveling, but then, I don't sit out much at night.

We said goodbye, and it felt like we'd shared a moment. I wanted to touch the woman's arm in her window but kept my social distance and wished them well. The man slowly pulled away as she and I waved to each other, lingering a little longer than need be. Masks didn't hide our feelings at all.

Wine Country Clinic

I finished folding down the Rancho and switched Mister from his porch leash to the walking leash. Then I asked if he wanted to get in the truck. I always ask because I need to know he's doing okay with this travel. He's a stoic dog and life on the road had its stresses. He is never off the leash. There is a lot of truck time and then days waiting in the Rancho while I work. For all the limitations, places I can't take a dog, time restrictions, pounds of dog hair, and a million other inconveniences, I want Mister with me. But I recognize he faces limitations in being on the road as well, so prioritizing his needs is at the top of my list.

When we're home, Mister plays bitey-face with the other dogs, barks at coyotes, and watches me do chores from a lawn chair in the yard. On the road, he's an only dog who gets more chewies than at home. We spend more time scratching and playing. We go on squirrel hunts, barking but we'd both faint if one fell in his mouth. But is it enough? He gives me the look that lets me know he isn't an only dog. He is *the* only dog.

Today Mister trotted beside me to the truck, and I opened the passenger side and asked if he wanted to load up. It's a choice. He gave me a wag and stood with his front feet on the running board. One day he may not, but today he does. I hoisted his backside as he gave a little jump with his hind legs to help me lift him.

It was mid-May and today we were driving north to a facility outside of Sacramento. We're on CA-99 traveling through the

Central Valley, a long flat area with some of the most verdant farmland I've ever seen. Winter wheat shimmers in the breeze as the combines roll, harvesting in the spring. Recently baled hay lays scattered through the fields. Corn had the greenest green, but the variety of crops seemed infinite.

After these recent days of driving in the desert, the abundance was overwhelming, and I stopped at a farm stand for some perishables. I was still thinking about the migration west over that devil of a stretch on Route 66. This land must have looked like a garden with enough for all. Like California could solve all their problems. There was more water then.

Skimming through small towns, everyone was busy at work. It was easy to forget this is how we live. Not in Hollywood, but here. These fields have so much barren land in other states to make up for, so many of us to feed. Pray for rain, and cross your fingers, that we learn to do better than we have. This planet has been so generous.

Our first stop was a facility in rolling hills with wineries on all sides. The vines ran in neat diagonal rows over the hillsides, and we set up under the arms of an enormous tree. It looked like a tree in a children's book, covered with huge knots that made it look like a gnarly old elf-human. We had three days of riding and writing ahead, and we got comfortably settled in.

Mister and I were practicing some dog agility on farm implements when the owner pulled up to give us a tour. Mister climbed into her golf cart, onto the seat next to her, and planted his big flipper on her thigh with blunt intimacy. He had avoided other golf carts, but today, he was very nonchalant.

We had neighbor donkeys auditing this clinic, lined up at the fence. And there were long-time blog readers taking part. There were lots of auditors at this clinic, so the questions were great. We had fine weather; the organizer was fabulous, and we had a wonderful weekend of riding lessons and honest sharing. As usual, I had a plan, but so did the horses, and we took their suggestions.

The participants really pleased me at this stop. We worked together well, and talked about what the horses were saying with their behaviors. It wasn't about correction, it was about listening and understanding. There were some fabulous rides. Some horses made quick beautiful changes that rewarded their rider. Others let us know their trauma was deeper, but even with that, listening and acknowledging was the answer that was needed. Their calming signals showed palpable relief. Sometimes that is the win. The riders were as inspiring as the horses in their willing, cheerful learning. The organizing had been impeccable, and my part was easier for it.

We finished with a writing day on Monday. The readings were amazing and heartfelt and inspiring. You could tell because Mister, sitting in a lawn chair in our circle, stayed awake all afternoon, watching the person reading with interest. He is a literary dog.

Then the three-day clinic ended, and we said goodbye with the genuine emotion of having come through an endurance test on the winning team. I was running on vapors. It seems most of my life I am at work while others are on vacation. Being "on" takes focus. Horses and people are subtle but in different ways. It's my job to listen, so no blinking. Then it's my goal to tie similarities together in horse behaviors and human, and then back again. I want us all to end up feeling more confident.

But whether I succeed or fail, I'll be footsore, and finally drag myself back to the Rancho so Mister can remind me it's all about him. I'm relieved to hear it. I needed the break.

Tuesday morning, Mister was ready to have a driving day, but I hadn't recuperated. We would have a couple of days off, but first, we had to drive two and a half hours to the Sonoma County Fairgrounds by Santa Rosa. I'd planned to stay a week at that location. The next weekend, there was a one-day clinic and a writing workshop with a day in between. It was Memorial Day Weekend coming up, so I reserved the spot, knowing it would be a busy camping weekend.

For now, we drove through more vineyards. Every mile I become less of an actor playing the part of a clinician and more normal, the usual profane and introspective me. Mister seemed satisfied to have me to himself and I listened to my current book, *The God of Small Things* by Arundhati Roy.

***

A brief history of my reading: We had no children's books growing up, but I would have never sat still long enough to read, anyway. My father sometimes cracked a Louis L'Amour book, but I don't remember my mother ever reading more than a rare article in Reader's Digest at a doctor's office. It was no surprise that I was a poor reader in grade school.

Shakespeare changed everything in high school. The class groaned at the assignment, but I could understand his language. I kept the secret at first. It embarrassed me and scared me at the same time. It was the first time I felt smart, but part of that was the English teacher who took an interest in me. Long book reports followed. I had discovered reading, and I wanted to talk about it. This outstanding teacher should have regretted the extra work. Instead, she gave me independent study and introduced the Greeks. I started cutting classes to read Euripides, cementing my fate as the least cool girl at William Winlock Miller High School. Ask me how I feel about teachers, and I will choke up every time.

College didn't work out, but I began a homeschool degree in literature by reading every classic I could find by English authors like Austin, Bronte, Hardy, or D. H. Lawrence. Not exactly a panorama, but when I'd ransacked England, I moved on to the greater world. When I wasn't reading, I was at the movies. I wanted stories in my head, no matter how they got there. Then I started making up my own.

It came to an abrupt halt when I had my midlife crisis. I

moved to my farm, where the work never ended, and by the time I fell into bed, I got no farther than reading the same sentence night after night. Exhaustion strangled reading.

Had I never heard of books on tape? Yes, and no. The technology was just developing then but slowly. I didn't live in town, and libraries were a block of time to be squeezed in while doing errands.

I stalked Audible like a romantic love interest. Finally, I splurged. I joined, just for a trial, and downloaded twenty free books to start, ones I'd wanted to read and some that I could have the luxury of re-reading. Like friends living far away, I'd missed them. I read new books by favorite authors; children I hadn't met from a beloved family. I read genres that wouldn't have been worthy of precious reading time before, but now I can read for sheer entertainment. I lounged in a gluttony of words. Words when I mucked. Words that commuted with me. Books that helped make sense of my life.

And here I am, driving long hours, with my nose buried in a book. This kind of reading gave me the contradictory feeling of reclining with a good book that kept me awake. Usually, both reading and driving sent me to sleep. Reading that didn't need my eyes and let me focus on the road while the story came to life. It made driving between long flat horizons interesting. It rewarded me every morning when we began our driving days until we parked for the night. I spend entire days in other worlds and times, reading as easy as breathing.

I've read so many wonderful books this year. They have informed, inspired, and been the very best company. Audible is a character as constant in the background of this trip as GPS Woman. There was always a story simmering in my mind, an escape door from stress and drudgery. Audible is my true vice. I smack it like a smart aleck with a sticky wad of gum.

Sonoma County Fairgrounds

The Sonoma County Fairgrounds felt nostalgic immediately. During my horse competition years, I camped in my horse trailer sometimes at shows, so this sort of location was bare bones but comfortably familiar. The bathroom was clean enough, there was a laundry, and there had been enough dogs there that Mister could sniff his way to digestive health. This place was affordable. Gas prices were averaging about $6.50 a gallon, and there was nothing I could do about that.

When I planned the trip, I did it online, planning every stop before leaving home. Coast to coast, I made reservations ahead because I have no sense of humor left by late afternoon. I think you've noticed that. So, I looked at my choices and picked ones that were lower priced but had easy access. My needs are few and travel costs add up. I never eat out. I pack my lunch and eat frugal dinners, but never cut back on dog chews. Most of all, first thing in the morning, I like to know where I'll be that night.

When I pulled into the fairgrounds, I could tell this RV park was different. There were older campers that people were living in. No feeling of affluent retirement anywhere. There were kids playing and dogs tied out. It was as lively as small towns used to be.

We unfolded and then unhooked from the truck for the first time since leaving home. Over the next week, we'd park here and drive to our locations. Then we took a nap, something Mister would cheerfully join me in, even after sleeping most of the day driving. By late afternoon, the air was cooler, and we walked out of the RV park and into the neighborhood toward a park we drove by on the way in. There was a soccer game happening and lots of family picnics. People were watching us, not overtly but not casually either. There were other dogs there, but few people who looked like me. A group of young men sitting on a parked car all stopped talking and turned their shoulders toward us as we walked past. We got to the far end of the park and sat down on a bench. The playground was down there, and the kids watched us, too.

It felt like I didn't belong. I smiled at people who didn't smile back. When I was younger, no place felt safe from aggressive eyes and catcalls, but I'm an older woman now and not on the meat market.

Maybe I was paranoid after the recent comments about traveling solo, but it was also pretty easy to pick up on general feelings. GPS Woman is neutral about destinations, she just points the direction. It doesn't show neighborhood lines. Or to be blunt, color lines. GPS Woman had an early warning system for poverty, noting the borders of reservations, but no lines are marked here. We sat on a bench for a few moments and then crossed to the far side of the street and walked back the way we came. I kept my eyes straight ahead. It was time for dinner.

More vehicles had returned from their day's excursions by the time we found our site again. The Rancho was always the smallest trailer, and it got lost between the other big boxy rigs. Across the lane, there was a large fifth wheel and now there were two construction vehicles with company names stenciled on the doors. A group of five or six men in work clothes sat outside drinking beer and talking in Spanish. There was more outdoor cooking going on and kids playing. Lanterns glowed as dusk came. No campfires allowed, but plenty of lawn chairs in arranged in circles. By ten o'clock, everyone was inside, and the camp was quiet.

The next morning, as I was sitting in bed writing just before dawn, I heard hushed voices and footsteps on the gravel. The two construction trucks quietly started up and rolled out, barely making a sound. It took until this moment to recognize that I'd finally found the other workers. At this RV park, no one was retired.

Some RV parks don't allow rigs over ten years old. They do it to keep the shabby people out, but I had the feeling a restored

Airstream could still get in. Some RV parks have mostly long-term residents and a couple of overnight spaces. I was figuring this new culture out, understanding there was a hierarchy of RV parks like neighborhoods in cities.

COVID-19 created a boom in the RV business, new and used. I had read that lots of people who had lost jobs or homes were living in RVs until they could settle again. People purchased them to park on their land for family members who needed a place. It was cheaper than building an addition. Others took to the road looking for work, and towing a trailer was cheaper than renting an apartment. And you could keep what you had for a home with you if circumstances changed, and they frequently did.

All were welcome at the Sonoma County Fairgrounds. It was affordable and clean enough. It was *Nomadland*, the movie, and I was living there for the next week.

Cujo and the Toddler

Memorial Day Weekend is usually a good time for a clinic, but the scheduling for this weekend had flipped twice. Locations shifted, then a late cancellation, and more confusion. At the last moment, another location opened. Scheduling clinics can take as much time as doing them. COVID-19 didn't help that equation. I thought about it before I left home, but now I was experiencing it in real-time.

In the end, there was a clinic day on Saturday, Sunday was a day off, and there was a writing workshop at another farm on Memorial Day Monday. I commuted from the fairgrounds with Mister and returned there each evening. A day off in the middle left us more out of rhythm than rested.

Getting back after the clinic all day Saturday, we found the RV park had filled with weekend revelers, and they squeezed in some extras on the wider lanes. There were neighbors five feet away on all sides. It hadn't been a problem leaving in the morning, but I could barely find our site when I got back that night. The crowd obscured visual landmarks; the lanes were overcrowded, and we didn't see our Rancho until we passed the site.

Mexican music boomed with the bass pumped up. There was a bumper crop of kids running and shouting, and even more vehicles double-parked along the lanes. The smell of chilies and onions on the grill filled the air, and I wasn't cooking any. My bag of salad looked not just unappetizing, but pathetic. They abandoned the nightly curfew. By dawn, there was so much trash that it was hard to get Mister's poop bag into the dumpster.

On Sunday, I broke down and drove to get Mexican food and cold beer. Then I settled in to answer yet more emails, while Mister was in a picnic table sploot, protecting the Rancho when he was awake.

Monday, we drove to the writing workshop, a farther distance away and down roads that made me grateful I didn't have the trailer along. GPS Woman kept her calm, but I knew she was confused. We found the farm, an impeccably kept older facility with a central pond. It was an ordinary writing event, meaning it was breathtaking and unique in every way, and the day passed quickly. One writer asked me to dinner, and I agreed but with stipulations. Mister had been waiting all day in the truck. It was a mild day; he was in the shade with a fan on him, but at five p.m., I was his dog. We had to go someplace he could come along.

At a restaurant with outdoor seating, we were conversing and finishing our dinners. Mister was happy to be out. He was quietly sitting under the table, not interested in saying hello to strangers but doing some casual people-watching, as one does. That was when it happened. This sort of incident was never easy.

Mister and I both caught an odd glint of light and a high-pitched squawk. Other diners turned their heads, too, with initial alarm. The glinty thing moved in jerky motions. Obvious prey. Maybe a bird with a broken wing trying to escape a cat?

What do you see when a little girl in a tutu squeals and dances in a street-side restaurant? Danger? How about when you hear bells banging on her little feet, tapping and twisting as she twirls? Her parents cheer. What's on fire? Do those tennis shoes light up? Can you hear her screeching laugh? She takes erratic, unbalanced steps because she's a toddler. Sometimes a knee seemed to give out, her arms swinging in an alternate non-rhythm. Is it a rabbit caught in a spangly trap? She squeaked in a high-pitched squeal again and again. Was it her battle cry? Was she attacking?

Mister was startled as he surveyed the scene. The crowd changed, too. He didn't understand, so he barked.

To be honest, it didn't start with this dog. Getting in trouble with parents is a constant if you have working dogs. Howdy, my Briard, helped with a little boy who went rogue. Briards herd, but rather than creeping along like a Border Collie, they use their head. You might see them move like a skid steer behind a resistant sheep, pushing them forward. You might feel their forehead pressing your back if you were slow to get out of the truck.

On that memorable day, a group of people were at my farm. It was fine until the boy's mom saw her boy trotting toward the pasture, with Howdy herding along behind. I knew because Howdy had just shot me a look of concern about the youngster leaving the herd of adults. Mom noticed a minute later and let out a panicked yell and the boy got scared and ran. Howdy saved the day by putting his head in the middle of the boy's back and bumping him to the ground. Then Howdy sat, ready for praise.

Did I mention Howdy was twice the size of the boy? The mom told me my dog was aggressive and needed to be punished, but he did a better job of watching her child than she did. I didn't remind her of that part. The toddler wasn't hurt and Howdy immediately came when I called him.

The blessing of seeing both the dog's side and the kid's side is that there's no blame, just understanding everyone was behaving naturally. Training against instinct is doable, but how often do we blame the animal, expecting them to subdue their instinct? We don't even consider that we could change ourselves in any fundamental way. Like the mom not yelling when she got scared because it might set off a chain reaction that would escalate the situation.

Back in the restaurant, it got quiet, except for Mister barking at the toddler. I looked around at the horror on the other diner's faces. Mister, who was "cute" a minute ago, had gone full-Cujo, vicious in their eyes. How dare he, they thought? Anyone could see the little girl was darling.

I've become non-human. Not that I see both sides, I've *changed* sides. I saw a little girl who was jangling oddly and moving like prey. Injured prey, actually. She might as well be a dying bunny who had interrupted our dinner. Humans try to be tolerant of kids. They like her dancing here, but probably not so much if they were on an airplane. Another idea I didn't share.

But her joy wasn't her fault, and her parents loved her. It isn't Mister's fault, either. He's not just a herding dog, but one tasked with the unreasonable job of guarding me. A habit I don't want to disabuse him of because I am prey myself.

I tell him he's a good boy because it's true, and knowing that scaring him with a correction will only add to the drama. Now the crowd thinks I'm wrong for not hitting my dog and they might turn on us. Mister barks again because now the ambient anxiety of the crowd is egging him on. He is at my feet, directly between me and the toddler, not pulling forward. And he lowered his voice to a mumble.

The toddler continued her dance, in blissful ignorance of the ripples sent out by that tutu. The crowd's anger with Mister seemed to grow. They had a vigilante glare. I imagined us on a hastily built gallows in the outdoor dining area. We both stood on chairs with nooses around our necks, looking soulfully into each other's eyes as we awaited our doom.

Take a breath, folks. She was thirty feet away and Mister was on a leash. He gave a few barks to express his anxiety, but it wasn't a crime. It was a nearly involuntary response for those who travel in a pack. Even a toy poodle knows that. Mister settled as I scratched him, quiet now. I got disapproving eyes, but it wasn't my job to give the crowd a show. The server, who looked like someone cool enough to have a cattle dog at home, hurried to bring the check and pave our escape. The lynch mob went back to their dinners.

Fair warning: if I'm attacked by a toddler from Mars in a sparkly tutu, there may be utter chaos, but Mister will stand his ground. In the middle of the conflict, I'll give an exhale to dull the roar and say good boy to remind him who he is. Any dog who barks at a kid doing an impression of a dying rabbit can't be all wrong. But in Mister's view, there was always more at stake than one sparkly thing.

By the time we got back to the fairgrounds, most of the weekend RVs were gone, and the ground looked bruised and on the way to a hangover. I had deflated a bit myself, aware that I protect Mister as much as he does me. Aware that I will always live in that unpredictable space between humans and animals.

Mister was tapping his toenails. Morse code for dinner time.

The Russian River

After staying in one site for a week, it felt good to hook up. We continued driving north, the land more familiar now. Coming back to the Russian River gave me pause. My boyfriend and I had planned a road trip from our hometown of Olympia, Washington, to San Francisco. It was 1972, and I had just graduated from high school and saved the money. Of course, my parents refused to let me go.

Not that they had something they needed me for, other than daily chores. It was just the habit of saying no to every idea I had. Teenagers always complain that their parents don't let them do anything. I was no different, but complaining about it doesn't mean it wasn't true. Besides, it was a little hypocritical. I'd been disowned and sent away the previous year. A family that I babysat for took me in for a few months. Then reluctantly, my parents brought me back, but it didn't heal the rift and they weren't happy to have me.

"No" was the primary language in our home. It didn't work, but it was all we knew. On this occasion, it felt a little short-sighted to refuse this trip. I would leave home in two months, anyway. By then, our family was decomposing. My siblings were gone, and the house was black with anger. I told my mother I was going on this trip, and we fought. She struck me, but it didn't knock the wind out of me that time; it let some in. My boyfriend and I left the next day.

Our first event on the trip was the Ashland Oregon Shake-speare Festival. That's how wicked and rebellious I was. Straight As on my report card, didn't do drugs, and my boyfriend was a geek. These days, a senior trip is a common way for kids to wander out a bit before leaving home. That was all we wanted.

The boyfriend moved on a year later. I didn't make it to my fiftieth-class reunion this summer. My parents both passed away over twenty-five years ago. I hadn't thought about that trip in forever, but now I was driving the same road we took in my boyfriend's VW Bug. There was a glimpse of the Russian River, and I recognized the place we skinny-dipped. The campground with the hot springs was nearby.

A totally unexpected bit of time travel, but there's nothing like quiet time driving for memories to return. Just like finding keys to an old diary, had I ever loved like I did that first time? Maybe because I was driving instead of flying over, or maybe it was seeing the road that took me away. Memories ambushed me and dragged me back to a time when another journey began.

I thought once I got away from home, everything would come right. It took a while to figure out the problem was more than location. I had been overly optimistic about the time it would take to heal. Disowning me became a new habit, even an improvement. Our fighting slowed, and we all progressed to holding angry grudges instead.

Driving north through the forests of northern California, I felt doused with conflicted memories of teen love and family hostility. Seeing that river, the scars from that time became tender again. How far I had gone since those days. And how far I had come. My parents repeatedly warned me how each and every wrong decision would ruin my young life forever. But seeing that girl through a tattered fifty-year-old veil, she was totally recognizable, totally loveable. She hitchhiked back then, and I picked her up now, glad to have that wild girl along.

***

Mister and I had one night of nostalgic overthinking camped in Weed, California. In the morning, we woke up feeling at home, belly up and safe in our world. No regrets, I claim all the times, good and bad. It isn't about forgetting, that doesn't happen. Surviving feels like a fresh miracle every day, says a gray-haired woman who might still have a rebellion or two left in her.

The trailer on the site next to us was an older twenty-seven-foot bumper pull with Wisconsin plates. A couple of bikes leaned against it, so I knew there were kids. They had a well-arranged area to sit by the fire pit and a cloth on the picnic table. There was a quiet, amiable dog sleeping by their door. They looked settled.

In the morning, as I was folding down, I heard a voice say hello. It was my next-door neighbor talking out a window, with a small dog in her arms. She asked me what kind of dog Mister was and we struck up a conversation. Their younger girl loved science and wanted to be a veterinarian and she was asking so she could tell her daughter when she got home from school.

It was she and her husband, two daughters, three dogs, and

a feral cat. I asked if it was crowded in there with teenagers, and she said it wasn't so bad. They were a religious family and living like this worked for them. Besides, she said, it's not like the kids could slam the door to their rooms.

The woman was cheerful and funny, sharing local facts and RV stories. They were long-term tenants in the park, which explained the comfortable site. Her husband had a great job through COVID-19 and hadn't had to miss a day. He did skilled, detailed welding and was always in demand. They had done well and had a contract on a new house. But after selling their previous house, there was a problem, and the contract fell through and left them high and dry. Then his job cut back his hours. So, they got this trailer and headed to more temperate climes for the winter. It was a risk; they had no fallback. Her husband was a strong worker, but the only job he could find was in a diner. She hit a note of pride, saying he'd do anything to feed his family.

The woman had a disability and couldn't work, so she took care of housekeeping in the trailer. The kids were in an excellent school and doing well. When I said they'd had quite a year, her face darkened for a moment. Then she said she hiked on her strong days. Now, she's my pandemic hero.

She returned the questions, and I told her I worked with horses. She made a note of my name so she could relay that to her daughter, too. I suspected they would Google me later and use it as a lesson. How much a part of life computers have become, both in education and in the RV culture.

Mister cautiously peered at a small cat underneath their trailer who had been staring, sneaking back and forth, until the woman noticed and introduced the cat. She said that when they arrived at the RV park, the half-starved cat had a litter of kittens that they had cared for and eventually re-homed. They had the cat spayed, and they all worked to tame the cat to bring her inside. The cat refused, while totally enjoying the tag game. The cat had the family just where she wanted them, crouched and chirping. Sometimes we get a little too earnest about rescuing animals from themselves. This tiny cat had a sense of humor. Kitty, kitty.

I had to marvel at the opportunities these girls were experiencing as the family got creative about their lifestyle. As much as I sometimes flinch at man-made religions, I couldn't help but think they were on a grand family adventure on a shoestring. I hope the daughters write about it one day. When I finally said goodbye, I felt a little better about the world for holding this family safe in a storm. But it was this woman smiling through a window screen I'll remember. Her family's home is where her heart is.

Jennifer: Walking the Herd Home

The next stop was Duchess Sanctuary. I've been here before. It is a haven (I mean heaven) for a herd of rescued PMU mares.

The drug Premarin was used for hormone replacement in menopausal women. PMU is an abbreviation of its source: pregnant mare urine. Canadian farms contracted to support the drug's production. At the industry's peak, about 50,000 mares were impregnated each year for the sole purpose of collecting their estrogen-rich urine. Standing all day in stalls with urine funnels tied between their hind legs, they kept the mares as long as they could breed. Their foals were an unwanted by-product.

North American Premarin production and consumption eventually decreased because of dangerous side effects and negative publicity for the pharmaceutical company. Not the cost in mares and foals.

But I want to tell you about the woman who cares for them. Jennifer was a horse girl. She would agree that loving horses is about the easiest thing. She grew up in Alberta, Canada, and in her teens, found her way to a barn. Jennifer showed a certain temperament; she was quiet in her body, introspective, and she listened with her eyes. Soon, she was warming up Quarter Horses for the trainer, riding horses she could never afford to own. The horses liked her soft hands and thoughtful approach. She'd say she got lucky, but trainers don't let just anyone on their young horses. There was a future for her there if she wanted it. It wouldn't be free, but the door was open.

She also volunteered with horse rescues on the side. Someone like Jennifer would. Soon she went off to college with a plan to get an MBA and make a lot of money so she could save horses. It was a noble goal, but also pragmatic. Anyone who knows horses understands that the financial side of care is expensive, even for a single horse. Money was realism. She was not prone to romantic notions, even then. Business school wasn't a good fit though, and she dropped out.

Soon after, she enrolled in "Horse College" in Olds, Alberta, where the subject suited her better. She got her degree in Equine Reproduction and Management. She loved nothing better than foaling out mares, and that was the goal for her future career. And just one of many ironies to follow.

Before and during college, Jennifer worked with a nonprofit, helping to adopt the PMU foals to forever homes. The numbers were never in their favor, but they tried their best. After college, she went to work for another nonprofit, caring for an entire herd of spotted draft mares and their foals. It was an ambitious undertaking; each horse weighed 1600-1800 pounds and had a good appetite. For three years, she cared for the herd in rural Alberta, learning something new every single day.

A plan was hatched to join forces with a larger organization to ensure a forever sanctuary for the herd. First, a benefactor bought a 1,120-acre farm in rural Oregon, and the Humane Society of the United States (HSUS) came on board. The farm had a house, a shop, a small shelter, and some barbed wire fencing. Not much of a start. With a few months of preparation, the herd, over 150 draft horse mares, traveled from Alberta in five semi-truck loads and a dozen stock trailer trips. That didn't include bringing the tractor, shelters, and tools. It took the better part of the summer of 2008 to move everything.

These are the dates and numbers, but the story of the herd and the woman who came with them is even more complicated than the logistics of moving them. Jennifer never had a plan to move to the United States. She loved being a Canadian, but by then she couldn't imagine life without the herd. She needed a work visa to accompany them to their new home.

Duchess Sanctuary took in other horses over the years, some from a mustang rescue, and several HSUS horses. A sanctuary had to be conservative on intakes because they are not in the business of adopting out horses. There was just one way to leave a sanctuary. The fervent hope is that it will be years after their arrival, thousands of dollars in care later, and after many seasons on green pasture.

Years passed, employees came and went, and Jennifer stayed. Each year, the budget for care got greater. They improved the land and planned for long-term viability. There were no more foals, but the elk and other wildlife thrived there. The facility grew and Jennifer continued working for the herd.

Jennifer's job title began as Ranch Manager, and then Director of Operations. In theory, it's a desk job involving planning, funding, and direction, but the care of the herd remained her priority. The woman who dreamed of a career foaling out mares instead protected mares who would never have to carry another foal for the drug industry. During daylight hours, the herd needed her eyes, hands, and skills as they transitioned from being under total human control to a life of liberty and space.

On my first trip to Duchess Sanctuary in May 2019, I gave an in-service for the staff. My reward was a trip up the hill to visit the big herd in a high pasture, out of view of civilization. It was late afternoon when Jennifer drove me up and we stopped at a distance.

Scattered over a high meadow, a vast herd of mares grazed in smaller groups scattered among the trees. It was a view of paradise; the dream made visible. We quietly watched for some time, and slowly the herd migrated, watching us just as quietly. They moved with strength and inner harmony, wanting nothing from us. They were healed of us, of the things we do, I thought.

A small group came close, one black and white spotted mare standing especially tall. It was summer, and she was shiny and fit. This is what normal looked like, I thought. This is natural. They had an awareness of their environment but no anxiety about us. An unforgettable experience. I return to this perfect moment often for hope as I struggle to help troubled horses.

I stopped again on this trip, happy to provide another in-service day, but I'd asked Jennifer if I could stay an extra day and talk to her. The sanctuary gets lots of good press, but I was more interested in her experience over the years with this herd.

Mister and I set up the Rancho under some trees near the donkeys and with a view of the pond. The sanctuary was busy with all kinds of animals. Mister felt that the ground squirrels, who stood right up and heckled him for being on a leash, were a serious issue that needed immediate attention. Jennifer shrugged. He thought the wild turkey population was excessive as he looked out a window in disapproval at a dozen who stalked us in the trailer. Something killed one overnight, leaving feathers everywhere, but Mister had no complaints about whoever was big enough to do that.

A Triangle of Mares

Duchess Sanctuary is an upside-down world where horses live the most natural life possible, with no work or love required of them. They are free of fussy humans with savior complexes who want to take them home. In a sanctuary, horses owe us nothing, not even companionship. What they share with us is by their choice. They've been fifteen years in Oregon now, and the median age of the herd is twenty-one. An aging herd requires more care. They have a precious and precarious mortal glow.

The next morning, Jennifer and I entered a distant pasture, a vast meadow with groups of mares standing in the shade of trees. It was the big herd I'd met on my first visit, their massive bodies at rest, their tails shooing flies off each other under huge shade trees. One mare was apart from the group and down on the ground, and as we drew closer, she stayed down. Not normal. The other mares were watching us now, not frightened but also not pandering to us. Their autonomy was regal and glorious. Jen walked an arc in one direction, as I stepped the other way for a better angle, knowing better than to think both of us walking up would be helpful.

Just then, a black mare left the shade and walked directly to the prone mare, and then turned to face me. I halted. She walked ten yards directly toward me. Instead of sniffing me, she turned and positioned her belly touching mine, her body perpendicular, blocking my view of the ailing mare and Jennifer. Silently, two other mares joined the black mare. They stepped quietly behind me to form a triangle around me, bending their ribcages close enough that I could feel each of them with my body. Each was at least as tall as my shoulder. No greeting, they weren't curious about me. Not friendly and not emotional. They were massive and immobile, and they contained me. My breath stayed intentionally slow and deep as I kept my hands by my side. I did not take a selfie.

After a few moments, when the mares were satisfied with my intentions, they dissolved back into the herd. I joined Jennifer with their permission. Jennifer had gotten the sick mare up and listened to her gut. It looked like colic, so after a slow, polite haltering process, the mare reluctantly allowed Jennifer to lead her to the gate. Another sanctuary employee had pulled a trailer there to carry the mare to the barn for treatment. There were moments when I wondered if the herd would let her go with us, but Jennifer's energy throughout the whole event gave the mare and her herd confidence.

It ended up being a mild colic, resolved in a few hours, and soon the big girl returned, healthy and whole, to her herd. She didn't say thank you and Jennifer didn't expect it.

Horses need us to survive in our world, but how arrogant we are to think the life we give horses is necessarily an improvement over their natural herd life. We offer horses love, as we claim theirs, but the more I watch and learn, the more I think horses have something better. After all, we fail each other as often as we fail horses. Our culture is nothing to brag about, but remembering those mares, I wonder if horses have had it right all along. It was never about domination; herd life was always about cooperation.

There is a word in the Māori language that I think might define what horses experience in herds. It isn't as selfish as individual love but lifts the ideal of community welfare:

whanaungatanga - Māori Dictionary (fa-nan-ga-tunga) 1. (noun) relationship, kinship, sense of family connection - a relationship through shared experiences and working together which provides people with a sense of belonging. It develops as a result of kinship rights and obligations, which also serve to strengthen each member of the kin group.

When listening to horses, the most important calming signal to learn is their baseline, their resting face. This was it, a herd grazing, breathing together, looking out for each other. It was their normal, beyond the screaming, hustling impatient world of humans. This was their understated natural home, even if they lived in cities. If we want to connect with a horse in their language and on their terms, we must be willing to let go of the things that create noise in our world and in our hearts. It's an idea as revolutionary as a sanctuary. We must let normal be enough.

Later in the day, we spent several hours trying to medicate a Percheron gelding. He came as a youngster back at the beginning. Watching Jennifer work with horses is a beautiful slow dance. She is perceptive and steady. No nonsense and all respect. She is a true horsewoman.

Jennifer and I had our extra day, but the actions were more eloquent than any words could say. That might be the truest thing about horses, too.

A rescue organization changed my career trajectory as one had Jennifer's. I hesitated to ask Jennifer the questions I struggle with every day in my career. What dreams had she given up in her life to maintain the herd? Was she lonely? Was the payoff worth it? I couldn't ask. It was too personal to me if not her. And if something was missing about Jennifer, I couldn't see it. Life was fair in hard ways. We all pay for what we have. Those questions were silly in the face of the big herd grazing in the sun.

A message from Jennifer posted later in The Barn School:

"Anna and I talked about this a LOT when she was here. Caring for an aging sanctuary herd means I am faced with making this decision often, and I know we've reached an intense period of saying goodbyes this summer. About 70 horses over the age of 20, many of those 25+. Not that 20 is really *old*, but stuff starts happening, especially with draft horses.

I have one euthanasia scheduled for next week, our regular vet day. But yesterday a different horse on the watch list let me know it was time for her, and she didn't want to wait until Tuesday. So the vet was out for her this morning. It took less than 30 seconds after the injection, after she spent about 15 minutes stuffing her face with oats and apples and cookies. Being there at the end is the final kindness I can offer.

Sweet Rhubari, she's been blind for a number of years now, but is the most trusting mare, letting us put ointment in her remaining eye daily, and willing to be caught and led and loved on, even loaded into a trailer in an emergency. Anna and I talked about her long-time companion horse too, similar in age, they both came from the same PMU barn in Canada long ago, and have been together 17-ish years, first out in a larger herd, then moving into a paddock when Rhubari's eyes started to go. Nitika doesn't really have any significant health issues except arthritis.

We agreed letting them go together would be kind. I couldn't do it.

Nitika wasn't upset until I went into the paddock with the tractor to remove the body, then she followed me calling a bit. I'm still going back and forth whether I did the right thing.

You're all going to think I only joined to tell you about dead horses. I promise that's not the case. But the universe is reminding me (again) that life is fleeting, with the loss of two more older herd members this past week. Both of these mares were the definition of stoic, and a lesson in leaving on your own terms. If they keep taking pieces of my heart with them, I'm not going to have any left! Of course, that's not true though. More than ever now, I believe I was put here to walk this herd home. I do feel like dragging my feet for a couple of days though."

***

People explain to me they love horses like it isn't the easiest thing in the world. They tell me their love is euphoric and special, as they talk about what their horses give them. And they share their frustrations, their fears, and the complicated quirks of getting their horse to do what they want.

Jennifer had always known it wasn't about what she wanted. It isn't humility as much as common sense. Horses come first. She says her biggest worry is that they aren't doing enough. If there were more staff, they could do more for the herd, but finding the right people isn't easy. Still, this herd had better care than most private barns can give.

It's been a few sad months since I was there. More horses have passed on and the business of running a sanctuary isn't getting easier. Inch by inch, the care level grows for the herd. Politics in the animal welfare world affects them, and against the odds, they hold on to their mission. It takes extraordinary people to maintain "normal" for a bunch of old broodmares hidden in the hills of Oregon.

Bless this old herd who have won their freedom, and this woman who stays to walk them home. It's the dream of a horse-crazy girl seen through to maturity. When I think of what loving horses means, I think of Jennifer and believe that sanctuary might be another word for an undomesticated life.

Jennifer says it's her hope that each member of the herd will draw their last breath there. I hope she gets her wish; I hope she is the last mare standing on that saddest and proudest day.

No Parking

Driving out of the sanctuary on the third morning was bittersweet. It was emotional to close the gate behind us. I hate goodbyes, but when is that news? We had a short drive that day and I tried to look ahead.

Mister and I are reading *The Call of the Wild* by Jack London. I've never read it before or any books by the author, and I'm impressed by his use of calming signals as he described the dog/wolf activity. That phrase for behaviors didn't exist back then, but describing body language brings life to the narrative. It's something I talk about when I give writing workshops. How had it taken me, especially me, so long to find this book?

Wolves, sled dogs, dog fights, or cold weather do not impress Mister. His civilized breed had standards and culture. He lectured me in a snobbish accent, his snout lifted so his double chin was less noticeable.

By late morning, we came to a small grocery store, and I wanted to stop for a cold drink and a snack. There was no parking out front and the road we were on was narrow. Just past the store, there was a turn, and I thought there must be a parking lot behind or at least a place I could pull over. GPS Woman scolded me for being off course. Practice what you preach, I thought.

I took the corner, but there was no parking lot behind or place to stop. I drove on, thinking I could probably just go around a block and get back to the road. But what started as a two-lane street quickly turned into a narrow lane. There were no places to turn, and the road got narrower until it ended at two driveways, with no warning it was a dead-end. Locals probably know that.

One driveway went off at a sharp angle with the house in sight but no yard to turn in, and one dropped steeply but no house was visible. It was a terrible choice either way, but the location of the house decided it. I like privacy when I tie us up in knots. I gambled on the steep one, thinking it would be easier to make a mess of this out of view. GPS Woman was mysteriously quiet. She must have been biting her tongue.

I put the truck in reverse and cranked my wheel to let the Rancho drop deep into the driveway. It jackknifed a little toward a ditch and I pulled forward. Then I turned the wheel the opposite way and reversed slowly, while the Rancho jack-knifed in the identical way it just had. I pulled forward, turned my wheel in the *other* opposite direction, and slowly backed up. But the Rancho jackknifed the same way it just had, and it didn't matter which way I turned the wheel. This wasn't the first time I thought the Rancho defied science.

I pulled forward again, as far as I could. Pause. Then I backed with my wheel perfectly straight, and the Rancho jackknifed the exact same way one more time.

Welcome to the thrill of single-axle trailers. I cranked my wheel and backed again. The same jackknife, but now I'm used to it. I gave up thinking that the Rancho was going to straighten out and cranked a few degrees more toward my escape and pulled forward. I cranked and reversed again, as I decided I would just reverse and go forward, reverse and go forward, until inch by inch I got out of this person's driveway. Hopefully, before they come and ask me to get off their property. Back and forth, back and forth, until the front corner of my truck only went into the ditch a bit, and we escaped.

I'm particularly parched now. I needed a stress snack for sure. But once we got back on the dirt road, GPS Woman tisk-tisked at us and sent us past the grocery store. I obeyed, without so much as a glance, and we continued on our way.

Toni: A Culture of Listening

The next stop was at New Purpose Farm outside of Portland. I'd been looking forward to this clinic. Toni and Rick and their herd have built a culture around listening to calming signals, taking it to heart more deeply than most. At this stop, I wouldn't be trying to convince participants that this affirmative approach works. Everyone already knows. With less explanation needed, we could go as deep as the horses would take us.

I met Toni and Rick at a clinic in 2019. Toni brought Samson, a young mustang gelding. I had a haltering conversation with him. He was shy and intelligent and curious, with a memory of Iberian blood visible in his conformation. He was a horse to remember, with large soft eyes. His head was a sweet chocolate color that slowly roaned-out with white hairs over his body, looking like a hard frost toward his hindquarters. Samson was cautious and thoughtful, and I took my time and enjoyed every minute. He was young, with so much potential, and I was smitten.

Toni sent him to a trainer for more work under saddle. Samson was green, and barely started previously. She hired a trainer with a solid reputation, but when she went to see Samson soon after, he was a totally different horse: terrified, frantic, and resistant to any contact. She almost didn't recognize him, and heart sore, she immediately brought him home.

Toni knew Samson was in a bad spot and wasn't entirely sure how to go forward. More of the method that broke him wouldn't be the approach to help him. More than usual, Toni used her new knowledge like a pair of glasses; she saw him only through that lens. Her priority was listening. He didn't need more training; he needed to recover from it.

We started working together in 2020 during COVID-19 doing online lessons. She was one of my first virtual clients, and she had a village of help. Rick spent hours videoing and being there, just in case. Samson wasn't a horse to work with alone. Then Toni enlisted Coral, a local trainer I'd met at that first clinic, to work with her for Samson. They were building a different culture in their barn. No one had been cruel previously; it was more that they committed to a better approach together. Toni told me initially she had to take a lunge whip with her when she went into the arena with Samson. I didn't want to believe her, but then I saw a video. Samson bolted around the arena was such extreme anxiety that he was blind with panic. He ran without awareness of hurting himself, much less anything or anyone in his path.

Samson was like a hysterical toddler on the floor screaming at the grocery store. He couldn't express himself any better. His fear and anxiety overwhelmed him. Maybe Toni took the Calming Signal/Affirmative Training approach to heart more deeply because she had a horse who needed help so badly.

To begin, she simply allowed him to express himself, and it wasn't pretty. Samson attacked things in the arena and Toni let him, partly with the notion that it was better inanimate objects than other horses or her. We knew these dangerous behaviors were emotions and keeping them inside would not do him any good. So, there were months when he got a halter on, slow and steady, and little else. Samson tried to regulate his anxiety and Toni gave him the time he needed. In watching him, Toni gained a deep understanding.

The exciting thing about calming signals is that it gives us a method to communicate in the language horses understand. Samson was being so demonstrative in his emotions. We both thought he had things to teach us.

Toni hung hay bags in the arena. Then Samson could release his anxiety in a healthier way and perhaps have a chance to not go so quickly into that panic mode, into his flight response.

Now when he had anxiety, he could run to the hay bag and get a bite. Samson had to articulate his poll to get the hay out, and then chew. In that process, he released tension in his jaw and anxiety in his neck. Samson knew he felt better and learned to substitute galloping frantically for grazing. It was no different than human stress-eating.

One day, there was a saddle pad on the rail, and he pulled it down. We thought he might tear it to bits. Like pounding pillows in Gestalt therapy, he took out his frustration on that saddle pad. We trusted his actions had meaning. Rather than seeing him as destructive and disobedient, we listened to him as if he was telling us a story. And we had the wonderful experience of watching him learn to process his feelings. He healed himself. His brief time in training had been traumatic, but he was finding his way back from it.

Two and a half years later, Samson was being ground driven. He could tolerate a saddle on his back. He was a calm communicator who had learned to trust that humans could hear him. That was the healing; the opposite of domination is trust.

When Toni asked me if I would come and do a clinic at her farm, I was beyond thrilled to meet this horse in his new state of confidence. But I also looked forward to going to a place where my methods didn't need a sales pitch.

I parked my trailer and got set up. Mister and I sniffed around and greeted the horses. I got a message from Toni that night that she'd be able to record the lessons the next day, and everything was ready to go. About an hour later, I got another text from Toni saying she was on the way to the hospital with a broken kneecap. It took a second reading of the text for it to sink in. What lousy news. She'd tripped in the house. I asked her if she'd like to cancel the clinic or postpone it. She said no, we would just go on with it as we had planned. She and Rick went off to the emergency room, where she spent most of the night getting her knee checked out. Toni had diagnosed herself correctly.

The next morning, the people who helped on the farm arrived. Coral pulled in with a horse in her trailer. Auditors trickled in and the group came together in a special way. Before riding his beautiful mare, Blue, Rick took his post at the camera. His night had been just as long as Toni's, and his good humor made the rest of us feel better. With mixed emotions, we began.

Coral stepped in and took Toni's slots with her horses, as well as her own slots. We had wonderful conversations, prompted by the horses. We had the time I'd hoped for, not being hurried by a larger number of participants, and there was fabulous sharing, with the horses directing the topics.

I kept referring to Samson as *the perfect horse* because he flat-out was. Coral even rode him in two brief lessons. So much had come back together for this horse and looking at him now, it was valuable to remember the state he was in when this all started. It was a journey that had changed Toni, too, and her next horses would all benefit. I smiled so hard my lips stuck to my gums. This is how the world changes.

At the end of each day, Coral and I went into Toni's room and sat on the corner of her bed to talk with her about how the day went. After that first day, she watched the lessons on the live cast in real-time with other members of our online group. She'd worked hard to plan and take part in this clinic, but now all she could do was watch other people work with her horses.

Toni's positivity held strong, her perceptions were amazing, and her spirit infused the group. I asked Toni how it was to sit inside and watch everybody work with her horses. She said seeing her horses respond so well to other people handling them was a thrill. We both knew it was the work that she had done that made it possible.

Sharing our horses is a thing most of us have gladly done whenever we're asked. There had to be trust and safety, but we know horses are a gift so precious that being without them is beyond our ability to imagine. So, we share them, as a way of paying it forward, hoping each time we do, it will add an hour of time with the horses we love.

I've always known horsewomen are not like other people. If you have four of us, we can do anything. We are persistent, opinionated, and we don't know how to quit. Generous and stubborn. Tough as twine but as soft as a breath when working with horses. With so much passion, we're nearly feral compared to other women. When the plan came apart, when help was needed, everyone in the herd, both horses and humans, pulled together like a draft horse team.

Sometimes the true partnership we build with horses looks like healing after a war. Samson will tell you trust has to be constructed gradually with patience. And if we do it right, horses return that favor. It felt like Samson filled in for Toni. He anchored the herd. He stood in her stead, undaunted and unbroken.

But in helping Samson find trust in humans again, Toni listened in his language. Samson's calming signals became her best aid. She worked outside the boundaries of the traditions that caused his problem. It wasn't that she tamed him or healed him. She became undomesticated for him. Toni became a mustang in her own species.

A Call from an Old Friend

After four wonderful days, we pulled out of New Purpose Farm and headed north. We crossed the Columbia River on I-5 and were close to my old home turf. I'd lived in Colorado since high school and my family had been gone from this place almost as long. Driving through memories as thick as the trees, I didn't stop to look at my old school. I don't have any friends or family living here now. Olympia had literally tripled in size.

It's the land that I've missed the most. The town felt overgrown with trees so tall they blocked the sky. That was the secret to dealing with all the gray clouds; hide them in a forest. Shrubs and blackberries threaten to claim the land back every moment.

I remember how naked I felt when I moved to my prairie farm. Like a bug on an asphalt parking lot, there was no place to hide. Now I'm claustrophobic when I can't see the horizon.

My horse, King, lived in our orchard. I didn't overstate the name, did I? He was a chestnut gelding that I insisted on calling a strawberry roan. I was obviously *A Teenager in Love*. We rode in the holly farm and at the grade school playground. I can still feel the warmth of his flank on my bare legs. Cut-offs and tennis shoes were my riding attire and babysitting money paid for the hay.

I got a call from King one day while I was in my high school economics class. Yes, decades before cell phones, but I got an image of him tied up or trapped. It scared me enough to cut the rest of my classes and drive home. He was standing in a blackberry bush, runners wrapped around his hind leg. He'd been pulling to get free. The thorns abraded the skin off the front side of his hock in an area the size of my hand. There was blood everywhere, but worse, raw muscle was visible.

I began carefully untwisting the coils of thorns. I could have protected my hands with gloves, and I could have used shears, but I did it by hand. It took a long time, but King stood still and didn't pull. When I was done, I cleaned and dressed his leg and didn't tell a soul about the call. I was far enough out on the fringe as it was, but I never thought I was psychic. The message came from my gut as a picture that was seen without words. That's the best description I can give. It's how I see messages to this day, but they can only come from listening with the kind of clear, empty mind a boring economics class provided. It's the place out beyond abject monotony, where peace lives. Messages from this far-off land feel like the opposite of making up a story, more like a present memory. It feels true, not a flicker of woo-woo to it. But it only works if you think of the horse; never yourself with them. If that makes it weirder, just call it intuition. I noticed the more I trusted it, the clearer my understanding became.

I got another call from King while I drove through Olympia that day. Even more strawberry-colored, his eyes had the glow of sunlight through honey. He still checks in with me now and then. Being haunted is one perk of having horses. The ghost herd always circles back.

***

When I planned this long trip, I set aside days for rest in between workdays. Trying to schedule the balance I wanted was about as easy as controlling the weather. My plan was to have time to write on the road, and days off with Mister, where we did less. Defining a day off while traveling proved to be complicated. Driving was work, too.

But trying to plan a trip that depends on others had challenges of its own. Things can change in the weeks between beginning the plan and arriving. On this trip between the planning and the arrival, organizers canceled three stops in Washington, but two remained. I couldn't go home early and miss those clinics, but I had more time off than I wanted or planned for.

Before COVID-19, this didn't happen. It felt more reliable back then. People wanted to plan ahead, but it was different now. There was trouble at their boarding barns, family members were sick, and others just changed their minds at the last minute. Even clinics that were filled with participants emailed to cancel with no excuse. This had never happened before.

Mister and I added days at RV parks, but too tired to go be tourists, we hunkered in. My thirty-day cancellation policy didn't help when trips were longer than that and had to be planned ahead. I didn't think that part through, and now I had some limbo time. Not really able to relax, knowing that too many days off would eat up my income. I'd been the in-demand clinician everyone wanted before COVID-19, but now we wandered some. Was this the new normal?

We passed God's porcupine and stopped in Gig Harbor for a night. The next morning, we headed north on a two-lane state highway into the Olympic Peninsula, a dense rainforest. I had a sour feeling that GPS Woman had taken us on another shortcut. I was learning to call them alternate routes because there is nothing shorter about these crooked paths in the woods. One more time, the road got narrower and narrower, with no place to turn around. The trees, overgrown to the edge of the fractured pavement, arched over the road and killed what daylight was left. I didn't know if we'd come out on a highway or if we'd get stuck in a ditch where no one would find us until spring. The next spring.

We rolled on, in a state of perpetual what-if, slowing for each blind corner, but never going up again to our previous speed. There were no signs, no mailboxes, and no hint when the GPS Wi-Fi died. You'd think I'd be getting used to it, but it was "fresh hell" each time, as Dorothy Parker would say.

Mister and I stopped for a moment. He needed a little walk. I needed some wine and stinky cheese, but moist, dense air would have to tide us over. We needed to find the RV park first.

This was Sasquatch country. Mister says they give off a fine bouquet of fish guts, rodent toes, and moldy ferns. He would roll on one, given the chance. He's wide awake and mumble-barking at something in the trees. We've blocked the road because there was no room to pull off, but it won't be a problem. We had seen no one in the last hour. Mister was playing it cool, so I took a cue from him. We went for a short stroll, then we climbed back into the truck and continued down the narrow road. Mister warned me it was getting close to dinnertime. It's part of his job description.

I was about to send up a flare, but we didn't have any. Finally, we glimpsed a sparkle of light. It would either mean we'd made it to a highway or water in a slimy ravine.

We inched along farther until we suddenly landed on a busy four-lane road, only a few miles from our RV park. We stayed in a town called Sequim for the next couple of days. I bought a crab the size of Mister's head to celebrate our imaginary Sasquatch sighting.

GPS Woman said I told you so. I suppose my panic was unfounded this time, but you never know. Maybe God's Sasquatch was the long-lost survivor of a practical joke their GPS thought was clever.

We had days where all the turns were perfect, and it was a smooth drive. It was GPS Woman's consistent inconsistency that fooled me every time. It was the kind of practical joke that Elaine would have cackled about. Did I mention that the woman's voice I chose for my GPS had a British accent? Maybe Elaine's ghost has possessed GPS Woman. That explains it; I could never refuse her.

A Country Club Trailer Park

We had one night before the next clinic, and we stayed at a fussy campground on the Olympic Peninsula. They warned us. One review said this RV park wasn't gay-friendly. I'm not gay but I tend to annoy the same people.

There were no pull-through sites, which I usually pay a couple of dollars extra for. It's no fun to unhook for one night when you have an option to just pull out in the morning, but I took what they had. Call it strike two.

I had to back my rig into an itty-bitty site and a man walked over to help me park. This single-axle trailer isn't the easiest and my truck is huge, but I have survived worse than this. The man came to my window, and I rolled it down. He said I must not drive on the grass, and I nodded. There were tiny areas of grass with cement all around them, each about the size of a picnic table. The driving lane was narrow and the sites on the other side of the lane angled in the wrong direction. A bad layout or maybe these sites were leftovers from some time when they didn't cater to Class-A rigs.

The only way into the tiny site is a backing jackknife turn, which sounds like an elegant dive into a pool more than a parking technique. I told him I had it, and he stood at the front corner of the truck hood and directed me with semaphore arm signals. Maybe I'm the smallest trailer he has ever seen, but really? I told him again that I've got this and began what will be several back-and-forth angles. He stood there, gesturing one way and then the other. Marriages have ended for less. I saw it daily.

I told him I meant it. He wasn't helping. Please, just let me do this.

He says it's his job, and he must, so I add him to my mental list of people working the wrong job. I've had the list for decades and now it's one RV parking lot attendant longer. It was clear he'd rather have me hit an electrical post than tread on his virgin grass.

I pulled forward and back, not listening. He got louder, and I wondered if he'd drop to his knees and sacrifice himself in front of the patch of grass. I am still not near it, but he's nervous that I might be. If he was going to be so touchy, they should make their sites farther apart.

Backing will never be easier when strange men direct me because all I can think of are the directions I'd like to give them and make it a two-way conversation. This guy was the crossing guard from hell. He was not kind, he didn't like me, or feel a need to be polite. He probably used to be an air traffic controller before he got promoted to this prestigious job with more power and responsibility.

His frustration was becoming contagious, so I rolled up my window, let out an enormous exhale, and started talking to Mister. I was in the middle of the lane, but no one was waiting. Dogs are the best for helping an attitude change. We scratched ears, and tilted our heads at each other, and Mister tried to roll over, which never works in his seat, as I finished my drink. The man was glaring openly now. I thought they might kick me out of the park.

In my own good time, I turned in my seat and backed into the center of my site, avoiding obstacles with inches to spare on either side. We couldn't unfold and get inside quickly enough.

All the RVs in the place were Class A tour buses big enough for a rock band. As if planned, they all had full-size American flags dangling on poles attached to their front grills. I come from a military family, and I like flags. This was different. There were no kids, no one who still worked, no music or laughter, and the fluffy white dogs were even smaller than usual.

The exception was one group of four impeccably tidy older Airstream trailers parked next to each other. One even had a fireplace inside. They were a group who traveled together and seemed to be good friends. Airstreams are vintage elite. My fantasy RV is an older "silver bullet," but isn't everyone's? I smiled a little too big, happy to see a line of them in formation.

Later, Mister and I were walking to the designated dog area, and I saw the parking man trimming a small grass area with hand clippers. Unbelievable. We are in a rainforest; growing grass here isn't brain science. The tiny, fenced dog area looked like a putting green. That was when I realized, not just that these huge buses cost more than my farm, but this was a country club trailer park. Dang, I didn't see this wrong turn coming. This place was all about privilege, politics, an elite lifestyle, and a narrow range of acceptable behavior that only the best people would have. It's their attitude that lets off a foul odor. No need to stare, I thought. My hair was as white as theirs.

Rather than feeling safe that night, for the first time, I stayed on guard. I'm usually good at finding commonality with people I meet, but no one even smiled at Mister. I longed for a mariachi band and the smell of chilies and onions on the grill.

Settling back on the bed, I read the camp rules. All camps have them, but their list was extra-long and stopped just short of a no-farting rule. I looked at Mister, belly up and softly snoring. Then I waited until dark and did a load of illegal laundry. Because there are some things you may not wash. Call it civil disobedience.

Leaving a Footprint

After this awkward and salty RV park, we moved on to the next stop. It was a clinic day with a couple who are both biologists and environmentalists, along with a group of their friends and neighbors. It was like a warm bath to find like-minds and kind hearts. They had a pack of odd, sweet rescue dogs, a herd of odd, sweet rescue horses, and a wonderful willingness to explore new ideas.

Driving to their front gate, I noticed the farm next door had a pasture of daisies. They were a stark white against all the green and I commented on their beauty. My new friends were concerned about the flowers taking over their pasture. Hay fields were being lost to heartier weeds like these innocent-looking daisies. I didn't know flowers could kill crops.

Between working with the horses, we had ongoing conversations about how the domestic farm world connected to the wild world. How the climate affected each life. My client's husband had researched a heat wave the previous summer that had killed a huge number of species of fish. The loss of food sources damaged the number of a certain bird species that lived on rocky cliffs nearby. I read his research paper, and the loss felt personal. It should feel personal to all of us.

I promised to bring up the environment more often at clinics. I had been, but after seeing all I'd seen at ground level on this road trip, the need felt even more immediate. Global warming isn't something people want to talk about. I don't understand our hesitation. Maybe we don't want to be bit players in a B-grade science fiction disaster movie. But horse people could be the heroes.

Global Warming is undeniable. The impact of climate change headlines the news every day. I wonder why horse people aren't banding together to help the planet. Why aren't agriculture people screaming loudest that we must make changes? We are the ones outdoors, in the simple sense. The people in high-rise offices who run the government and big business don't get their shoes dirty. They act like they have no children or grandchildren. Like they don't owe a debt to the world that gave them dinner and a home.

We see the impact on horses already. Now we vaccinate for West Nile, because of more robust insects passing this disease on. Other diseases are on the rise. Mares are cycling year-round instead of seasonally like it was twenty years ago. Research shows that horses are living longer but in worse health than ever.

No matter where I am, the weather is the same. It isn't normal, people tell me. It can be in a foreign country, in states far and wide, and on my home farm. This isn't our normal weather. More drought and more floods, more unnatural disasters. Hay prices are higher than anyone can recall.

I know I'm part of the problem. Sometimes the clinic groups were large but sometimes small, and still, I traveled by air and caught rides from airports to hotels or farms. I want to think one person traveling is better than a group traveling to me, but was my presence worth the environmental cost to get there? The ethics of how we work matter now that more is at stake. We found out during the pandemic that more of us could work from home. Maybe I'll be training online, but at the very least, I must do all I can. We must take responsibility for the mess we have made. Horses are not cockroaches. They will not be the long-term survivors in this new wasteland. Are we sitting back, waiting to see who all dies before we do?

It was with a bit of guilt that I drove the country this year. The world is changing quickly. What does my career look like now, says the woman who won't retire but doesn't have a cockroach's survival skills either. Conscious that I left a footprint again, I am sorry, but also stronger in my convictions.

My truck uses too much gas. I know it and hope that changes soon. The Rollin' Rancho is a house of conservation; the travel version of less is more. I use less water, buy less packaging, and recycle. Using fewer resources, I can manage a small space and take special care, be frugal with utilities, and use fuel additives so gas burns cleaner. I am aware of the close intimacy I share with the natural world and strive to be a better steward, understanding that all things are interconnected. It's up to each of us to do what we can, even if it's small. Or maybe especially if it's small.

I don't know all that this couple knows. They've committed their lives to studying the environment and I have such respect for the work they've done. It was a day that I learned as much as I taught, and those are my very best days. I left with some fresh eggs from the hens we parked next to, and a jar of blackberry jelly that tastes just like sweet dew, soft clouds, and evergreen hearts.

A horse trainer isn't qualified to address this global warming in the grand sense, but this is what I know. The major lesson in training is always how can I give up predator-like domination and create a healthier, more sustainable way of working *with* horses rather than *against* them. Speaking softer with my body and voice will draw a horse closer. Waging peace works but first, we have to recognize the war we've been fighting. It's time to stop fighting against Earth, as well. How can I use less and get more? That had to be the bigger question for the world, too. The Earth depends on us to learn its language and become a partner, but that isn't a loss. Call it affirmative evolution. It will be the biggest gain since the gift of this planet.

Killed by Kindness

We had another break for a few days before the last clinic of this trip, so we took the ferry to Orcas Island in the San Juans. It was dark, trapped between semis on the lowest level of the ferry, and Mister and I stayed put in the truck. People used to cross the ocean this way. I was thinking of those sailing ships my ancestors took for their journey to the New World. Our trip was only an hour long, but Mister and I were already claustrophobic.

We unfolded in the parking lot of a client's recently closed business. It was a good location. We had electricity, and I recently dumped the black water, so we were set for a while. It was a good neighborhood for walking.

The island was a jungle of forests, its roads narrow, with the stop signs conveniently hidden in undergrowth. In the village area, there were upscale shops, contemporary condos, and restaurants that all looked out over the water. The streets were narrow and crowded. My truck and I both felt awkward. Me because resorts always looked like wealthy slums to me, too curated, too artfully arranged to hide the things they don't want to see. The truck because it took a grocery store lot to find a big enough parking space.

This water is the Salish Sea. The Salish tribes have lived in this area for 11,000 years. These tribes, especially the Lummi people, have carved totem poles for generations. Their art and design are integral to the Pacific Northwest and personal to me growing up on Puget Sound. But this area is a fancy resort, not a reservation.

Washington state has twenty-nine indigenous reservations in all. The Nisqually tribe was closest to where I lived. Sport fishermen had been fighting with them over their fishing rights all my young life. The words in the treaty said, "usual and accustomed areas." This meant net fishing during the salmon runs and the sport fishermen didn't like that promised privilege during the 70s Fish Wars.

I remember for a time, The Quinault Indian Nation on the Pacific coast shut out tourists who had damaged their tide pools. Then they carefully brought the tide pools back and the surrounding area was rejuvenated as well. Then the tide pools were opened again to visitors and monitored closely, setting a beautiful example. This tribe that had walked those beaches and hunted the same land as their ancestors did centuries ago gave the land a second chance. Fifty years after reclaiming the tide pools, the Quinault Indian Nation is facing possible relocation because of an "evolving" environment. The rainforests and coasts of the Olympic Peninsula are facing the same threats and damage as high-rise hotels on the East Coast, despite their concern for their environment.

The soft cloud cover in the Northwest is not quite constant. Tourists complain about the lack of sun, but locals know all the diffused light makes the natural colors more intense. My client there took me to visit her horses, two fine gentlemen I'd met before, who now live on a vintage farm. The original family built the house and barn from lumber chopped and milled on their land. It was as if the horses were living in another era, primal and as natural a place as I've seen horses in captivity. Except owning horses on an island is challenging without a large animal vet or local hay.

It's hard to balance all the landscape from Arizona to Puget Sound like an environmental profit-loss statement. The assets and liabilities are hard to quantify, but human qualities are not. We all lose when we don't plan and gluttony rules. It is hopeful here. This land especially feels alive with its mossy breath.

We had almost a week of writing and visiting there, restful in some ways and not others. By the end of this week, Mister and I had been gone from home for forty days, and this trip wasn't over yet. I could feel us getting closer to turning into that kid kicking the back of your seat on a flight from Des Moines.

***

This is how I will die. The kindness of strangers will kill me. How is it even possible to be so ungrateful as to complain? I'm overwhelmed by people's kindness. Others might find it flattering, but I shut down. I say I'm an introvert to explain my behavior and they agree. They are, too, they insist, and then in the same breath, they ask if they can invite another person to join us for dinner. I dread this conversation for its unstated question: Can you be different just this once because this is a special occasion for us?

In setting up a clinic with an organizer, often she will ask me to stay in her home. If I'm flying, I'll pay for my lodging in a hotel. If I'm driving, I inform her I'll stay in the trailer with my dog. This detail usually takes more negotiation than any other in the entire event. They want me to be comfortable. Then I do a miserable job of explaining that their beautiful home will not be comfortable for me. And it's not personal. *No-thank-you.*

But there's a spare bedroom and a bathroom, and they say it's no trouble that I get up in the middle of the night to write. Everyone knows I do that, and they tell me to turn on the lights and make coffee. Could you do that in a stranger's house? I'm too conscious about flushing the toilet much less using the kitchen. *No-thank-you.*

They say it's fine to bring Mister in the house, and that their dogs get along with other dogs. Do they understand he doesn't deal with change any better than I do? That he might not get along with their dogs, but both of us will worry about it.

I thank them for their kindness and confirm that I prefer to keep the routine in the trailer. *No-thank-you.* They immediately ask again.

They invite me to share their dinner and then make a fabulous meal. With the best intentions, dinner is rarely ready before seven p.m. because, of course, they take care of evening barn chores first. Just as they should, but that means we're probably not done eating by eight. I won't share my digestive challenges. It's enough that I'm still on my feet and I'm still talking, and the next day's clinic begins in twelve hours.

I need to be polite, but I'm worn out. Not new to this job, I know what I need. After years of crowd surfing between clinics, not having a car, or any other escape, I have only gotten worse at sleeping in strange beds. It isn't about being rude; it's about self-care. I need alone time to be conscious the next day.

So, I thank them kindly. *No-thank-you.* I see their disappointment, so I don't mention how Mister feels about cats.

More than once this year, I've been a bad guest. Of course, I try, but the things a good guest should do are just beyond me. After work, I'm drained to my dregs but I try to give more; I stay a bit late, and I come out early. But still, people seem nervous around me and I'm not sure why. I try to tell them I'm not the pseudo-famous person who doesn't eat brown M&M's but now I worry I've failed their expectations. If that doesn't scare me enough, then they might rant about it on social media. Because criticism always comes easier than praise.

Everyone wants to be the exception to my rule. When I was younger, I believed things would go easier if I told my date at the beginning of the evening, there would be no sex at the end of the date. A simple *no-thank-you.* It was very naïve; they belligerently didn't hear me. All it really did was paint a target on me. It was as if the date became a competition; would he be the one who hit a home run on that first date? But surely this wasn't the same thing.

Each host assures me there are no expectations, but unstated expectations are exactly that. Expectations that no one needs to mention are just as easy to read as the unstated disappointment that follows. I know by writing this, I might make people more nervous and visits more awkward. I don't want to make others feel as awkward as I do. Truly, people are so kind, I should be nothing but grateful. Then I think of the horses who struggle under the cloying love of their owners, and I wonder if this is how they feel. As stoic as they are, I stuff my feelings, determined to play my part better.

I realize that I have borrowed patience from the future, and it might be a finite commodity. I'm no fun. Too exhausted to hang out and too much of an introvert for small talk. I'm an outrider and only good company for a dog who sleeps a lot.

***

Leaving the island a few days later, we arrived early for the first ferry. I saw a bald eagle perched high on the top brace of a boat hoist next to our line to load. It isn't unusual to see bald eagles in this area, but this one seemed to stare at me. Or I wanted it to. She was a huge pillar against the gray sky, her head as bright as a searchlight. She was being heckled by some seagulls who were dive-bombing her, but she ignored them. It was impossible to look away for the next hour before boarding. Words failed me as both Mister and I stared at this immense, proud bird amid the harbor noise and trash. Was seeing her a metaphor or is she an analogy? Everything felt like a contradiction of something else. And I think too much. Just let her be beautiful.

The final clinic of this trip was held at a Snohomish farm I hadn't been to before. Three women worked together on organizing the event, and it was an easy, friendly clinic. There were several Lipizzaner horses there that reminded me of my Iberians at home. The participants boarded there mostly, so the group knew each other. They were a barn family. I spent my best years riding at a boarding facility with a talented trainer and a group of like-minded friends, just like this. Horses are always better when shared.

The clinic went off like an obstacle course. The horses threw us some curve balls and the participants each faced challenges from them and me. It was an intense two days, with every emotion on display. It wasn't perfect, but it was art and beauty and inspirational. The participants, led by an amazing trainer, rose above the fray and took my breath away. I was proud of them and a bit dorky about it, but I do love this dance between complicated horses and women who do the best they can, in every moment. This passion we share is a thing to behold.

I even had a few moments with a foal. I work with so many traumatized adult horses that when I get to work with young-sters, it's a rare privilege. Training foals was where my career started. They are the *before* version and it's our job to keep their precious faith and curiosity intact throughout their lives.

At the end of the last day, we had a wrap-up meeting. We were a few minutes late, and the meeting would last awhile, so I asked if Mister could join us. I do this if it's a safe place. He'd been in the Rancho all day and he truly excels at chair-sitting. We were all in a circle. There were some extra bar stools, and I asked for one, thinking I'd use it and then Mister could sit in my chair. Before I could stand, Mister climbed up and over me, onto the bar stool. It didn't have armrests, just a back, and he's a very long dog. Somehow, he got himself situated, a bit taller than I was, and sat listening to the conversation for the next hour. He was patient and attentive as each person made a final comment.

Herding dogs are famous for being bad at dog parks because they have no tolerance for chaos. They believe it is their Type A, God-given right to put it all straight. For Mister, every day on the road is a new dog park. His job looks simple from the outside. But I'm no sheep, not easy to herd. I'm half-deaf and I wear glasses. Without his senses, I'd be lost. If I wasn't a big enough challenge, Mister needs to tolerate meeting new people daily. There is an argument that his job might be harder than mine. But here he sits, listening to people talk. Consistently better behaved than I am.

Sitting in the circle, I worked to tie the events of the weekend together one last time. Telling everyone how well they did, how grateful I was to be invited, and how truly wonderful it's been. It was the absolute truth, and I realize even as I say it, that I can't wait to be alone with this enigma on the bar stool.

The Long Haul Home

We folded down early the next morning, and I was chirpy. Mister doesn't know we're heading home. For all he knows, these weeks on the road *are* home. We have traveled beyond counting in dog time, but the home dogs know I'll come back. Sometimes I talk to them on the phone, the Dude Rancher holding the receiver so they can hear. Their reaction is no surprise. Barkety-bark, ye-howly-boof, yip-yap-yip. They recognize my voice, but it's a mixed blessing. Would it be kinder to not remind them? I miss my own horses, I say in less than a big girl voice. I worry about the elder llamas.

We headed east through the Cascades to the farmland in eastern Washington and Oregon. The land is open to an endless sky. I wanted to ride here. That's always my first judgment of land as if my senses work best through a horse's hooves.

The miles go slower on the way home, and I wonder if GPS Woman tampered with the odometer. These days are good for talking with the Dude Rancher on the phone. I need to check in for my sanity. If I call in the evening after clinic days, I can barely focus enough to answer. It's not much different when I'm home. My IQ fades at dusk and then sets with the sun. Midday is a quiet time on the farm. When I'm gone, we talk longer, almost like we did back when we were dating.

The road cuts diagonally across Idaho toward Caldwell, a long five-hundred-mile drive to the Country Corners RV Park, where we stopped for the night. It felt easier knowing there were no upcoming clinic workdays, but traveling was a different kind of workday. Still exhausting.

We unfolded near dinner time, and I didn't care what I would eat. Mister would never be so complacent, but I was too tired to find groceries. Dinner was a spicy cup-of-noodles and the last apple. The night walk was longer because I needed to walk off the extra hours sitting. It felt like a strange limbo of not working and not being home.

Early to bed and off at dawn, we pulled in behind a semi as we watched miles burn by. Our only goal was to cover ground.

I remember a client who came to my art gallery years ago, Claire. She and her husband traveled. She taught me to use that word. They were retired and avoided tourists by going places like India, and when I asked about recent vacations, she corrected me. She said travel was an action verb and vacationing had to do with chaise lounges and swimming pools. She had an unusual manner of speaking. I can still hear her, though she and her husband have surely traveled from this place years ago.

Driving isn't a chaise lounge vacation. It required me to hold a keen focus on my energy within a still body. Anyone can stay awake in their environment while walking. Driving was definitely the most tired you can get while sitting in one place. These days were good for reading, good for being still and quiet. But I can't do it forever. I cranked up the music and car-danced a while.

Now the land was changing to gray, more arid. Some of it was the drought that was dramatically affecting the Colorado River basin, which provided water to southern areas. In every direction, the land looked too dry for June. I worry about our amazing Earth. I fear the future is going to look like a trashy science fiction movie.

Our park for the night was on the outskirts of Green River, Wyoming, the starting line for the I-80 drag race east. I took the exit for the RV park, and sure enough, the edge of town looked like an old set from a Mad Max movie. Both sides of the road had rutted driveways with broken-down single-wide trailers with their windows blown out and doors swung open. Rusted-out cars parked at angles with their hoods up and various piles of trash were scattered, only those pieces heavy enough to stay put in the wind remained. Nothing was green. It looked like everyone caught a bus and left in a hurry. Anything with any value had gone long since.

There are horses here, some kept in tiny pens made of wooden pallets in the backyard of mobile homes. Farther along I see dry-lot horse yards hidden in the shade of run-in shelters. It's riding country, but there isn't enough ground cover for any natural grazing here, just like my farm. The Green River, a tributary to the Colorado, runs through the town with a well-worn path next to it. I hoped the horses got ridden out often. God's horses, not mine.

I stopped for gas because I wanted to launch away early. There was no decent gas station food, no grocery store I could find. This little town on a river seemed to be only a gas stop with an old motel, and this RV park up on a mesa.

The Rancho held steady as a squall rocked us and spit rain at us while I unfolded the Rancho. I had a breakfast bar and some nuts for dinner, missing my usual stock of bagged salad. Neither Mister nor I wanted to go squirrel hunting. He was unsettled. His senses are much better than mine and I trust him as he takes his guard position, standing with his front feet on my chest. Slowly, his legs splayed wider until his chest touched mine. From there, his body took a slow-motion slide, until he draped around my waist like an inner tube. I stayed awake listening to the things I couldn't quite hear.

I must have slept, but it didn't feel like it as I rolled out early in the morning. Today was homecoming, a day I never understood in high school. No fancy dress for me, no cummerbund for Mister. Just coffee in a travel cup and we were on the road early enough to get to squint into the sun for the first hour.

If the wind isn't blowing, you aren't on I-80. I remember driving this freeway during a blizzard in a four-hundred-dollar VW Bug back in the day, hydroplaning when trucks passed me, and they all did. My car was so rusted out that ice water splashed through the floorboards. I felt like such an adult now, but for the weight of this monster truck, it felt powerless as if we were dragging rocks. Like a giant child's hand toyed with us. Soon traffic slowed to a walk, and we came upon a jackknifed semi, a common sort of Wyoming roadkill. The cab twisted like a broken wrist and flipped its cargo, half of a modular home, sideways with the tarp-covered side up. Just beyond, the other half had pulled over to the side, waiting for its twin to stand up again. Back up to speed, the Rancho was steady in the wind. Steadier than a modular home, anyway. Another good day for a flat trailer.

We stopped in a few hours for a walkabout. Mister looked like his unflappable self. Particular about the facilities. He sampled the water I offered and got a new pork chew. He had borne the white-hot glare of my full attention on the road with good humor. At home, it was easier. He shared the love spotlight with Lulu, Peach, Preacher Man, Jack, Belle Starr, Sebastian, Clara, Nube, Andante, Namaste, Bhim, Arthur, and Edgar Rice Burro. A lesser dog might have crumbled from the one-on-one pressure. Mister stopped chewing, looked at me, and tilted his head, the upside ear rose in the air like a catcher's mitt.

We followed the road toward the horizon east and never got there. We turned right at Laramie and took the back road south to hitch up with I-25 a few miles sooner. The landmarks were familiar now. The freeway traced the Rockies south toward home for the longest three hours of the trip.

Home Stay
June 30–July 15

July Is Too Hot

July is just too hot to schedule clinics in the northern hemisphere. There might be an indoor arena at the clinic venue, so there is shade, but I hate the idea of hauling horses in this heat. And I need a break between the extended spring and fall travel, so I've made July my summer break.

There are a couple of online classes to teach, and I did some local talks. I got to judge a virtual dressage show, which is about the best way to compete ever. The camera at "C" has the same view as sitting there live, but if the ride comes apart, the rider can have a do-over. Everyone sends a video that ends up being a fair representation of the horse and rider on a good day. This show was a group of junior riders in Canada who wore little white shirts and rode costume quadrilles, too. Judging horse-crazy kids riding a dressage test is a job that doubles as rehab if I'm feeling a bit cynical.

July is also the month for farm upkeep, not by choice so much as by default. The fences needed repair and the gates wanted adjusting. Weeds were attacking the riding arena. I can't grow a decent pasture, but weeds threatened to steal the corners of the arena, and inch by inch, shrink the riding area. So, I weeded early or late in the day, which made my muscles ache, and was nothing at all like being at the beach, other than the sand. I repaired things, usually with found pieces, and built things I didn't have the skill to build. I loved these days of marking my territory.

The chronic issue has always been erosion in my pens. The wind had torn away my topsoil, and the long drought hadn't helped. We are on a high desert prairie and erosion is constant. My horses live in large dry lots with friends, with a thoughtful, healthy feeding and horse management plan. That means they are active, running and rolling, and there is always a cloud of sand in the air. So, my pens were all a few inches lower than the ground on just the other side of the fence, with constant negotiation to keep it from getting worse.

I bought a few dump truck loads of fill dirt and pea gravel delivered in huge piles in the north pen, along with a rented skid steer. Then I spent some time driving something much less comfortable than my truck. No dog hair, just grit splattered on my face and scum on my teeth from smiling, along with the satisfaction of using the right tool for the job.

It seems I have a light touch with rocks and dirt. It felt good to scream across the pen, peering under the bucket, take a quick turn, and dump my load just a little at a time while backing up. Really, you'd think backing that trailer would be easier the way I dance with a skid steer. The Dude Rancher on the ATV did the smoothing out. At the end of a long day, we hoped the pea gravel would help us hold our dirt. We recuperated, hanging in the tree swings, cheering our accomplishments with cold drinks. Being home was hot and dirty and very sweet.

Meanwhile, Mister enjoyed playing chase games with his brothers and hanging out in the yard in a lawn chair. The farm was a place where a dog could bark at will. He had zoomies with a bright green stolen Croc in his mouth. I surrendered it. Mister asked me for that Croc quite a few times before I gave in. Those were his now and he can tell the difference. He doesn't take the others.

But soon, it was time to start the leaving process once again. Prep took more time each trip, or maybe I dragged my feet more, cleaning the barn and our house. The dogs recognized it immediately and the ambient anxiety went up a few notches. I upgraded some things in the Rancho for the next trip. Knowing more about my preferences, I replaced the microwave with a toaster oven, but I doubt I'll use it either. Most people don't trust the water at RV parks, so I bring my own, but to be safe, I added an extra five-gallon container and a smaller inside water container that was easier to use. Customizing feels like self-care.

And I bought a larger capacity toilet. The old one needed to be dumped every three days and this new one holds twice that. Dumping is yet another RV park "frill" that private homes don't offer. This plastic toilet is comfortable, it flushes, and the tank deodorizer breaks down waste. It doesn't smell or tip over and it's easy to empty. I have it beside the bed, so Mister has a step up. Besides, who wants to leave the trailer in the middle of the night to find the loo?

People seem uneasy about these toilets, but it isn't much different from cleaning up after dogs or horses, a pretty normal event. Or maybe it's a hangover from growing up on our family farm. We didn't get indoor plumbing until I was four or five. Using an outhouse or chamber pot was a vivid childhood memory. Even now, my farm has a septic tank to deal with rather than a city sewer system.

But it gets weirder. Once we finally got indoor plumbing on the farm, they turned the old outhouse into a playhouse for me. Now that I think about it, that playhouse was an extremely rustic version of this little Rollin' Rancho. It became my hideout, with a tiny table and a chair. I didn't have dolls, but I kept stuffed animals there, like Mister's on our bed. Oh my, they say your childhood follows you through life, but this seems way too literal.

Exhausted from the time off at home, we were ready to head up to Wyoming, where long clinic days would make for a comparatively easy work week.

Wyoming
July 17–21

Joni: The Barn in Cheyenne

Joni's barn in Cheyenne was less than three hours away, which, after driving to the West Coast, feels like next door. They are not strangers to the infamous Wyoming wind, but Joni's indoor arena is as snug as any I know, tight in the wind and cool in the summer. Horses appreciate the layout. The length of one side of the indoor has a half wall with ties on the far side, in a wide alleyway. So, first thing in the morning, we kindly halter and bring all the horses in. There is no separation anxiety because the entire herd is there. We turn them out to lunch when we break. We bring them back in again for the afternoon and then turn them out at the day's end. This method resolves so much herd anxiety right at the start. It also gives the participants a chance to do thoughtful haltering, a fundamental too often overlooked, twice a day.

Joni has a circle of riders in the area who join us, and Joni will sometimes lend her horses to visitors. But if you want to listen and learn, it's a wonderful spot to audit. Some of the best conversations happen here because Joni schedules the clinic in horse time.

Best of all, because I go there at least twice a year, I get to see the horses develop. When I trained locally, often seeing a horse and rider weekly, I got to watch their progress and be more involved in day-to-day questions. As a clinician, I meet more horses and riders, but only briefly. I wonder about them long after clinics end. Clinics are like having serial first dates, but here, Joni and her horses are becoming old friends. I can do better if we all know each other a bit.

Besides, Mister liked the obstacle course behind the barn that doubled as an agility course for his visits. Their pasture has mysterious rodents to stalk during night walks. And there's an RV spot down by the barn with a thirty-amp plug. We feel right at home.

Joni is a lifelong horsewoman. No, she didn't have horses as a kid, although her North Dakota mother claims Joni was raised by aliens behind the barn. She started with horses at age thirty-nine, but she made up for lost time quickly by working with challenging horses.

Joni is the sort you'd expect to see on a nice Quarter Horse. But somewhere along the way, she got hooked on Peruvian Pasos, a gaited breed. She has been involved with the breed long enough now that others know her skills. People offer her "giveaway" gaited horses. I am not sure how they differ from rescues, but Joni prefers that word. Each horse has a story. Some were show horses, and some were not, but they all fell into trouble. Our conversations between rides are as valuable as the lessons themselves because training is about what the horse felt or understood, as much as how to fix it. We prioritize what the horse says.

Gaited horse training methods are traditionally accomplished with harsh shank bits. Not everyone, but most follow that old habit. Anxiety in the horse raises the energy of their gait, so for the best gait, the horse gets pushed harder. A frightened horse's gaits are more visually dramatic, but the stress affects the horse mentally. They can lose confidence and become unreliable. Horses get the blame when they come apart, but it was the training method at fault.

Joni and I agree that rough hands and strong bits create memories the horses can't forget. The muzzle and mouth are the most sensitive places on a horse and that sensitivity never deadens. A horse's mouth and muzzle are where any partnership is built or destroyed. Or when necessary, rebuilt.

I always ask all my riders to ride with a neck ring. It's a loop of rope that is knotted loose around the horse's neck. When the rider holds the neck ring, it touches the horse at the base of their neck, and we use it in conjunction with long reins. It's meant to leave the horse's head as free as possible, so we cue with our seat and legs. Few riders like the idea initially because it feels like the rider has less control, which is the exact reason to use one. Over-control makes horses crazy, and the neck ring encourages riders to use their hands less but also gives a feeling of safety, with lots to hang onto if needed.

Initially, I misunderstood Joni. I explained all this to her on my first visit and she said, okay, they will need to get used to the neck ring. I thought it was a strange thing to say. Most horses welcome the room to breathe they get with a neck ring. What I didn't know was that Joni rode with no bridle or any rope at all. There she was, on a "giveaway" with her arms folded over her chest. That way, she couldn't use her hands, Joni said. She was ahead of me. I'm used to having resistance to adding a neck ring, but she proved the point even better. Her horses didn't toss their heads or fight her hands because when you lay down the weapon, there is no fight.

Watching Joni, I could see her no-hands approach improved her riding position, too. She sat centered in the saddle and balanced with her shoulders back and in alignment with her pelvic bones. No leaning, no twisting, and with this neutral seat, she aided her horse's balance.

Position is important, so I complimented Joni, but she was focused on listening to her horse. For that moment, I am only background sound. This was exactly the priority I liked: the rider listening to the horse first. She was riding the inside of her horse with the inside of her body. It's another word for true dressage, not that Joni aspired to dressage. But the beauty of dressage is that it's just good riding.

Joni credits a hearing loss for her ability to *listen* because it makes her *see* things better. It's a distinct advantage, she says, because it's easier to naturally block out the external chaos. She uses technology when she wants to but makes choices about what she wants to hear and sometimes it's just the quiet conversation with a horse. My hearing loss gives me the same advantage, and I know others who'd agree. Maybe the other senses compensate and add up to more awareness. Or maybe we like the sense of feeling alone with our horses.

Joni knew that step one with her giveaways was to begin the slow process of rebuilding trust. We must give the horse time, by going slow. Encouraging calming signals was more than a training technique. We calmly gave the horse a voice, and then full autonomy. When they felt a wave of anxiety, Joni let them soothe themselves. When horses get the experience of humans not acting like predators, they notice something *didn't* happen that they expected. They began to feel safe in hindsight. Joni let the horse experience the lack of a threat by riding as she does. We can't make the horse forget his past, but we can let him reason his way to a different future.

Meanwhile, we talked about ways to ride with a seat and legs. It was a day of lessons where we worked toward a way of riding that engaged the horse's intellect. Riders offered horses confidence rather than the lower language of predators. We rode with true liberty.

Traveling to Joni's barn is becoming a habit, in the best way. Less first-day anxiety, more understanding on all sides and we are developing a culture with a language of our own. The horses are amazing, and the humans have hit a very nice stride, too.

Joni credits her "long-suffering horse husband," without whom she couldn't do her horses and accounting business. Bill says she married him under false pretenses because she didn't have horses in the beginning. I'm just an observer, but he doesn't make it look like a burden, happy to help if needed. He's always smiling and his dog, Bailey, is close by with a wag to match.

Joni is a woman of a certain age who wears long gray braids and jeans and has a bold marching kind of walk that horses appreciate. She is a bit of a fringe-dweller; an independent thinker, and capable of leading a horse to trust. She leads by going first, offering bite-sized bits of trust, and letting the horse chew on it.

Some would call what Joni does rehabbing horses. I call it a process of undomestication. A move away from aggressive human methods and a return to a more horse-centric way of working together.

Southwestern Skies
August 25–September 13

Better Than I Thought

It was halfway through August, and I was setting out on the road again. This trip would be a loop through the Southwest, my expanded neighborhood. I was hungry for the road, but leaving was hard as always. Preacher Man is a one-woman dog, and his age is slowing him down. Still barking, but with a little moan in it, like he's singing the blues. Edgar Rice Burro brays when he sees me in a window, he follows me closer with his head pressed to my back. I've been told he stares at the driveway when I'm gone. Missing home is an anvil I carry in my heart, sometimes even when I'm at home.

The llama elders are stoic and well beyond their expiration dates. I wonder if I'll see them again. They don't show distress as visually as horses, and by the time something is noticeable, they are almost past help. But all animals are fragile in one way or another.

At Equidays in New Zealand a few years ago, just before I went on in front of a large group, I got a text that a donkey was down and couldn't get up. That time, God's donkey was one of mine. I could do nothing. I had to trust that all was working for the best, even if it didn't seem that way. The donkey rallied for a few more months. God's animals don't all die right then, but they are beyond my help.

Now, as I prepared to leave home, I asked the horse gods to watch over my herd and the prairie moon to protect us all. I tried to strike a karma bargain that I would do my best for other horses if mine could be safe while I was gone.

After days of prep, we finally took the last load out to the truck. Mister had his harness on and knew the drill. He was enthusiastic about being clipped in. The Dude Rancher got the gate. We said goodbye again. Tears blurred my vision as I rolled past the mailbox and onto the washboard dirt road. Finally, I took a breath. I'd crossed the no-man's-land by the mailbox and took a sip of my coffee. It tasted like poison.

It's a half-hour until I reach the freeway south, which seemed like the first hurdle. I'm filled with doubt. Why do I do this? It's a job that gets harder, not easier. COVID-19 has backed people off. There were fewer invitations this year, and it's still as competitive as ever to get the work. I remind myself I'm good at it, but my methods contradict old ways. I remind myself again, that there are good people who want to do better. Soon the miles are churning past.

I'd been doing some research for this book. When I began writing my first memoir, *Stable Relation*, I checked into other memoirs about people who had moved to the country. I wanted to know what other writers were saying. Most of the stories had to do with women who were mad about getting horse manure on their pumps or not having Starbucks Coffee. They whined in an updated version of *Green Acres*, a sitcom starring Eddie Albert and Eva Gabor as a couple who moved from New York City to a country farm. Sometimes I think it's funny to watch city folks tiptoe around the farm. Other times, the books seemed like one long blonde joke saying all we cared about were our nails. They were insulting and demeaning, in that way women are often the butt of jokes. Are trivial concerns our only skill? Asks this woman who can hang a gate, level and true. Drive a skid steer with the rhythm of a tango. Back a recalcitrant trailer into a tight space.

My research is different for this memoir. I'm reading about reservation life, stories of immigrants, and courageous women. I continue to be haunted by a book called *Heartland* by Sarah Smarsh, a truer story of what it means to be poor and white and a woman in America. It was a secret in our family and one the country doesn't want to hear. We're too proud to ask for help. Smarsh weaves the stories of her mother and grandmother, and the politics of poverty, and brings them forward all the way to her never-to-be-born daughter. Some of us change our family narrative by stopping the traditions that need to end and then living as orphans for complicated reasons. Reading it felt like reading my diary. Great books give us a feeling of kinship, and more than that, validate our choices.

I'd passed the halfway point this year on the road with the Rollin' Rancho in my rearview. Mister was asleep because only one of us thinks too much. My truck roared south as I listened to a podcast article by a New York Times contributor about spending a week traveling in a van. She didn't want to be alone, so she brought a friend along. I'm sure it's supposed to be a comedy of errors, but it rang a bit snarky to my well-traveled ear. She was living on Cheez-Its and unhappy with everything.

Any long-haul traveler knows the approved road trip snack is sunflower seeds and oranges. Sure, sticky fingers afterward, but worth it for the juice and air-purifying qualities of the fruit. I want to tell this writer the roads we travel had better add up to more than bad snacks. Perhaps if she'd traveled alone, she might have heard what I have on the road. The voice of the Earth telling her story, part memoir, part mystery, part science fiction. I can't put it down, wanting the next chapter to come into view at the place just up ahead where the Earth meets the sky, the sun pulling us forward. Earth's story was written in mud and dead bugs on my truck as I steered my way, sometimes slammed my brakes, and other times, sped away. But always looking and listening.

When I first bought the Rollin' Rancho, I joined online

groups. They shared photos of upgraded interiors, but mostly long-winded how-to techniques for repairing what's broken. They made traveling in an A-frame sound like a vale of tears. So much to repair and so few skilled repairmen. The posts were all cautionary tales, like the *Times* article, and nothing but complaints.

Early on, I had trouble with my trailer hitch, but I adjusted it to work. One lock on a storage area stopped working, and I took it apart and fixed it. I didn't post about it. It took time to figure out power issues and how to level the trailer. Opening my giant notebook of instruction manuals, I forced myself to understand the extraterrestrial scribbling. After lots of trial by error, I learned how things work. I did it myself. Those were the first words I spoke as a kid, and my independent ways haven't changed.

On godforsaken land with no gas stations for miles, I've argued with GPS Woman. I've managed to keep rolling over long stretches of alternate routes. There were exhausted moments when I pulled into an RV park or somebody's ranch for a clinic, and it was raining or blowing or egg-frying hot. But I opened that repaired lock on my storage compartment, and I pulled out my drill to set the drop-down jacks. Moving around the trailer, I stabilized the Rancho as Mister supervised. I pushed the roof up, using the strong muscles in my arms, and jumped for the last bit to catch. I build my house every day.

I felt capable and strong, not old. Or worse, irrelevant. I'm on the path to something worthwhile and I won't trivialize the experience. Out here on the open road in this land of ours, there are no small things. From deserts to rainforests, we are alive. Mine is only a tiny insignificant life, no bigger than a speck on the backside of a gnat. But we matter, all living things are expressions of the whole and it is never clearer than when we leave our comfy homes. I say yes to being part of all of this land, all of this technology, and all the loose screws. It isn't about holding it together but riding the fast expansion of all we know.

Honestly, I'm better at this than I thought I'd be, and so is this dog. Mister opened one eye but reconsidered.

***

We crossed the border to New Mexico and arrived at the first work location near Taos for the clinic that was canceled earlier in the year due to fire. There was a particular light here, often seen in paintings of the area, that was warm and surreal at the same time. We landed at a therapeutic center with a large group of horses. The founder and I had so many similar experiences that I felt an immediate connection.

As she gave me a tour, we shared stories about having jobs we both loved, but that were definitely not as romantic as they seemed to the public. When we're told we're lucky to work with horses, we both smile, nod, and bite our tongues. Our conversation ran the gamut from laughing out loud to quiet, sad realities we didn't want to put into words. Keeping horses is life-altering for individuals, but programs like this are so complex. The founder must find a balance between the needs of the horses and the desires of the people. They had wonderful volunteers who were up to the job, but the herd was large and their requirements were many. There were always tough decisions to be made. In some ways, she might have carried the horses more than they carried her. And she would probably disagree with me on that because that's how horsewomen think.

A few of my clients attended this event, and that was always a joy, plus longtime blog readers and people who had been brave enough to try an online course. We shared a great day with the horses. I know. Any day with horses is great.

How to Attend a Clinic

Gray Mare memories: It was one of the first clinics I ever attended. The clinician was world famous; I signed up for three fifty-minute lessons that added up to more than I paid for my horse. It was a huge amount of money at the time. It still is.

The night before the clinic was to start, we all went to dinner together. The clinician, who smoked and talked with an accent, explained that if a person didn't get lessons as a kid, it was too late to learn to ride as an adult. Did I hear that right? We were all around age thirty and so shocked that he'd said this aloud that we just stared at each other. I bit my tongue and nearly swallowed it, choking with my outrage. I'd show him.

The next day was our first lesson. I groomed my horse to a shine, oiled my tack, and even put on the white saddle pad and polo wraps. I spent less time on myself but wore my tall boots, full-seat breeches, and my good helmet. We entered the arena and halted, waiting for instructions. The clinician was talking to the auditors, smoking, and being charming and foreign. Americans are suckers for an accent. I don't remember when I stopped breathing, but finally the clinician came over, exhaled some smoke, and baby-talked to my horse, who nearly spun out from under me. Maybe it was the smoke, the baby-talk, my collapsed lungs, or maybe all three. I tried my best but (here come the excuses) I was embarrassed, couldn't hear well, and it was scary riding in front of the auditors. On the high side, I don't think I blacked out. The clinician dismissed me ten minutes early. My horse and I stumbled back to our stall, and I cried.

On the second day, I put on the white saddle pad and polo wraps; I'd washed them overnight. Then I tidied my red eyes, took a deep breath, and rode into the arena again. My horse didn't spook this time, but the clinician didn't greet us as kindly. We got the same lesson as the day before, but in full disclosure, I was so nervous that I barely remembered the previous lesson.

I tried hard, but then I remembered that he'd told me I was too old to learn, and I was starting to believe him. We weren't better than the previous day and got dismissed early again. When we got back to the stall this time, I was mad. Too mad to sleep that night.

For our third and last ride, I had a change of attitude. My horse was clean enough. I pulled out a purple patterned saddle pad and purple polo wraps. I dusted my tall boots and wore a purple polo shirt. Dressage riders enjoy dressing like their horses. As I rode over to the clinician, I noticed I wasn't so awestruck. I didn't stammer, and I held his eye.

"Sir, my horse is small but very athletic. Could you give me some advice about how I might use his strengths to my advantage in competition?"

In the almost forty years since that day, I've seen about every side of a clinic. I've lost count of the number I've attended or audited, keeping notes after each one. Eventually, I organized clinics, attending to the details needed. I competed, but I also planned shows for my dressage chapter, worked in the show office, and scribed for judges as often as I could. I've seen the horse world from all perspectives. It's easy to complain, to judge an unfamiliar discipline unkindly, especially from a chair that can't buck you off.

Some riders are defensive. "I don't compete!" they confirm. "I just go to clinics." As if there is a difference. They both have all the expense and stress, and there's an audience of auditors, something we rarely had at shows. Most of all, you're riding for someone whose opinion you care about. How is it different?

Either way, it's valuable to get out with your horse for the weekend and see who you both are off-property. We can be our own worst judges and horses would like us to quiet the railbirds in our heads.

It's natural to have growing pains. Sometimes when you arrive at a different barn, the horse who comes out of the trailer is one you've never seen before. His hooves barely stayed on the ground, and he was twice as tall as the one you loaded. The first day is usually a little rough; a strange trainer, a strange location, a strange person inside your breeches. You want everyone to know how your horse behaves at home, but the clinician can only work with the horse in front of them. Clinicians know it isn't his usual behavior, but at least it happens when they can be of some help. Meanwhile, you wish you'd never left home. Assuming there is no actual abuse, please stick it out and give your horse a chance to cope.

Shows used to give a "Most Improved" award and I've won my share. You must have a lousy start to land one of these awards. It's the best feeling you can have with a horse to transform a hard ride into a good experience. Keep breathing. Things have to come apart so they can come back together better.

Traveling is stressful, so keep it simple. Let the horse be your only priority and mean it. If a fire-breathing dragon comes off the trailer, put a big smile on your face and say, "Good Boy!" First, you can't scare a horse out of being scared. Second, it throws people off guard. Take my word, someone that seemingly irrational is capable of anything.

So, how did the last lesson go at that long ago clinic? For the first time, the clinician gave me a genuine smile as he told me what our strengths were. It was as if he'd been wandering, but he zeroed in now. The canter was fine, he said, but our trot needed work. I had no awareness of anyone but the three of us. His advice was spot on, and the lesson was intense and affirming. But the real lesson I learned was to ask for what I want. Clinicians aren't psychic. They need a bit of direction, too.

If you live long enough, it all circles back. Now I'm the clinician. It's like being a drive-by shooter, stirring things up, and then you're gone. You get to meet so many more horses and riders, and your learning curve is continually growing. You also get blamed sometimes if someone has a challenging day. In that way, it's like any customer service job.

Here in Taos, a woman entered the arena with a halting

stride. She was a long-time reader, and we'd worked together online. I was happy to see her. Are those tears coming? How can she be nervous? It's just me! But then time blurred, and it was me with those twisted feelings. If my job title means too much, it will damage the lesson. Awkwardly, I smiled and told her to snap out of it. We laughed, and her horse exhaled, moist and loud. Then it's my favorite thing; just a horse, a rider, and me.

***

On the last day in Taos, there was a writing workshop. The attendees' talent was astounding, as usual. The founder had published already, and each person had a writing voice that was unique and strong. How can this experience be as dependable as it always was?

I hope everyone who comes to workshops keeps writing. Yes, our lives are over-scheduled, and our resources are limited. None of us are reclining by the pool evaluating our nails. The challenge of work, family, and keeping horses gets harder all the time. The objects in our lives that need to be juggled are so oddly shaped and weirdly defined that the thought of it all is disabling before we even start. We do what we can but never feel it's enough. Then it doesn't help that we're hard on ourselves about that, too. There's just no time to write. Pause. Because that's the best reason to write. To throw a wrench into the screaming rush of the day, to slow down the frantic patter of life, and spend some time with our thoughts. It's a way to poke our creativity and all kinds of things happen when that bear wakes up.

As usual, the experience of the writing day flipped both ways and I came away inspired, too. We had one more night here. We had parked the Rancho between a couple of horse trailers behind the barn. It was the perfect hideout. This stop had been a good one, so much diversity of experience. As we took our sunset walk, the sky was all the unnatural colors that sherbet comes in, layered over the graham-cracker-colored ground. Mister and I felt that same glow.

There are always horses who steal the show, but at this stop, especially great horses. I know. I always say that.

Amanda: A Voice for the Horse

From Taos, we drove northwest to the corner of Colorado and to a facility outside of a town called Hesperus. The barn that was available for the clinic was near another dead-end on a remote county road. Amanda, the organizer, lived a few miles away and she'd meet me there later. I had directions on where to park, and when I got through the gate, I saw there was an actual RV site. Who has these on private farms?

I backed my Rancho into a paved spot with oaks and shrubs all around. There was plenty of water, electricity, and even a black water dump. The land was sandy with scrub oak, and this corner of the southwestern sky had a new set of colors all its own.

Mister was on his long leash just outside the Rancho. He isn't much of a lover of the great outdoors, but he can enjoy a native sploot after a day of driving. He was not quite awake when it happened. This was serious. I could tell because he stood up.

It was high drama in the Rollin' Rancho camp as three strangers meandered in at a slow stroll. First, the Border Terrier, who had an enormous head and kinky hair. He acted cocky, like he was a tough guy. A Boston Terrier with weirdly long back legs followed him. What nose he had left looked like it had been on the losing end of a few barn fights already. Then, following after his lieutenants, the barn guardian dog, a Yorkie, swaggered into camp with a very serious stare. He seemed much taller than you'd imagine, up close like that. He stopped and looked us up and down in a judgmental way. His eyes inspected the trailer, assessing if there might be loot inside. They were clearly outlaws of the worst sort.

It was a standoff. I could hear the theme from every spaghetti western ever made, all at once. Mister glanced at the sun to tell the hour. Not so much as a breeze interrupted the standoff as the dogs took stock of each other, waiting for the sign. Mister was positioned at the entrance to the trailer, his legs squared, and his ears were, well, monumental. Such trophy ears as his have intimidated dogs who wear inconsequential ears themselves.

He did not go to welcome them. The intruders got bored and left, and Mister bounced up and down, and sneezed twice. When it was safe, he quietly mumble-barked them on their way and wagged his tail, the clear victor. He jumped into the Rancho and barked at me until I sat down. Climbing up, he filled my lap and held me down, so he knew exactly where I was. It had been quite a day so far.

***

The clinic went well. I am confident in my job. Again, I met wonderful horses, and yes, I think they all are, but that doesn't mean I'm blind. I helped the riders listen, and it wasn't always easy, being in between a horse and what a rider wants to believe. I understand that side, too, because I've been in trouble with a horse and in a confused way, almost defensive of him to clinicians. We're complicated about our horses.

People are certain that working with horses requires a mystical bond of some kind. It isn't true. If it was, I couldn't get results with horses within minutes of meeting them. The secret is listening with your eyes. Horses are always searching for humans who can communicate, and they recognize it at a distance. It's written all over us, just like they recognize fear or anger. Their behavior is my reward for a lifelong effort to understand them. It's how I know I'm on the right path. But often the thing they want us to know is that they are in pain, so it ends up not exactly what I'd hoped.

The days went quickly, and the people at this stop were particularly engaging. Some old friends came that I hadn't met in person yet, and I was happy to work with Amanda again.

Amanda is a younger trainer, but most trainers are younger than me at this point, I guess. I first met her when she came to a clinic in California, and I liked her right away. Initially, it was her smile and sly humor, but as soon as we began with a horse, I could see she wanted to go deep. She was much less concerned about the horse doing a specific task and way more interested in what the horse was experiencing.

A year later, I went to Amanda's barn for a clinic stop and saw she had made serious progress with a couple of challenging horses. We did some more brainstorming. Later, she sat in the back of the group, smiling as I spoke to her clients. I was probably repeating what she told them, in different words. That's always my hope.

I wish I could work with younger trainers more often. There is so much normalized abuse in training, but she will be part of the future. I want her to stick it out. At best, training horses isn't a high-paying job, but more than that, Amanda is one of the good guys.

California was expensive and getting a toehold meant working in other people's barns. It was easy to get forced out, and buying land there was nearly impossible. Amanda found a place in Colorado where she could afford a farm. Just barely, but she could, and soon moved. A small supportive group of friends came along, as well as a Cattle Dog named Lily who lives in Amanda's shadow. The property had a house and not much else, so she got to work. This woman built every inch of fence on the place and is working on building the shelters now.

She brought a herd of horses from California along to the desert prairie. Some are old and some are lesson horses. Some she has been trying to heal for years but still aren't okay. They all eat hay, they all require care, and most have no other place to be. She also has a talented horse with emotional challenges; that's how horse trainers get athletic horses that would normally be out of their budget. Amanda boards a few horses, but not enough to pay for the horses who can't earn their keep. It's always the way. They all share this new farm.

Like me, she often gets hired to fix damaged horses. It's slow, challenging work. She commutes to the location of the horse and that takes more time. Sometimes there is a colossal success and the horse blossoms. Then the owners move to a more well-known trainer, forgetting who got them there. They have no loyalty. The people, not the horse.

Sometimes Amanda tells the owner that the horse is unsound and that the cause of the behavioral problem is pain. Someone else who hasn't seen the horse recently might disagree, and for the cost of vet care, the owner doesn't want to believe Amanda or the horse. The horse says one thing and the humans say another and Amanda stands in the middle to translate. But the horse gets shipped to a trainer more interested in results.

To the clients, it's a choice between possibilities. Sometimes the new trainer makes promises or there is a thing they want more than their horse's welfare, but they wouldn't admit to it. Most times, the owner just doesn't know any better.

But a good trainer just got fired because she refused to ride a horse in pain. It's undeniably depressing to work so hard, achieve so much, get so little acknowledgment, and still lose the horse. That's an understatement. It's soul-killing.

Years ago, I had a client with a horse who was frightened and damaged by his first trainer. The horse was about twelve years old when I met him. He stood still for his owner to mount, but then wouldn't take a step. He was that afraid. They had sent him to a trainer when he was too young, and he came home in an extremely harsh spade bit a month later. You wouldn't walk forward into that pain, either.

She wanted to ride him now, after years off. He would not be a quick fix, but over the next year, we made good progress. Just when he was beginning to feel safe enough to offer a bigger try, his owner got frustrated. She told me off and then fired me. He was not mine, but good trainers have to let themselves love the horse to do the best work. The wisdom is questionable when you lose the horse, the client, and a bit of your heart, but it's still a choice I'd make every time.

Recently, I saw a post on social media saying that the same horse had died at a respectable age. The ex-client was heartbroken, saying that every day of that horse's life was perfect. I was glad she felt that way. She might have forgotten our work or just been too sad. I didn't expect her gratitude.

He was a horse with an enormous heart behind that memory of pain. I know what I did for that horse. Our experience together is mine forever. And sometimes this beautiful gelding still drops by to help me work with a lost youngster. I see him out of the corner of my eye, and he breathes us on. He's grazing just over my shoulder as I write.

Amanda, please stick it out. Despite those who don't share your ethics or those whose commitment to their horse isn't what it could be. Look for the hope we kindle in the fearful eye of a horse used hard by cruel humans. Stay for the horses who will never be sound, the ones who will never be yours. Listen and continue to understand horses so deeply that you begin to see yourself through their eyes. We're a little bruised, but being inside looking out was always the dream.

Resorts and Reservations

We spent the last night at Amanda's new farm and got a worried start the next morning because a prairie dog barked at Mister at just the wrong moment. Mister got nervous, and it ruined his morning constitutional. We folded down and drove to the next gas station to resolve things there. It was a hospitable location and lots of dogs had already relieved themselves there. Gas stations have public dog bathrooms. Some travel advice for you from Mister, at last.

For most of this trip, we would travel in and through Native American reservations in the Four Corners area, where Colorado, Arizona, New Mexico, and Utah meet. The Navajo Nation is the largest, comprising 27,000 square miles. The combined area of the reservation is greater than the states of Massachusetts, New Hampshire, and Vermont.

Mesas framed the view from one horizon to the other in all directions, rising straight up, their flat tops bracing the sky. The canyons were just as long and deep as the mesas were tall. It was as if the stone was lifted out of the ground and stacked at the canyon's edge in horizontal stripes in this gravel pit landscape. It's impossible to measure distance, but maybe moonscape-large is a good approximation. The sedimentary rocks shared the same colors of gemstones: garnet, topaz, amber, or pale rose quartz. Sometimes the rocks took on the color of the clouds, turning purple or misty teal. We passed arroyos washed smooth by a flash flood, either days or years ago. The soil was a rusty color, as if infused with blood. There was something timeless and familiar and uninhabitable, all at the same time. A land of memory and a monument to survival.

There was little green and less lawn. Maybe a small burst of spring color in the desert plants, but like my farm on the high prairie, harsh weather can easily strip the ground of plants and topsoil. Once that happens, nothing grows back soon. The balance of life was fragile, be it wild or domestic.

We followed a state highway south through small towns with too many stores closed, and too many empty parking lots. Fewer gas stations even. Sometimes a dirt driveway trailed to a handful of single-wides or small pre-fabs strung along a short frontage road. Red dirt bordered the houses and stained the bottom few inches of their walls. Some homes had small hogans next to them, much better suited to the environment, made of adobe, sun-dried mud bricks. Abandoned homes decomposed in this unforgiving wind with windows broken and doors ripped off their hinges. They sat next to houses with plastic toys in the yard.

Only a few thin horses stood slagging flies out back, with no shade in sight. A few wiry short-horn cattle wandered, looking to graze, with especially prominent pelvic bones, as if their ribs didn't say enough. They might be a Mexican breed. They looked as tough as they'd had to be to survive on this land. There was almost no roadkill, but high above, turkey buzzards were soaring arcs.

The cars parked close to the houses in yards with no visible boundary. Old tires, kid's hot wheels, broken appliances, and rusted flatbed trailers with dogs underneath fanned around the front. Some piles were trash with no place to be thrown, but other things were being stored for repurposing. Recycling has always been common in poor areas, but tourists call it something else.

The same kinds of piles are behind my barn. I keep a stash of used fence parts just in case. If I might need the linoleum leftovers or the plastic buckets, those are in the garage. I am frugal because I know things can always be worse. When I was little, I was embarrassed wearing hand-me-downs and worn shoes to school, always trying to look like we had more than we did. People here know it's no use. Poverty isn't a secret. There's no one to hide it from.

A few miles farther, I saw a sign spray-painted on a broken piece of plywood tied to a barbed wire fence next to the road. The house was a way back from the traffic but with the same red dirt stains and parked cars. Someone scrawled "please don't litter" in letters that trailed off.

The sign read like a plaintive call, a desperate plea. We have enough to deal with, it seemed to say. Fast food wrappers and plastic bottles clogged the ditch. It was never as obvious as here, under this sign. The residents hadn't littered their land, of course not. These families were just getting by. Tourists ate that kind of food. Maybe they asked how could people live this way, shaking their heads as they powered their windows down and tossed a Starbucks cup out. Throwing it was the same as name-calling the people living here; a bully's nod before speeding on. It was a privilege to have that kind of trash to throw away.

The sign said please.

There were long stretches with no towns, no life visible, like a third-world country. At the edge of one town, I saw a pickup truck with a few bales of pale hay on it and a sign that said $23 a bale. It's one-and-a-half times the amount I pay at home. The hay can't be local, probably from Colorado. Then I realized there would be no local produce, either. Nothing grew here. All the food had to be hauled in from elsewhere. Was it different than the commodity food their ancestors were given?

It's been thirty-three months since the pandemic and here on the reservation, everyone wore masks, from small children to adults. Even now, after most places have quit and there are no more signs up. On the reservation, even teenage boys comply. I remember reading that the death toll on reservations was especially high. The Navajo Nation had a higher per capita rate of infection than any other state. There are many reasons, including a prevalent lack of quality health care, poverty, and community behaviors. The masks they wore were mostly dark colored and looked like they doubled as a symbol of mourning. Even passing through, the loss seemed palpable. Ravens perched together on a fence like mourners waiting and watching.

Economists on the news have talked about the widening income gap for years. The dwindling middle class, the extreme inequality. It wasn't news to me, I noted the increase in expenses in my business and didn't raise my prices because everyone's expendable income was down. Horse people had to be conservative about how they spent on their horses. It's held organizers back from inviting me, but on the reservation, the survival line is even lower. I didn't expect it would be the most overwhelmingly obvious thing I saw traveling all year. But the reservations are worse. I can't look away. The trickle-down from the one-percenters has not made it here. It never will.

I was driving across the Navajo reservation the day that Queen Elizabeth died. It was sad but expected. She was at Balmoral Castle, her favorite Scottish retreat. It was a brave choice in her condition. They say she hung her crown on the gate; it is a remote and beautiful place. The place she chose to die. There was something about having seen the area that made it even more personal to me. But I have always had bittersweet conflicted feelings about the Queen. She was a horse lover; she started riding as a child and rode until the end on her beautiful Dartmoor ponies. That makes her part of our barn family.

I've never envied her at all. She lived a life of service with honor, and that involved both the requirement of managing children and the affairs of the state. She never had the freedom I do. Arguably, she needed to ride more to counterbalance that weight, but the Queen had enough staff to make it safer and easier. We'd all ride into our nineties if we had that kind of help.

I held a grudge against the Queen after Diana, the Patron Saint of Bad Marriages, died. It took me years to grow to understand the Queen beyond her royal stiffness. Her job was to play a part, just like I do, but on a much bigger stage. She became differently relatable as my life changed to be marginally more public. In the photos, she was impassive, almost cold. Except where she shared the frame with a horse. Then her eyes twinkled, and there was genuine joy on her face. I think that's when my smile is the most genuine, too. Did she hide from the world in the barn like I do?

As long as we're talking about her, Mister would like me to mention that the Queen was the Patron Saint of Corgi dogs around the world. They are independent dogs, often called the Queen's dogs, and she had a decent-sized pack, more than a polite number. They toddled down from state vehicles, lounged around in the palace, and they routinely bit the press. Mister considers himself a royal by birth.

There was footage of mounted riders, just people who brought their horses to the road for a special goodbye, looking on as her body traveled back to London. It was the acknowledgment that meant the most to me. The Household Cavalry Mounted Regiment, the Queen's Guard, was fancier, but this was a salute to a horsewoman from horsewomen, some of them my clients.

It also has to be mentioned that she was a white woman of extreme wealth and privilege. Her country colonized many others, assuming British occupation was better than the indigenous civilizations. Wars over land greed have had a foundation in racial inequality throughout history. Perhaps not her personal choice, but her inheritance was a history of plunder. At its height, Great Britain was a world power, but in the last few years, they have been divesting themselves from their colonies, and now the monarchy is in doubt. Many believe it's high time.

How to balance both extremes on this year-long road trip through elite resorts for the rich and Native American reservations. It was a line that was impossible to ignore, great wealth and cold poverty, with a narrowing strip of middle ground between them. Is it sustainable to defend the status quo and continue as we always have? When does privilege at the expense of others get tossed in the ditch with the Starbucks cup? It sounds so out of style, but what about the Golden Rule?

I am a white woman of privilege, but I'm not wealthy. I keep horses and teeter on that ever-narrowing strip between rich and poor. Prices go up and I hold on with white knuckles. I worry that the day will come when ordinary kids like me won't get to have horses growing up. Or maybe ever. But my skin color gives me more opportunity from the start than most girls living on this reservation. Poor white farm girls are still white.

Am I poking a touchy subject? It might be smart to hold my tongue on this whole topic of privilege, but every day it nearly burns my eyes. Road trips make the view indelible. Our history informs the present as much as the land does. I'm reading as much as I'm driving and many of the books touch the edges of what I see. Books like *The Night Watchman* and *The Sentence* by Louise Erdrich, *Empire of the Summer Moon* by Gwynne, *The Oregon Trail* by Parkman, and *Horse* by Brooks. And when you think about it, add every other book, from detective procedurals to science fiction. Privilege is so interwoven, so ingrained, that we don't notice it. That doesn't mean we're immune to the effects.

The American Indian Wars, which lasted 313 years, were mainly over land control. Like England, we thought we had the right to claim the world for ourselves. Our country was founded on the idea of Manifest Destiny. We learned it in history class. White American men were divinely ordained to settle the entire continent of North America. It meant we were justified in removing or destroying the native population. But it doesn't take a genius to make the connection between Manifest Destiny and white supremacists.

Here's where horses come in. As a teen, I loved Appaloosas. In the northwest, there is an annual progressive trail ride, sponsored by the Appaloosa Horse Club. One section per year, following the route taken by the Nez Perce attempting to escape the calvary. My romantic dream was that one day I'd own an Appaloosa and be able to go.

Instead, I dug into the history. Chief Joseph led eight hundred people, mostly women and children, in a fighting retreat known as the Nez Perce War, to avoid being put on a reservation. They headed for Canada, where Sitting Bull and the Lakota found refuge. Their skill in the face of incredible adversity won the Nez Perce admiration from the army and the public. Even their native horses, Appaloosas, got credit for their tenacious stability over rough terrain. We still labeled Chief Joseph a "savage" despite his brilliant and effective battle strategies.

The US Army finally stopped the tribe forty miles from the border. With too many lost, and too many weak, Chief Joseph surrendered. An officer of lower rank wrote that they only caught the Nez Perce because they had families with them but could not have beaten them in battle. The cavalry prevailed by outnumbering them. We took their land, not with honor or skill, but as thieves.

"Hear me, my chiefs; my heart is sick and sad. From where the sun now stands, I will fight no more forever." Chief Joseph's words at their surrender, October 5, 1877. I never forgot this quote and used it in teaching affirmative training. It's the promise I make to horses. It's also how a horse-crazy girl became politically engaged.

We fought a civil war over slavery and still debate civil rights daily. Even saying the words "Black Lives Matter" will incite passionate arguments in our divisive time. The books we grew up reading confirm stereotypes and beliefs that deserve reflection. Can I still cheer for *Gone with the Wind* and acknowledge the truth of slavery? Each time I read it, the meaning cuts deeper. I can't swoon over Rhett anymore. Is it the same plot as practically any Western movie made in their heyday? Do they all leave a sour taste now, like rodeos and horse races? Am I the one gone with the wind?

History is a living thing, present in every book we read, every movie, and every corner of life. Women were late to the conversation. A gentle reminder: Women got the vote in 1920, in the 19th Amendment fifty-two years after African American men got that right in the 14th Amendment. It was 1900 when every state had passed legislation modeled after New York's Married Women's Property Act, and we won the right to own our wages and homes. Before the 1970s, marital rape was legal in every US state.

It isn't the first time I've wondered how white men won the lottery. And I certainly didn't get into horse training to be political, but I've always worked in traditionally male jobs and felt the uneven squeeze. Women are a minority, even if there are more of us. When I talk about debunked training approaches, I know I'm stepping on traditional training toes, connected to political toes on the same foot.

So, my clients are women mostly, and already privileged to have horses. Many like me have stopped listening to the false science about herd dynamics and outdated fear-based training methods. We see intimidating horses into submission as a failure. We understand being hurt or frightened never creates trust or love. Is Affirmative Training a #*MeToo* movement for horses?

From that point, things can get extra touchy. Humans are born predators, but women can become prey to our own species. Having the experience of both sides gives women a unique insight into working with horses. We understand dominance will not bring mutual trust. And we are excellent negotiators who allow horses to volunteer. Rather than force them, we trust their intelligence and allow them autonomy. We are having wonderful success training horses with kindness and understanding, both in our home arenas and in the competition arena. The horse world is changing and becoming better for horses. Women lead that change and we should be proud of our contribution.

As much as we try to separate horses from the world, everything we do bleeds into everything else. For me, it's easier to learn a thing from horses than from the news. I'm not saying that horse training is the same as world peace. I'm just saying it's one place to begin.

The tank is low, and my thoughts are cooling down. Reservation dogs slink around the gas pumps with arched backs and visible ribs. Their fur is almost always charcoal brown, dry, almost burnt-looking. They are like coyotes, smart scavengers. They stalk people in cars with eyes peering from submissively lowered heads. Tourists give them scraps in the same way they might feed wild animals. It's a thin line of domestication with these dogs. I wonder if the workers try to send the dogs away, or if that is even possible. We are all creatures of instinct and intelligence, but would animals think we were the pinnacle of intelligence? Filling my tank, I watch people come back to their vehicles with arms full of snacks in bright packages sized larger than their contents and drinks in monster plastic cups. I wonder if the tourists will toss their trash out of their cars a few miles down the road.

I don't engage the dogs as I fill up. I kept my eyes to myself and they didn't ask me. We read each other too well. They know me. It's something I learned from horses.

Still, I don't let Mister out at this stop. I worry that Mister might get defensive and do something we'd both regret. Besides, we can stop a ways down the road. Mister is a dog who belongs to a white woman of privilege. We have choices.

Barb: The Elderly Cowgirl

The last clinic stop on this southwest trip was in Flagstaff, Arizona. Barb, the organizer, was a long-time client and hero of mine. The clinic itself was at a facility a few miles from her home, but Mister and I unhooked in the field behind her house. In the morning, Barb and I were each driving to the clinic location. She needed to haul her mare, Scooter, and I needed to have the training gear in my truck.

At our agreed-upon departure time, Mister and I were ready to go, waiting in my truck. Down the hill, at a small distance, I saw Barb and Scooter in the pen, haltering and preparing to leave for the day. She had the trailer hitched and parked in the driveway with the back door open wide. Barb had prepared well, which is smart because last-minute fumbling affects horses. Preparing ahead like this can avoid anxiety on both sides and create a rhythm. For all we can't control, this part can be easy.

I'm not sure why people think it's so hard to get horses to load. Humans might be the ones afraid of trailers. At the end of the last day of clinics, it can be a challenge for some. People think the horses should know they are going home, but unless horses trailered frequently, they don't know. Mainly, everyone is tired. I help if I'm asked, but I don't loiter, always knowing that feeling watched makes the job a little harder.

This morning, we waited where we were. I hadn't started my engine. Scooter would see me, of course. The truck hadn't been there previously, but we sat back to watch the Barb and Scooter Show.

Barb finished checking the halter and lead rope, opened the gate to Scooter's pen, and led her out onto the drive. Scooter stood quietly as Barb closed the gate without pulling on her mare's face once, and then, on a long slack lead, the mare followed Barb's feet. It's instinctual with horses. Barb wasn't being a genius. Yet.

Barb is a woman of a certain age, but always lively, with the brightest eyes and a quick laugh. She's had a lifetime of experience. All the best and worst things have happened, and she's survived with a kind heart, strong political opinions, and a great sense of humor. Barb refers to herself as The Elderly Cowgirl. I wouldn't mind if other horse people emulated her version of "elderly."

One thing Barb and I have in common is hearing loss. She recently got cochlear implants. I have hearing aids, but from first meeting her, when she clipped a special mic onto my collar at a clinic, I knew I liked her. She asked for what she wanted and did it with a smile. Being assertive is a wonderful thing, as any mare will tell you.

After a few strides, Scooter halted thoughtfully and looked up the hill at us. The truck didn't belong there, and concern about the environment is a mare's primary job. She paused, thinking about us for a moment. Barb gave her time to process what she saw.

Scooter is a mare of a certain age with a chocolaty color, and she has tiny ears hidden in a thick mane. She is an Icelandic horse, tough and independent. Smart and steady. There are some physical issues now and then, but Barb gets them sorted. They are not quitters. Scooter's favorite color is red, and she and Barb like to dress to match. It isn't cute, it's their partnership made visible. They are on the same team. Barb also makes up songs in praise of Scooter, and she isn't afraid to sing them right out loud for you. But don't underestimate their skill; it's not that they haven't hit some bumps over the years. It's just that they keep working on understanding each other.

Finally, Scooter exhaled, and they moved toward the trailer, the lead still slack, looking for all the world like they were dawdling. The art of being with horses is to go slow, even if a clinician is watching.

Then Scooter saw something on her right. She stopped to look, and Barb slowed to a stop; the lead remained slack. This wasn't a big visible action. Barb didn't look for what Scooter saw, but just kept breathing and looking ahead to the trailer. She stayed on task.

Barb and Scooter trail ride in the hills around Flagstaff. The greatest skill for a trail horse is to be curious, and not fearful. To stay steady and process what they see, rather than spin and bolt. Barb and Scooter show the quality of their relationship in quiet, small moments. Does this trailer conversation seem more impressive now?

When Scooter was ready, the mare brought her head back, and they walked the rest of the way to the trailer.

We don't need to cue a horse when the back door of the trailer is open. We take ourselves so seriously that we think we need to train common things every time we do them, but horses are intelligent. They can understand an open door on a trailer. Worse, when we make a big deal out of ordinary things, horses wonder why we're focused on something they don't see. Our worry is palpable to a herd animal used to depending on the senses of those around them as well as their own. A horse is right to think twice if the human has trailer anxiety.

Barb trusted that Scooter knew what the task was, and the mare paused again, thoughtfully taking her time. She considered the tall step, and then, without swinging ropes or popping whips, with no fanfare at all, Scooter got up into the trailer. Barb gave her a pat, secured her for the trip, and closed the door.

Haven't we had enough of chasing horses in circles, baiting them with food, or flooding horses with sticks? Horses have certainly had enough; they are often more afraid of the ground behind the trailer than the trailer itself. Afraid of the scene of the crime, where the fight happens.

We let horses always be right because there is no upside to making them wrong and punishing them. If a horse has unpleasant experiences around trailers, it will take time to win their trust back. We stay affirmative in our minds and are ready with praise. They will load when they feel safe. Aggression should never be an option; that's how we train horses to be afraid. When we intimidate horses, we damage their trust in us.

Watching this pair was not just a great start to the day. It was one of the best trailer-loading demonstrations I'd ever seen, a conversation without drama. If Barb felt pressure, it didn't show. The mare never once said no, and Barb never once corrected her. They simply continued with their task.

Had five minutes passed? Ten? Time has no power over this pair and that makes the task go quickly. It's all the micromanaging and bickering and flapping and circling that takes time.

Is there anything more beautiful than choice and consent? Ever notice how those good at what they do make it look ordinary? The proper goal with a horse, at the trailer or out on the trail, is to see peace as the win. It's common for people to say their horse is better for the trainer and not the same for them. We aren't magic; this is how we do it. Good trainers have learned to quiet their body and mind. To stay focused on one request and not confuse their horses by changing the question. Horses give better answers when we ask calmly and simply.

It isn't *what* we ask a horse, it's *how* we ask. A partnership doesn't happen just because we say so. We must perish the thought of a fight. It isn't enough to think peace, go deeper. It's holding a consistent embodiment of a soft and fearless confidence in asking, so horses can trust us.

If you have problems loading horses, I'd suggest finding an

"Elderly Cowgirl" to help you. They make the art of partnership look ordinary. Horses love that.

***

Some of us in this Flagstaff clinic were a reunion of women who used to meet at Heidi's, who passed away the previous year. I was coming home from a clinic at her ranch when I met that face talker on the airplane. Heidi's energy seemed to blend with the shadows as we remembered and missed her and her beloved Arabian herd now.

New people and horses came to the clinic, as well as previous participants. There were long-time blog readers; we knew each other by word more than face. As usual, I had a plan and a schedule, but it went off the rails in all the best ways. The horses inspired us; it's as dependable as dawn. It was a time of vulnerable sharing and interesting questions. We are women with a passion to do better for horses. Miraculous and ordinary for our sort.

When it was all done, I was sharing a glass of wine with Barb and her wife, Ann. We talked about the weekend, but mostly we appreciated each other's company. I got a good recommendation for support hose from Ann. Yeah, it's time.

On Monday morning, I began the drive home to Colorado Springs. It's a two-day drive, but I've been on this road before. Soon we were in our home state, and I recognized the town names on the signs. We can coast home from here.

We spent the last night at an RV park outside Durango. Mister and I watched a movie on my computer. One of us snacked on a few too many liver treats, and then we dozed off in a dog pile. It was a celebration, not that Mister cares. He never knows the plan, and he does just fine without it. Or maybe we're always on his plan.

I returned home a year older. It was my birthday during the Flagstaff clinic. I didn't tell anyone. Age is in my thoughts more, not with bravado or as an excuse. It's that I know this is my swan song. I was always so young for what I did, whether leaving home at seventeen or showing my work in New York galleries at twenty-five. I have always made alternative decisions, worked unusual jobs, and struggled to relate to humans, but now I'm the old one doing it. It's taking some time for the backside of my eyes to adjust.

Home Stay
September 14–15

The Season of Letting Go

The autumnal equinox is about change. There was a miserable fog today, dense and so uncommon on my high prairie. Chilly enough for a sweatshirt, the dog bellies were all muddy, and the geldings were skidding and careening about, itchy in new winter coats. Dusk comes earlier each day, and we had frost last week. The leaves are hardening and letting go.

If there is a New Year, this is my time on the calendar to assess the old year. Fall is a season of remembering those who have gone on ahead while taking a reckoning of those who are still here. Then I put my wolf skin on and pondered the meaning of being the only predator my animals have. I stand motionless, stalking at my elders, weighing their strength against the cold months ahead.

I am a bit of an expert on death, so this subject comes up often with strangers and friends all year through. But be clear, this isn't about you, it's about me. Death has been an oversized part of my life from an early age. I used to fear the best parts of me would chip away with each passing of a cat or horse or human I loved. So much loss would take too much of a toll. Instead, loss has given me grace. It isn't that I welcome death now, it's just that at a certain point in frequency, I gave up denial and began making peace with death. So, I welcome sad conversations because the words need to be said. Because scary things shrink when we drag them out into broad daylight and pick away at them. Death is as ordinary as dirt. Living is the art that I hold highest.

Fear of death blinds us to a more important question. Why are we so unwilling to see their pain? Every week someone tells me they have a thirty-something horse who acts young and happy. They proudly brag that they still ride. What are they thinking? Every week there are horses half that age struggling with some undiagnosable malady and in more decline every day. Is it possible for an animal to separate physical pain from wild anxiety?

What does it mean to a horse, a flight animal, to lose the ability to escape? To not lay down for fear of not being able to get up. To constantly pretend to be strong so others won't see their weakness. Their senses may fade, but survival instinct doesn't dim. How mentally damaging is a physical limitation to a prey animal?

Sometimes it's a slow game of attrition. Each year there's a health crisis, and the animal recovers about 85% of his old self. We saved him, but he's not like he was before. Then, year after year, the elder loses a bit more ground, but we think there hasn't been a hard line when we know it's time. Just increasing cruel frailty while we cling to the nebulous, waiting for an even bigger sign. How much suffering is enough?

We praise that special sweetness in elders. For all the decline I've witnessed, I recognize a gentle eye is a sign of shutting down, frequently a sign of pain. Sometimes I wonder if they are just exhausted to death.

Why do we act like death is a failure? Why do we act surprised and make the elderly prove their pain? Do we blame ourselves because we can't stop time? Do we blame them because they got old? That's the last thing I'd want them to feel.

We need to separate our emotions from our animal's

experiences. We think they're aware of what's happening, but if anything, they can become anxious about our emotions. Animals have a powerful survival instinct but don't struggle with existential life-and-death questions. Humans are the ones stuck with that.

I met a man who said he spent $160,000.00 on brain surgery for his young Great Dane. He lost his dog but took comfort in that he'd done what he could. No one wants to talk about money at times like this, but I need to be pragmatic. I can't risk the entire farm for one of us, so I have a kind of DNR amount for each species and then I trust it. Animals aren't capable of understanding money or guilt. I follow their lead on that.

On the poor ownership side, so much damage has been done: mournful neglect, hollow ribs, animals whose eyes are blank. It's ugly, but I wonder if sometimes we hang on too long, compensating for all those who neglect animals. If we try to make up for their lack by keeping our animals alive too long. We go too far to help them, sometimes making things worse. We keep the animal alive past when we should, unconsciously overcompensating for the others. Anything is better than admitting what no one wants to know.

We can easily recognize their pain if we let ourselves. But if we can acknowledge their pain, then we must weigh it against our own.

Finally comes the day when the worst thing starts to look like a relief. I've seen too much suffering to believe that a natural passing is always peaceful. They struggle if organs don't shut down in the right order; they don't just "fall asleep." I've seen animals grapple with pain and fear when "letting nature take its course." And that happened with my father. When I declined to help my father kill himself, he spat out, "If I was a dog, you could shoot me." I just nodded. It wasn't fair.

I'm watching three elders on my farm now. One is an ancient llama who is almost blind and frightened. One is an ancient ginger cat who has outlived her contemporaries by years. Her meow sounds like a bird chirping. And one is our heart, our Edgar Rice Burro. His passing will be like a long train coming; I'll see it at the farthest distance. At least, that's what I hope.

I won't say their ages because it isn't a contest. If one cat lives twenty years, we think they all should, and most fail. Time is a phantom thing. As uncontrollable as winter storms, it goes slowly until it goes fast. So, like taking a spoonful of poison a day, I will prepare myself and be ready. There are worse things than death. I cannot abide the suffering of animals.

The end-of-life decision is never easy. Knowing that we will mourn them forever, is there a way to make this easier *for them*? Once a visitor, a friend of my assistant, overheard plans for an upcoming euthanasia. She played out a melodrama that scared a couple of old geldings who were trying to graze on one of their last sunny afternoons. She felt a need to pile her own feelings about death on them. I regretted ever letting her on the farm. Now I keep the dates a secret.

Here's my plan. The vet will come out. We'll let it be like any other shot. There is no reason an animal who's had vet care before would worry about an ordinary shot. It isn't that I won't mourn them; I'll just wait until they're dead. Anticipatory mourning makes animals nervous; besides it isn't like I stop loving them. That would be a serious cause for concern.

Just breathe with them. Let our breath be enough; breath was their first memory. Let it be the last.

Sometimes, looking around, it seems the entire herd is on the way to dying. Life here is a one-way ticket; the best care I can muster until the end, with the promise that I won't abandon them to death. Better to go a week too soon than a day too late. I will give them that ultimate gift that is not promised to me.

Until then, I won't shame my companions for getting old. I'll leave a steady warm hand on their neck, pull on a smile, and tell them all the best stories of our bravest adventures.

Back to Wyoming
September 16–19

A Festival in Laramie, Wyoming

After being home for three tiny days, I headed back to Wyoming for a festival that also had music, a quilt show, llamas, and a local horse rescue group. They had invited me to give two presentations on Calming Signals, an hour long each, and have the rest of the day for general question answering and schmoozing.

I stopped at the Cheyenne barn on the way up. Joni invited a group of riders, and they watched us work with her horses. It was the kind of collaborative day that horses like and the people enjoy watching. I felt sharper afterward, more tuned up after a day with horses. And it was always good to be with a group that really supported the horses and each other.

Then on to Laramie and day one of the festival. The location was at a state historical site with rustic log buildings. The music was legendary, and the gourmet ethnic foods were irresistible.

A small group watched me and listened to the ideas I shared. I wish I could say the crowd went wild, but this area was conservative about horse training methods. I understood tradition was comfortable and change was not. My farm was in the same sort of area with a commitment to "the cowboy way." It always seems odd that I'm more known in foreign countries, but days like this remind me.

My demo was in a large pen with three mares who were in varied stages of rehab. They had much to say, and I listened. We all think we listen. We all think we go slowly, but I showed what patience looked like in real-time. It doesn't match the high drama of a rodeo.

Just before my demo, I met a volunteer at the fair. The woman was from another state where she does search and rescue. She works with a reservation dog, black with a spangle of white on her chest and pointy stand-up ears she wears very close together. In her photo, the dog positively beams with intelligence. And she climbs ladders. The woman said she was the oldest handler in her group, and the other dogs were well-bred German shepherds and Malinois. But this woman and her rez dog were the top pair. When I thought back to the dogs on the reservation in Arizona, it did not surprise me.

This woman was my like-mind here, my kindred spirit. The horse conversation blew her away when I'm sure a couple of others wondered if I even knew how to halter a horse. She and I worked with opposing natures in our animals, but the way we worked was more similar than different.

An animal's language is easy to translate if you give yourself up to it, if you don't think you are superior to your animal. I looked for her in the group as I carefully pointed out each eye movement and ear flick, then translated the meaning of looking away, the meaning of grazing. Calming signals were first discussed in the dog training world, and it changed our understanding of the popular domination methods of the day.

At the end of the day, I walked to my truck to find Mister wasn't there. No, I didn't bring him. This wasn't his kind of gig. Too many people running loose. They didn't allow dogs at the festival. Still, I was just stricken that the dog I didn't bring wasn't there. More dependent on his wise council than I knew, I couldn't shake it off.

Instead, I picked up dinner and headed back to my room with a king bed and way too many pillows. There was a spa tub, but I didn't feel I should use that much water. The drought never leaves this land, as my flaky skin reminds me, and I take a Navy shower, toweled off with a scrap of terrycloth, and hit the sheets.

On the second day of the event, my demo came later in the day, an affirmative riding lesson. One horse just wasn't safe to ride, upset at the strange surroundings and tired from the day before. The mare had paced most of both days and now just couldn't do it. We listened to the horse. The audience might not have agreed with me, but being a horse advocate means putting the mare's needs above the audience's expectations. It happens just as often to well-loved horses. Sometimes *not* riding is as important as any riding lesson I give.

The second rider had a wonderful ride, her horse getting softer and more relaxed with every stride. The pair deserved so much credit for surviving the anxiety of the other horse, as well as all the challenges of being a demo rider in front of an audience. So brave. I am still proud of that good pair.

And then it was done. The horses were exhausted. This would have been a tiring weekend even if they were seasoned show horses accustomed to traveling to new places, but they were rescue horses who'd had lots of recent changes in their lives. Sometimes we expect horses to work like dirt bikes. In a situation with expectations, it's hard to acknowledge the horse's needs. Peer pressure is a motivator for bad behavior when our ego needs a result. It was good that things had gone a bit sideways for the first horse. I hoped my actions spoke louder than words.

What Did the Old Gray Mare Say?

Later in the day, a man approached the horse rescue booth. I was sitting there with a volunteer who stood and cheerfully greeted him. He was the sort of man who had a joke for all occasions and shared them as a habit.

"What did the old gray mare say?" he asked. He leaned into

the booth and without a pause answered himself, "I'm down and I can't giddy up."

Then he laughed at his wit, waved, and was gone. He wasn't interested in the rescue or the horses. We just reminded him of a joke he knew. The volunteer laughed to be polite, but I didn't bother. A horse who can't get up wasn't funny to me. Must we laugh to be polite? Add it to my list of shortcomings. I'm a party pooper.

A horse down on the ground can be a dangerous situation. It might mean a long rehab if we're lucky and have the funds to assist. It might mean a gentle euthanasia, which will break our hearts and still require some cash. I know the man didn't have evil intent; he thinks he's funny. Or he doesn't think at all.

My mother told me my problem (one of many) was that I had no sense of humor. It was after a group of my uncles circled me, put a bag over my head, and then made fun of me for being a hippie. I had a beaded anklet that offended them. They held my arms and taunted me while pulling at the anklet. I retaliated by swearing a blue streak, trying to cover my fear with bravado. I kicked one of them, but it got back to my mother that I was silly to be mad when they were only teasing. Jokes in my family always had a wicked edge, both physically and mentally. Jokes were a way of saying something intentionally mean but then saying they were kidding when you knew they weren't. The recipient was supposed to smile. But my family was all about if you could take the punch. My mother was right. I was humorless about it.

I'd gone to the rodeo a few times growing up and I hated the clowns. You are supposed to think they were heroes who saved cowboys from bulls. As if bull riding wasn't doing the gene pool a favor. Clowns used that same humor as my family and I thought they were mean, too. You could see the evolution of bad jokes in their skits. I am old enough to remember watching racist skits. They evolved to ethnic skits, then misogynist skits about dumb blondes and wives. At the last rodeo I went to, and it was decades ago now, the clown skit was ridiculing gays. The target changed over the years, but the intention still felt more cruel than funny. The humor of my people.

I'd like to say I stopped going to rodeos in protest of bad clown jokes, but the cruelty didn't stop there. I'd seen too many animals being jerked around. Horse's mouths gaped in pain, with their heads tied down. Cowboys aren't such heroes when the calf dies. The problem with learning about calming signals is once you see the anxiety and fear, you can't unsee it. The party ended when I saw the rodeo through the horse's eyes.

Part of my job is being amusing while talking about hard, sometimes ugly truths. Call it the rodeo clown aspect of being a clinician. My rule with comedy was that jokes should be more sophisticated than rodeo clown jokes about asses or rescued horses. I'd be killed if I joked about old horses on the ground. I hope we describe animals by understanding their nature without demeaning them. If someone has to be foolish, let it be us. But if jokes are too self-deprecating, they can become a knife that can do some self-harm. It's better to find affectionate humor, the fun in a twist of words, or brag about something counterintuitive. I try to balance myself on the tightrope of not taking myself too seriously and finding humor between difficult topics. Then I let myself laugh, hoping to cue it in others. Laughter is a human calming signal. It makes us feel better, and that makes horses feel better, too.

"I've fallen and I can't get up," was from a commercial for a gadget for independent elders to call for help. The slogan hit popular culture over *thirty years ago*. I like dark humor, but this one struck a different chord. Was the man at the festival making fun of old people who were losing mobility? He wasn't younger than me. Does acting like we are in on the joke make it less cutting? I could hear my mother's ghost remind me of my lousy sense of humor.

Maybe they haven't been out in a ground blizzard at midnight trying to get an old horse up on his feet. Maybe they haven't tried to deadlift their cancer-stricken father back onto his bed. Or maybe I'm just no fun if that makes it easier.

The day ended, and it was time to pack up. The weekend was a big success. The organizers had to cancel this festival the two previous years because of COVID-19. Now it was at a new site, and organizing events like this was a huge juggle of a job. For this festival to happen was a tremendous win. As I was learning this year on the road, things were different now. The pandemic created a ripple effect with an undertow that will take some time to understand.

One more night at the hotel and I headed home very early the next morning. The passenger seat of my truck was empty except for a snowfall of dog hair. I hurried home so I could wag my tail in apology. The dogs and I all take our jobs too seriously and then celebrate our geeky weirdness. Jack lifted a lip to show teeth in a sideways sneer. He's nervous that way. Preacher will shriek until next Thursday, and Mister flew up on my lap and dropped like a rock. Once I was good and truly pinned, he gave me the side-eye, the "I told you I should have come" look. Right again.

Home Stay
September 20–27

Goodbyes Don't Get Easier

I had only nine days to get ready for the longest of the four trips this year. We're heading to the East Coast, so I started prep by going out to the barn. I mucked for hours each morning, resting on the fork, and talking to the horses. Edgar Rice Burro took the most conversation because he misses me the most. Donkeys are territorial and protect their farms. It's his job. He just can't figure out how to protect me from leaving.

Midday, there's a dog pile nap. Then, date nights with the Dude Rancher. I spend my days at home just being home. I practice *be-here-now-ness*.

In the middle of being here, I began the plan for not being here. Before the pandemic, organizers used to plan clinics six months in advance and now many can't decide until the last minute. I can blame COVID-19, but it doesn't help. See me as that man on *The Ed Sullivan Show* spinning plates.

My personal Catch-22 has become obvious. Planning has always been time-consuming but for the first time, they are canceling late. I can't hold up scheduling the entire trip because I'm waiting for one lagging confirmation. But one would-be organizer ghosted me after we exchanged a dozen emails. I sent a few more before I took the hint. It's just business, I told myself. Still, I felt jilted.

A cancellation at the beginning or the end of a trip was easy to work around, but within two days of leaving for this trip, I had three last-minute cancellations for clinics in the middle of the trip. And now it was too late to fill the dates. That was going to mean no work for several days, not counting the days that I'd scheduled off. I was going to be spending money while making none.

This is where I remind you one more time I'm not on vacation, not on a trust fund, and I am certainly not retired. But I'd promised Mister both oceans this year, not that he cared. And I would hate to disappoint him. Again, not that he cared.

Knowing that I was going to need income immediately once I returned, I spent hours scheduling classes to start in the online school as soon as I was back. The online school had become as important a job as travel. Being self-employed was a roller coaster ride, and it wasn't slowing down. And yes, I got to work with horses. They say we get what we pay for, but I think it's the opposite. We pay for what we get.

Physical preparation for this trip was familiar. I don't leave a mess, so I did a thorough cleaning and dusting, more laundry, and if there's time, some baking. There was no joy in getting ready to leave. It almost felt like it wasn't worth the effort when the preparation took so much planning and work. These tasks are necessary, but they don't get faster.

Then it's the rest of the farm prep before leaving, giving the water tanks a special scrub, cleaning the barn, and checking the fences. I restocked the supplements, feed, and hay. Then I re-checked everything that I just checked three more times.

I'd been worried about Lulu all year. She was my ancient, matted skeleton of a cat, with either blindness or dementia or both. She was so old that neither of us could do the math, and she ate less every day and drank more. I don't need a vet to tell me what was wrong with her.

Lulu was a feral barn kitten, wild and intractable when I brought her home. She stayed in the house but was out of sight, in closets or under beds, for a couple of years until my dog tamed her. It was long after that when she finally sat with me. Her long ginger hair made her look larger than she was. She had a crack in her meow, a half-silent gacking noise like she swallowed the sound. And she had outlived her dog for many sleep-in-the-sun years.

I write this as if I have to justify my affection in an obituary, as if I must defend my actions. Lulu would never question me. Here is the truth. I knew she would continue to fail. Her best days were not ahead, and the Dude Rancher wasn't as good at seeing pain or dealing with death as I am. So, before the trip, I called my in-home "transitions" vet to euthanize her. My vet understood my choice, and we did our best for Lulu.

It's not the first time I've made this choice and timed it before a trip. Each time, I felt guilty and heartbroken. But I do it with no apology. She became my responsibility the day that hissing wad of fur came home with me. In the end, she was a freckled, loose-skinned, cloudy-eyed elder almost as light as a kitten. She is God's Lulu now, in moth heaven, I hope.

I didn't tell the horses I was leaving; they knew. My mare looked away more when I was close. Edgar Rice Burro took it the hardest. He had aged over this year, almost twenty-five now. When he first came to the farm, he'd bray every time he saw me. It settled into just heaves of a few pre-bray throaty moans at feeding time. In old age, he was back to calling when he saw me in a window or when I opened a door. He's losing confidence. His health is changing. When I'm in bed at night in the Rancho, hundreds or thousands of miles away, I think I hear him. His voice carries.

Maybe Edgar picks up on it from the dogs; they are the first to get anxious. Preacher Man gets barkier, and Jack gets clingier. Mister, who has never rushed the gates, starts breaking out of the yard. Then he bolts to the Rancho door and waits there, looking at the door and back at me and then the door again. He may have to break out for a couple of weeks, but disappointment will not deter him. He'll keep breaking out until we go.

The Sunrise Side
East Coast
September 28- November 7

Wading in Crocs

When we finally pulled out, Mister gave a satisfied moan as his head dropped to the console between us. He told me so. We headed east for our first stop in Kearney, Nebraska, driving familiar roads across the Colorado prairie. I let the semis pull us along like a reluctant child leaving a birthday party. When I could no longer see Pikes Peak and the Front Range in the rearview, the call of the road kicked in. There were dozens and hundreds of wind turbines in all directions, their blades lumbering through the air, polluting the view. And hopefully saving the planet. We pay for what we get.

GPS Woman takes us away from I-70, cutting across county roads, heading northeast to I-80 and Nebraska. Acres of prairie grass tossed by currents of air were almost mesmerizing, as the sleek blades capturing the wind's energy held formation on the horizon. The native grass gave way to cornfields and hayfields with the same towering windmills standing guard all the way to the next horizon. Cattle grazed by antelope in fenced pastures. A grain elevator in the distance meant there was a small town ahead. We passed feed lots black with mud, manure, and Angus cattle. This land is our actual grocery store.

Today is the death-aversary of my Grandfather Horse, gone seven years now. Some of us try to please our fathers and fail for decades of our lives. I've given that up for the goal of impressing a dead horse. It's a debt I savor more with each payment. For the thirty years he gave me, I pay it forward working for other horses now.

GPS Woman got us off the freeway and sent us down a country road. It looked exactly like you'd expect in late September; the cornfields were all near harvest. We drove a few miles, taking the turns we were told to, right until GPS Woman told us to turn right, and the road wasn't even a road. This was worse, even more unkept and narrow than the usual one-lane mistakes. This looked like the one the tractor used to plant the field last spring. It was more like a path in the corn. Miraculously, I didn't turn.

GPS Woman has a great sense of humor, but I know how this ends. I kept driving and eventually left-turned my way back to a version of civilization, and then asked her again. This time, GPS Woman sent me on an overpass in the opposite direction from where we were, and the campground was not even a half-mile from the freeway. I could have seen it from the road. What a comedian she was. And so smart to crack a joke so randomly that she drew me in every time.

It could be worse. An hour ago, we passed Prairie Dog State Park, and if we had somehow ended up there, I can't imagine the night Mister would have had. The stink alone, not that I am evolved enough to smell it. Mister always gets a bit constipated when there are varmints around. He wouldn't have blinked all night and I would have had stress fractures on several ribs from his protection.

We pulled into the RV park. This one was friendly and green, not very full on a weekday. There was a slow-moving river next to the park and after we set up, Mister and I took a nature stroll. We took the cement sidewalk, which is Mister's idea of close enough. That way, he could see what was ahead and venture off the pavement when he felt the need for sniffs and business.

***

It was a three-day drive to the Chicago area, and on night two, we were on the outskirts of Des Moines. Our RV site was at the edge of a large pond. It had been a hot day, and as usual, we were both sit-sore, so we set up the Rancho, easy and quick by now. I hadn't pinched a finger in a while.

We strolled across a lane to the pond. There was a wide, gradual downhill path to the beach, and the water was shallow at the shore. There was no choice. I rolled up my pant legs, waded in a few strides, and smiled at the eternal practicality of my Crocs: soft, plastic, and holes everywhere.

Mister glanced both ways with the look of a disapproving church lady, but we were using the extra-long leash. I left it slack and by the time I was about five feet from shore, the greenish water was lapping around my ankles. My Crocs let the water flow in and soothe my toes.

Mister hates the water. I do not coax him. He walked a few slow steps one way, and then the other on the shore, avoiding even looking at me now. I wouldn't be long.

Then he stopped, faced me, and in a moment, waded in toward me. A few strides and his chest was wet and his ears almost horizontal. Was it his personal fire walk?

Words came to my mind, "Whither thou goest..." I don't know the Bible, but I know this one. Did it come from him? No, Mister quoting the Bible was a bridge too far. I came right out of the water. Back at the Rancho, I carefully dried his flippers. He has thick ankles and enormous feet with long hairs between his toes. Mister patiently held them for me, in the way I've seen queens allow servants to dress them in movies.

Then Mister jumped up on the bed and rolled into a double-reverse sploot. If a sploot is that belly flat to cool linoleum lay-down, it makes sense that a reverse sploot is belly up. With his neck kinked so far to the side, that counts as a double. He was air-drying his belly and flippers.

We don't know a rescue dog's birthday or even their age for sure, so we mark the day they came, so we can at least know how long they have lived with us. Mister's one-year mark came the week before we left home. It was such a rush out of town, but a year had passed, along with over 9,000 miles so far.

When our lives intersect with other lives, we never know what it will mean in the beginning. We don't know how much time we have with them, whether it's a passing moment or long sweet years. We might become attached at the soul, and other times, it's closer to the surface. Neither Mister nor I knew who we would be for each other when he came. We didn't know A-Frame trailers either.

It started simply; we met in a hotel room. He was shy and a bit nervous. I sat on the couch with liver treats, waiting. He slowly came closer and accepted the treat. Then he climbed over and covered my whole lap, releasing his muscles to become dead weight. It was all over but the tattoos.

Now is as good a time as any to admit I'm having problems in Mister's agility class. I can't keep up with him. When I run, my feet slap the ground, my body lurches, and sometimes I lose sight of him and nearly trip because he's under my feet. I am not gazelle-like; he has twice my physical ability. Agility class leaves me feeling unflatteringly old and awkward. Often, he must stop and wait for me to catch up. I cheer him on, I yip and yap, but I'm a poor partner.

Still, I know agility class was why he risked his very life, against his better judgment, and waded into that horrible pond. He thought I asked, and he always says yes. As he woke up from his nap, I reached over to the far corner of the mattress where he liked to bury his bones. I handed him one, still belly up. He gave me a wag. Just one.

One More Question

At the end of a clinic day, after I've asked if there are any more questions and we've finished, someone might come forward. They meet me off to the side and I stop.

Sometimes it's to share something important for them to say. It might be an insight or a personal breakthrough. Often women want to thank me for something I've written or tell me private experiences that they've never shared before. Because we talk about the horse's emotional state, they think it invites sharing their own, so they tell me about lost children and unfaithful men. I am that safe stranger. Some people are heartfelt, and some insist on sharing the ugliest pain as if they meant to shock me. As if it's a contest.

Their words put pictures in my mind when my mind is already full of images of more pain and blood and broken bodies than they can imagine. My clinician costume is smiling and accepting. I can't be rude, but I can't help. I can't carry their pain, any more than their horse can. It's an experience that leaves me a little more committed to, and exhausted by, my job.

Other times, I never figure out what they want. The person had a question about her horse. She spent a few minutes explaining everything about how her horse came to her and then finally got to her question. She doesn't like the way her trainer does something.

This is a common quicksand complaint, complicated because many of the horses I meet are being rehabbed from fear-based training methods. That experience can be as hard on riders as their horses. In training an alternative, I've heard all the human complaints, too. When it should be about the horse.

Still listening, my feet feel tighter in my shoes, and I suggest a resolution. Find a different trainer. But no, she says, that wasn't really the problem. It's something else, she says, and the story changes. Then I gave another suggestion, but it wasn't helpful either. She corrected me and went on to tell me one more fact that contradicted the previous facts.

Now we're talking in a circle. I'm not sure if she wants help from me or if she wants to rant that she knows more than her trainer. Maybe she does. Over the next fifteen minutes, the story changed a few more times. Every time I tried to clarify the question, she pulled it back. Since I didn't understand her, she went into more unrelated detail.

She doesn't need to agree with my answer, but we can't even agree on the question. Finally, I told her it's been a half hour. Mister was waiting for me. Ask me what you want to ask me. She said never mind, and explosions went off behind my eyes. No, I say. I am here, ask your question. She went back to the first idea, and I repeat that she still can't tell her trainer how to train.

Maybe she wants attention. Or maybe this was her souvenir to tell friends about. Perhaps she wanted me to realize we could be friends.

If she was a friend, she'd know my throat was sore from talking. That my eyes were tired from watching each detail so I could give the same quality lesson from the first to the last. She'd ask me if I wanted to sit. Perhaps she hadn't noticed that I had only one bathroom break, and it was at lunch, where I took questions as I ate. But if she was truly a friend, she'd ask about *my* horses.

Holding me here was not a good start to a friendship, and now having my full attention was not as flattering as she had hoped. I got a few degrees blunter every minute now. I worried I might go full Jack Nicholson on her, yelling out, "You can't handle the truth!" all red-faced and spitting. But I took another breath and thanked her for the question, whatever it was, and headed home to Mister.

May I share something? I have worked hard to succeed in this work I love. I'm grateful. And because it is the human condition to whine about our blessings and our troubles, sometimes I complain. Please understand whatever notoriety I have comes from sitting alone in a room writing. I have lifelong experience in the study of horses, and I have considered ideas deeply and written about them. Some days, standing in front of a crowd that's waiting to hear me speak, I don't recognize myself or know how I got there. I didn't read Dale Carnegie's *How to Win Friends and Influence People* to come up with a logical plan for fame and fortune. It was hours spent with horses and then hours spent typing that got me this job. When the opportunity appeared, I ran with it. But I am never comfortable in a group. I play the part of a charming clinician, but it's a mystery how I ended up here. With just enough fame that some people know my name, but not enough income to hire staff.

Awkwardly, I'm the most popular person at the clinic and not a friend in sight. If I said this aloud, volunteer hands would fly up, but I don't want an entourage. It's my fault; I write in an intimate voice. A reader might think I'm their friend already. Luckily, Mister has my back. He would never prioritize a stranger's conversation over his dinner. He is my living, breathing excuse to escape.

Meanwhile, the authors, musicians, and artists who have shaped my life don't know I'm alive. There's a proverb: Never meet your heroes, they rarely live up to your expectations. My side of it is that it's still no fun to fail people.

Sometimes I refer to myself as a couple's therapist for horses and humans. I loved my years in therapy because there were clear boundaries. I paid someone to listen to me figure things out, and it was meant to be non-reciprocal. Not my job to worry about the therapist. We didn't go for drinks after. It was a relief to know.

Now I'm on the other side, and people pay me to listen. I do that job to the best of my ability but without the same professional boundaries. I envy the businesses that have strict rules against personal relationships between co-workers. It changes the group dynamic for everyone. I want to uphold ethical standards, even if I come off sounding like a Girl Scout.

Gosh, I sound ungrateful again! I am treated like a queen. Oh. Looking at Britain's royal family over the last few years, I wonder if being treated that way was really such a good thing. Like them, I have all the potential to make mistakes and disappoint people, followed by judgment and criticism shared on social media. But I don't own any of the Crown Jewels. And there I go, complaining again.

The World's Largest Truck Stop

Most days, we hung with semi-trucks. Semis ran, nose to tail, from horizon to horizon out beyond the city limits and we nestled in and cruised at their speed, like a hound, tracking along with them. Not one of them, just a hanger-on.

My dad used to tell me if I ever got in trouble to ask a trucker for help. He made it sound like truckers were where all the knights worked now. Maybe he listened to too much country music, or maybe things had changed since he drove trucks in the Forties. It didn't take many road trips to find out that wasn't always true. Not to say truckers are bad, but no group is all one thing.

Running the highways with truckers means developing a taste for truck stops. A good one should offer room to park a rig, have bathrooms the size of locker rooms, and make a great plate of eggs. They should have the smell of grease, both motor and cooking. They should be an impression of a hardware store crossed with a drugstore, along with the usual nasty treats and fried burritos of unknown origin. The snack that levitates in the air above all others is ice cream on a hot day.

The Iowa 80 Truck Stop in Walcott is the world's largest, and the signs advertised it like a national landmark, so we pulled in. It was disappointing. Lots of light and was more like a mall or an airport, with a fast-food court, racks of clothing with their logo, and a section of tech gear to rival Amazon. There was so much tourist trash you'd think the place was a Walmart by Mount Rushmore. The bathroom was altogether too clean. The parking lot was at least five or six times the size of my farm. As a truck stop aficionado, it did not impress me. The truck stop experience isn't complete if you don't get at least a little nervous or wonder if you've been transported back in time.

I didn't need gas and the rule of the road is if you use the bathroom, you buy something. It was such a clean normal place, that I almost considered getting a T-shirt so I could make fun of it later. I settled for an overpriced candy coffee and headed back out to my little rig and Mister.

As I got there, a couple in a car pulled up. The man with an accent politely said something. If he wanted directions, I wasn't the one to ask. I didn't wear my hearing aids that day, so I was rolling the sounds, trying to tie them to words as he continued quietly talking. I gathered they were having traveling troubles. His wife in the passenger seat held a young girl who was crying, and they all looked exhausted. I couldn't make out his words, but I read their faces. I didn't want to make him repeat their troubles.

I understood he was asking for money. I am not sure where the accent was from, but this was Iowa. How much of my life have I lived as "other?" Even now, I feel like an outsider every day. How many times have I lived on a shoestring counting pennies? I'm far from rich, but I'd gotten a cash tip a while back, so I grabbed a few bills and handed them to him. It was a bit more than what a tourist T-shirt would have cost.

His gratitude was overwhelming. Now his wife was crying with their girl. She might have felt embarrassed, or relieved, or both. The man nearly crumpled, then twisted slightly toward me, but the steering wheel stopped him. He bowed as low as he could, his palms together to his forehead. Now I noticed I had something in my eye and took a step back, but he offered his hand, so I extended mine. He didn't shake my hand; he touched his lips to it.

Shauna: Steely Dan's Soft Eye

Back on the road, my thoughts were still spinning. It might have been the most intimate moment I'd spent with a stranger since I couldn't remember. I felt raw and "unstuck in time," as Vonnegut writes, thinking of the vulnerability of travel. How near impossible it was for me to ask for help coupled with the ease of offering help to others. It's classic horsewoman behavior.

We cruised along until the roadkill became nearly unbearable. It was strictly raccoons, but in huge numbers, many times in pairs. The road was littered with their smashed carcasses as if they walked blindly into traffic like lemmings. So many that I wondered if there was a suicide pact. It didn't make sense. The sheer numbers were awful. Passing into Illinois, it was beautiful farmland in all directions. Huge green pastures filled with cattle that nearly glowed with health. The land was fertile, and pastoral in all the best ways, except for that bizarre number of God's raccoons on the road.

We were here to see Shauna, a vet by profession and a horsewoman by avocation. She's had horses her whole life, and these days, she leans towards gaited horses. She has a pretty spectacular herd and has studied with everybody who's anybody. Shauna was no slouch.

She went to another state to look at a horse named Steely Dan. He had a winning show record and was perhaps the most valuable and well-trained horse she'd ever considered purchasing. When she got there, she saw something entirely different. Steely was a beautiful horse, but his eyes were too still, darkened with dread. He vibrated with tension.

Steely told a different story than the seller. He wasn't the horse she came to see. Not the horse she wanted, but sometimes the path takes a curve. She knew better than to think she could evangelize the seller into awareness; she let the rant go and began the purchase process. The seller required her to copy and perform some maneuvers with Steely. He must have wanted to make sure Shauna could handle this horse, who, she later discovered, had to be tranquilized to get his feet trimmed.

I think I've seen more gaited horses in the last three years than all the years before. They have smooth gaits and are comfortable to ride. They conserve more energy than they would if they trotted, so they have greater stamina and endurance. With dogs or horses, I get nervous when a breed's popularity peaks, knowing that those who benefit will not be the animals.

In what can only be called a graduation picture, Shauna was required to ask Steely Dan to lie down, and then she sat on top of him. She did it against her will and the seller took a photo. Shauna referred to the look on her face as her dead Elvis smile. She bought this expensive rescue horse, knowing he'd be a project. True horsewomen are nearly allergic to common sense in situations where a horse is in trouble.

Steely Dan was a beautiful, smoky color, as gray as a rainy day. His face was intelligent, and he was smaller, but so strong in his body. He probably got started too young and, with his good looks, no doubt pushed too hard. He'd had success for his owner but at a cost.

Maybe it was all fear and no reward, maybe just the traditional training methods for gaited horses. Steely was so fearful and defiant that his body went nearly catatonic, his eyes totally black. He didn't blink or breathe if a human was near; he was stiff and braced. His only release was when he bolted.

Shauna and I worked together online. We shared ideas and Steely gained tiny bits of confidence, a little at a time. The very last thing he needed was more training; that's how he ended up where he was.

Shauna slowed down, then slowed down even more. Finally, he took a deep breath. He taught her to stand at his hip and wait until he was ready for her to come closer. She spent lots of time there.

She hung a hay bag at the location where she groomed,

and the farrier worked. He never took a bite in the beginning. When horses are in their flight mode, the heart rate goes up and digestion slows down. It's why hand-feeding treats doesn't work on frightened horses.

Eventually, he took a bite of hay, a win, and then he paused for a few seconds. His eye softened. The chewing released his jaw; it was like a cue to calm himself. Every good thing needs a relaxed start and now change has become possible. Steely was learning it was safe to take a moment and think.

He stands to have his feet trimmed with no force or medication now. Shauna rides him, but she's smart and rides out with a friend. She used a gradual process so he would feel safe. If he gets anxious and needs to release it, she lets him have some free strides and he can come back. Bolting is no longer his only option.

While I was there, they had a couple of really short rides, each one a dramatic improvement over the previous. Now he could settle and be present without panic. Shauna had done a fabulous job. Steely's body was visibly different. He had a new softness, his muscles were smooth, and he was warm to the touch. His body seemed even stronger now that he was relaxed.

Shauna had an offer for Steely, and she considered it briefly, just in case. Sometimes she worried she was not the best person for him, but that's a thought that doesn't cross Steely's mind or any of the other animals there. He was cautious still, maybe always would be. It's taken a few years of patience because there is no miracle cure for trauma, even if you're a vet. But a horse's eye will always tell the truth, and he softens his eye for her.

I marvel at my clients and their commitment to their horses. That's an understatement. It's all I can do to not jump up and down screaming for their victory over the past. But I'd scare the horses.

It seems the people who should be the most concerned about doing better for horses never blink at their cruelty. But those who go to hell and back to help horses always think there might be more or better they could do for their horse. Shauna was too humble about their results. Steely was alive again, brought back from purgatory. Nothing less.

***

There was a small group here at Shauna's. We ate well and laughed loud and long. The herd taught us much, and it thrilled me to celebrate Steely's good fortune. The house pets were the weird diverse group that might get dumped with a vet who can say no, but doesn't choose to. Shauna's Mom made us all small red crocheted hearts, capturing exactly how we felt, and mine has a permanent place in the Rancho.

Before Steely Dan came into her life, Shauna had always been able to solve training questions that came up. But none of what she knew worked for Steely. She had to find a different approach. Later Shauna quipped she wasn't happy to call somebody as weird as me, but she just didn't have any other options.

And I smiled like a Cheshire cat. I hear that often, and it's a compliment. Sometimes I work with beginners, but more often it's good horsewomen trying to get better. Continuing to stretch and learn is another way of getting back on a horse.

Over at the far edge of what we can learn is where the art of horsemanship begins. It's where we know what we know, but it isn't enough. It's when we must go beyond judgment and begin truly understanding. Finally, confident enough to give the horse their voice without fear of losing our own. We break strict old rules and don't make new ones. It's better to relax into thinking less and seeing like a horse, listening to their language, and becoming a deeper kind of vulnerable.

Steely was immune to kindness when he arrived. Shauna was incapable of continuing the previous aggression, but her sympathy or compassion didn't connect with him either. Horses don't understand those nebulous emotions. So, Shauna took a leap of faith and landed in the undomesticated territory of listening. The true art of horsemanship is like floating in midair.

We Let Our Minds Graze

Leaving Shauna's, we drove for an hour and then made a quick stop to stand in a field with some horses. Two women who audited Shauna's clinic boarded their horses at this lovely old farm, and I'd wanted to meet the horses since hearing about them. Or maybe I just wanted the pleasure of being there. Standing in a pasture will cure just about anything. The horses didn't need us and we didn't rush around petting them. The air was especially nourishing.

Then Mister and I started the long drive through Illinois, Indiana, and Ohio to the next stop in Pennsylvania. This was farm country, with food crops as far as the land extended on both sides of the road. Corn and soybeans, mainly. The ground was as rich as the Southwest was dry. Seeing such abundance could trick you into thinking that the planet was thriving. If my farm hadn't become a dirt bowl, it might have fooled me. If I hadn't seen so many densely populated areas, so much urban sprawl, and so many mouths to feed, it might have fooled me. There are birds everywhere and still more raccoons. God's raccoons.

How can this all balance? Farms are crucial to feeding us all, but many of these smaller farms are failing, edged out by corporations. There are vast buildings for chickens who never get to eat bugs in the morning light. I know huge slaughterhouses are beyond brutal, but it's the chicken factories that get to me. And with all the advances in machinery and technology, how come it's not easier to make a living on a small farm now than it was when my family lost ours decades ago?

I put a load of washing in this morning. This time it's agitating in the bed of my truck in a simple ten-gallon bucket with a lid. The quiet agitation cleans way better than you'd imagine. Tonight, I'll hang the net bag holding my laundry outside the Rancho and let it drain well. I'll do the rinse cycle tomorrow as we're driving and then hang them from my high ceiling. My clothes dry easily overnight. I bet pioneers used wooden barrels and did the same in covered wagons. I've thought of them every day on the road, often wondering if that was where I belonged in history. I'll be too old for the next pioneer migration.

Mister started the day with a nap, but it was hard to get comfortable. He tells me every day about how much he hates his harness. This one is his third so far and he's strapped into a dog bed attached to the seat. It has that thick rim, so when I stop or turn, he can use it to balance. Sadly, not enough room for a reverse sploot. So, he twists into a canted diagonal position and falls asleep with his head tilted back and his mouth quietly opening and closing like a beached carp.

It's his third harness because none of them fit as he would like. Getting into his harness is the only resistance he ever gives me. Understandable as can be. As soon as we park at night, his harness and my bra come off in practically one motion.

We stopped for one night in Fort Wayne, Indiana, and we checked in early, so I took some time to clean the trailer. I have a miracle dog hair roller for the bed and then I pick up the rug and do the floor. That might make it sound like picking up dog hair is a special occasion, but it's a daily task. Then I aired up the tire with the slow leak.

The next morning, we drove through the rest of Indiana and across Ohio with beautiful pastures looking refreshed in the morning as I squinted into the sun. Someone planted deciduous trees and a few evergreens in close arcs around the houses back when they were first built. Hopeful for the future, knowing they wouldn't give shade until generations later. Farmhouses all look like an oasis because there are no telltale trees in the fields that have been groomed for planting. Sometimes there are low walls made from all the stones removed from the field, along with the tree stumps. The ditches were wide, and the houses were set back from the road. There was no line where the lawn stopped, and the public ground started. The large open green areas were as well-kept as a golf course.

This was Christmas Card America. The farmhouses were two stories high with peaked dormers and always a wrap-around porch with wooden rocking chairs on it. Back behind the house was a big red barn with livestock. Maybe some horses in the pasture next to the barn and some Holstein milk cows in fields close by. Peaceful and pastoral; this moment in time could be any decade in our history. This was a picture of everything good about us.

Literally on the other side of the road was a farm with a bitter slogan painted on the barn roof; hate speech spelled out in letters as tall as the man who painted them. No way to miss it. This America was just as real. It should have seemed out of place, but maybe there will always be a dark shadow edging close to a bright light.

Not a mile farther on the road was a one-room white church with small stained-glass windows and a tall spire. Behind it was a sweet cemetery with the headstones of those who planted those farmhouse trees. A sign welcomed the congregation for a soup supper next Wednesday.

The trees were changing now, and the bottom half of the corn plants had dried. Soon corn cribs would be full and these fields would be put to bed for the winter. Harvest time.

The next night was in Emlenton, Pennsylvania, and now we were in the deep woods. In forests filled with trees. What else would we fill them with, you ask? No, this wasn't your West Coast kind of forest. Here, the hills were covered with trees, deep valleys with creeks and trees, and high bridges crossing deep tree-filled ravines. Long bridges over wide rivers with currents circling and trees at the very edge of the water. It seems like nothing but trees and no open ground to the horizon in every direction.

The nights were frosty now. Leaves crisping into a botanical paint chip display to rival any hardware store. A dozen shades of gold, rust, copper, lemon yellow, hot pink, cranberry, salmon, burgundy, mossy green, forest green, army green, and lime green. It's an abundance of color and an even greater abundance of trees. As far as the eye can see, not a windmill in sight. The flies are almost tame this time of year.

Mister and I are taking this trip together, but seeing the world through Mister's eyes is a little more interesting. My jaded eyes miss some of the best stuff. The squirrels at this RV park told us that tourists feed them. Like I need hungry demons scurrying about, says Mister. Anything could happen, and he poked his nose through the curtain to guard us. It was going to be an awful night for an evening constitutional, but off we went. Curious and primal, Mister stalked a place to pee and reminded me to inhabit my senses, feel this air settle, and let the moon glow light our way.

Finally, Pennsylvania and we're in Amish country. Mourning my romanticism was a common experience now. My eyes are wary of seeing what I don't want to see. Yes, there are quaint carriages on the road, pulled by thin black horses, trotting on pavement, their eyes too quiet. We have a polite curiosity about the Old-World habits of the Amish. I respect them for holding onto a culture as the world changes. But some have gotten a reputation for harsh training. People purchase horses that struggle in similar ways that Steely Dan did at first but have never competed. The Amish use these horses hard. I also knew this area was a hotbed of puppy mills. Many of the rescue dogs I've had were mill puppies who grew to have chronic health issues that morphed into behavioral issues.

Aren't we asked to be good stewards of the land? I don't understand why this often means domination and hard use. I don't know why they aren't leading the fight to save the planet instead. Okay, I know why, but I hate it.

This Amish community probably makes some of the best

driving tack available and I own some. There are farm stands with young men in white shirts and suspenders selling produce. Some have signs for puppies. It occurs to me that religious communities who live separately in our country aren't so different from indigenous people on reservations, except for the obvious quality of the land.

But it's still farming, depending on the whims of the weather. City people talk about the weather as the most meaningless small talk. "Isn't it pretty out today?" In farm country, the weather reports top the international news. "Will the crop get in before the storm?" or "Will we get enough rain for the seeds to grow?" or "Can we survive the drought for two years in a row?" Farming seems dull to city dwellers, but it's more like Las Vegas than sleepy Pennsylvania. Nothing but risk in all directions. The farmers routinely throw the dice. Earth does as she will.

Mister Redefines Fetch

The first stop in Pennsylvania was at a private barn for a one-day visit. I can't say these Barn Visits always work well. The experiment has been worthwhile overall. It's been wonderful to meet clients, and the conversations have been great. But the horses don't always have enough time to settle. It's still too rushed. I wanted a visit to be affordable but one day just wasn't enough time.

Even a traditional clinic can be amazing or not, depending on a bunch of things not in my control. I don't want to see a group of horses stressed out at the beginning of a clinic, but if there are a few days, they settle. However, a few days might be longer than many clients can commit to.

I wanted to give folks an entry into organizing a clinic by starting small. But there was no outguessing the horses. For all the time we spend overthinking ourselves and our horses, it was always a guess. We have a plan and then figure it out as we go.

One rule will never apply to all horses, but I still struggled to let go of the hard days.

Some visits weren't about riding at all; there were days brainstorming about horse care and barn design. On other days, we talked about end-of-life choices. It could be anything. Sometimes there was discomfort with one-on-one intensity between the client and me, and sometimes our time together was illuminating. I try to read humans and horses, and sometimes I get it wrong.

In one-day clinic or Barn Visit, there was so little time for horses who take alternate routes, and many do. The changes in their familiar environment will spook some horses, while others shut down as a survival skill. Every horse has a story of their own and it usually isn't the one we tell about them. They may move as a herd, but each one will find a different path to being okay with humans.

Meanwhile, Mister sat on people. If they didn't grab at him, if he got to take his time, he climbed up and fell asleep on strange laps as a matter of course. He is longer and heavier than you'd think. He doesn't fit on laps, so it was a minor sport to watch when I suggested sitting in a "man-spread" position. I took dozens of "Mister Sat Here" photos as the trip went on. Mister gained confidence, as he found a spot he wanted and tilted his ears, looking as sincere as an airport lounge singer.

After the long day ended, the organizer stopped at the trailer with my check, and I invited her in. I knew her as a long-time blog follower. She had two horses and was active in the online school. I enjoyed her humor. She also brought a few more toys for Mister. He can pick the actual dog person out of a crowd of dog lovers quicker than a lick. He jumped up on the bench seat beside her, and as we talked, she played a little game with Mister, trying to engage him with a toy.

Before Mister came to live with us in Colorado, I'd seen a video of him decidedly not fetching. He obviously thought it was a game for dolts because it always ended the same way. That was fine with me, but as the organizer and I talked way too late, she kept at it. She started with what looked like an invitation to play tug, a game he loves. Not bringing it back was more his style.

Eventually, Mister took the toy in his mouth and then dropped it to the floor. The organizer picked it up and offered the toy again, with the patience of a mother with a toddler pushing food off their highchair tray. We talked on and after an hour of Mister dropping the toy, I finally understood what was going on. I'd had Golden Retriever dogs who lived and died for retrieving. You can miss things if you've had dogs that play fetch in the traditional way, but I'd gotten the entire game backward. Mister says it's the person who retrieves.

The new toys joined the stuffed zoo on the bed. Sadly, this alternative fetch game became part of our going to bed routine, no matter how tired I was, every night thereafter.

"Here, Anna. Fetch. I'll bark at the toy until you find it."

The organizer must be pleased. It's the practical joke that keeps on giving.

Family and Friends

The next week, Mister and I leapfrogged between Philadelphia and Washington, DC, where a bald eagle followed us by flying above for a few miles. Thinking of the eagles we'd seen on the West Coast, "from sea to shining sea" never seemed truer. I will never tire of eagles. It felt like I should pull over and stand with a hand over my heart.

It was my wedding anniversary on a day I spent talking about end-of-life decisions at a Barn Visit, but I got back in time to call the Dude Rancher. Depending on the time zone differences, I can miss it entirely.

What's left of my family does not live close, by design probably. Sometimes the best way to put out a fire was to spread the embers. Most of my parent's generation are gone now, along with a fair number in my generation. Choosing to not have children can be an odd position in a family, and it was one more reason I never fit in well.

I hadn't seen my nephew in Philadelphia since his wedding, and he and his wife have two kids taller than me now. I was nervous as I invited myself for dinner, but he and his family welcomed me with warm hearts. It delighted me to see him as a man, to see him cook dinner with his family around him. He teaches English and Lit classes at a charter school; a stressful job during COVID-19. His wife was kind and inclusive. Someone I liked immediately when we met years ago. Their kids were engaging and had unusual and creative hobbies. Young teens now, and so like him at their age. I missed the conversations we shared then.

They made a home to be proud of and there were bits of my family revealed in his children. The best bits. The conversation was wide-ranging, and as always, we talked about books. He said he taught *Braiding Sweetgrass* by Robin Wall Kimmerer in his classes but let kids skip chapters. I started the book the next day. The hook didn't catch on to me, and because he gave his kids that permission, I skipped two-thirds of the book.

A few days later, I visited his sister, my niece in Virginia, who was the family member I saw the most often, meaning every few years. She is the single parent of a busy little boy who has very little interest in me. But why should he? My niece showed him photos and reminded him of me, but I'm a stranger. They lived in a suburban house in a cul-de-sac. It wasn't the place I'd expected from this woman who was a little wild herself, but I soon saw why. Packs of kids ran through her house, shouted greetings, and grabbed snacks in passing. Semi-feral boys dumped their bikes in the yard, played baseball with a soccer ball, and got to have the old-fashioned fun that was scarce these days. "Please" and "thanks" rang out, but they made other rules up as needed. My niece and I toasted each other with champagne and sat back to watch their fun.

There were a couple more Barn Visits scattered in the DC/ Virginia area. Then, just before I left, I went to visit Tessa. She is intelligent, funny, blunt, and always a bit ahead of me. I will read anything she writes. We both loved Elaine.

Tessa met Elaine in that writing group around the same time I did. Tessa writes and often photographs her dogs at play. Quinn, the boneless flying Cattle Dog, was the star. We found Tessa's farm, and Mister napped in the car as Tessa introduced her brilliant dogs who each had better manners than I do. It was a perfect bright morning. We strolled out to meet the horses, and we remembered our friend.

She and Elaine used to post blogs back and forth, sparking each other for inspiration. Cake was a favorite topic. It was a quiet writing group that didn't post often, but for almost a year, we all got to share their fun. When Elaine died, Tessa tried to carry on posting. We both hoped someone would step forward, but eventually, Tessa stopped. I would have done the same.

Back in her kitchen, Tessa brought a tall cake out of the fridge. Not just a cake, but The Legendary Cake. She made the cake she and Elaine wrote about. It was a Russian Burnt Honey Cake with about two hundred layers and a frosting made of air, hummingbird spit, and love. It was the best cake in the universe. We toasted Elaine with cake.

Elaine died in England during the pandemic. Sharing this moment with someone else who missed Elaine was something I needed more than I knew. Sometimes I forget what a gift it is to share mourning.

When it was time to leave, Tessa gave me about half the cake in Tupperware. Later, I emailed and thanked Tessa again, saying I knew she made it for Elaine, but my new cake diet was going very well. Mostly, I tried to thank Tessa for remembering our friend. I worry Elaine will be forgotten.

Tessa responded, "Cake is healing and nourishing! And you're right, I did make it for Elaine, but I also made it for you, and for me (because I never got to make it for her), and for us.

I loved seeing you and having you here and the dogs are also clearly in love with you and that's my best-ever measure of a person. Thank you for coming here."

Mister hates this about me; being dog popular. Tessa's dogs flattered me to distraction, but I brought the stink of infidelity back with me to the truck. On the way back to our RV park, Mister pouted a little while I thought of Elaine. We were immediate forever friends as if we had agreed upon it as children living a world apart. We were late meeting. She had a parched, ironic sense of humor, always a little dark, but in the cleverest way. Elaine delighted in responding with an extra layer of posh on top of her enunciated English accent. Followed with an innocent eyebrow lift, she added an "isn't it?" or "don't you think?" to the finish of her remark. It was a slam-dunk response to foolishness, and you'd be ridiculous to disagree.

I had received an acid-spiked hate letter from someone I thought was a friend after I wrote a blog about death. It's common for me to talk with a few clients about euthanasia and loss every week, but the ex-friend was certain I was suggesting she kill her horse. I wasn't. She called me a liar and vented her rage. As intended, it hurt my feelings.

Elaine frequently teased me about my minuscule fame, called me FP for famous person, and then watched me squirm with embarrassment. But when I told her about the hate mail, she immediately understood, as few would, that I was constantly on the brink of an unknown betrayal. I was a monster or a genius, but always standing on black ice.

She shared the opening line in a poem by Brian A. "Drew" Chalker with me. "People come into your life for a reason, a season, or a lifetime." The ebb and flow of friendship had always baffled me. Our talk helped me put the incident in a less per-sonal box of acquaintance friends that I could store on a shelf. Without a moment's doubt, Elaine and I knew where we were on that spectrum. We joked it was like getting married before the first date. What I didn't know was how soon she would be gone, or that I'd be living our friendship without her.

Elaine had a peaceful death in hospice after a wildly courageous life. Without an instant of regret, I skipped a year of my writing to complete her book with her husband, Mark, and publish it.

Of course, I have squirreled away treats for Elaine in this book. Secret messages, a line of cake crumbs with drops of frosting that she would love more than anyone else.

The older I get, the more I value my genuine friendships. I have not known many. It's not just the work I do or that my life changed over the years. I traveled as much as I was home but most of my friends don't live near enough to meet for coffee. And like relationships with co-workers, getting personal with my clients was precarious footing and most are too one-sided to hold. I've been wrong about people too often, and like a rescue dog, I am slower to try now.

Elaine called it. Our friendship would be forever. As much as I like to think she checks on me, I hope she's off doing something *infinitely* more interesting. I hope she's leaving me cake crumbs, too.

The Outer Banks

Driving south from Washington DC, the land was still all woods. It seemed the freeway cut through virgin forests. Maybe I thought of the East Coast as overpopulated, one city limit crashing into another, but it wasn't true. These forests, with broadleaf trees shifting seasons, made for the best travel company. Even if it was impossible to tell what direction you were going.

The state lines came and went so quickly, like speed bumps: New Jersey, Delaware, Maryland. Finally, heading south in Virginia, the landscape settled, and we were back in roadkill country. I still don't look away. It's a kind of acknowledgment, a prayer at the speed limit for so many cats here: black cats, tabby cats, orange and white, oh-so-domestic cats. All God's cats.

The fall color change seemed to match our stride coming south. We had been riding a wave of color that was just beginning and in no hurry to break out ahead of us. Now on a North Carolina state highway moving towards the coast, the roadkill transitioned to God's skunks and God's foxes as we left the urban areas.

We were at the part of the trip where the clinic cancellations had happened. Having the Rancho really mattered now because a week in a hotel would have blown most of my income so far. I could be frugal, tuck in, and bide my time. And I truly loved being inside it. It made us feel sustainable.

Sometimes I pause the audiobook and write for a while, using voice dictation on my phone. I tell a story when I drive, having fun setting the scene. But that day, during a pause Mister woke up and let out a bark. The screen showed the word "what." So, I guess he's writing a book, too. I can't wait to read it.

We stopped at a farm stand about forty-five minutes from the next RV park and got some fresh veggies, bread, and ice. And then on to our reservation at the Outer Banks KOA campground. I'd heard of the Outer Banks before, probably in a novel, but the name was all I knew. It would have been fine, but GPS Woman didn't know any more than I did. Or it was another of her side-splitting practical jokes. I could never tell.

We drove a full hour, nearly an eternity, in the wrong direction, at a measly thirty miles per hour. But rather than taking me to some lost and overgrown Sasquatch-lurking dead-end, this time she took me to a very elite beach neighborhood. Each of the homes was three or more stories high so they could see the ocean and not go outside. The houses looked ready for their glamor shot for Architectural Digest. I unwisely trusted GPS Woman; the directions still had a confident sound. Then she had me pull into a fancy shopping area that was more like a frilly traffic circle. Everyone parked their expensive little cars diagonally, and the dogs looked like they all had hair stylists. Driving there was a squeeze for a Ford F-250, much less one dragging a trailer. The affluence was stifling, and I had better not rub one of these imports.

We inched our way around the loop of narrow road. Tanned people in Bermuda shorts and flip-flops wandered on the side-walk, nearly as wide as the traffic lane. They moved slowly past seafood bistros, art galleries, and wine stores. I still couldn't find the turn that GPS Woman insisted was right there. It was our third lap looking for the RV park in the middle of this pastel ghetto. They had managed to stave off Walmart, fast-food restaurants, and any parking lot big enough for us to stop.

We finally got back to the road and found a gas station, where the attendant told me there was no KOA there. I knew it was a ludicrous question the second I asked.

It was getting to be late afternoon. Surrendering to GPS Woman's clever deception with a scowl, we headed back to the mainland. The speed limit was still thirty miles per hour, and that made backtracking more punishing. It had taken forever to get to another wrong dead-end. The private beach homes mocked us as we drove past them, back the way we came, traffic circle after traffic circle. This community did everything to dis-courage tourists. It might well have been a private golf course, I thought, as the Rancho's tire bounced over one more curb.

Once we finally got back to the mainland, I typed into GPS Woman again. Without a trace of sarcasm or remorse, she suggested a turn close to the farm stand I'd stopped at earlier. It was still miles behind us and when we finally got to our turn, the pavement stopped after a couple of blocks. Always a bad sign. Then it was miles of partly washed-out single-lane road. I wanted to strangle GPS Woman's chirpy little neck. We drove farther. This was where we'd get killed, I thought. Probably by snakes. A couple of miles later, I saw a dead-end sign. Just beyond that, the entry sign for the Outer Banks KOA camp-ground. I didn't know which to believe, but it was almost dark and there was no place to turn around.

I parked the truck to check in and left the engine running.

The people in the office told me they had my reservation for a three-day stay… but it was marked for a different date. That bit of information landed like wet seaweed on the counter. I could not speak. The woman behind the counter was born for her multitasking job, held one finger up as she smiled at me, checked sites, and answered a question from another camper. This late in the day, there was a line forming behind me. It was a popular spot and other people's GPS Women had apparently gotten them there on the first try. I can't imagine the look of exhausted desperation on my face, but it was nearly inspirational to the woman helping me, and she found a space for us. Hallelujah, it was even a pull-thru because I knew for a fact that I had no reverse left in me.

I added her to my list of people working their perfect jobs. Someone has to keep track of these things.

We learned that Halloween, still two weeks away, was a special holiday at RV parks. I might have seen it mentioned before, but I didn't expect every RV to be decorated with orange lights and blow-up skeletons. We were surrounded by pumpkins. There was a haunted house out in the woods on the east side of the park. The place was swarming with kids in costumes. I looked at Mister and said a small prayer that everyone would survive as we crawled into bed to play fetch.

At dawn, we went to the beach for a walk. Dawn on the East Coast was as breathtaking as a sunset on the west. Mister and I walked out on a dock to the very end and sat on a bench. He jumped up beside me and dropped his flipper on my leg and we watched the sun lift off the horizon. These precious moments hold me forever. Then we walked along the sidewalk next to the water to the end, where a path led over to the pond in the woods. There was great walking in this park.

I wrote the rest of the morning and Mister, on his long leash, did some splooting on the grass just outside. People silently rolled past in golf carts because it was a big park, but also because Americans travel with little vehicles inside bigger vehicles. I was no exception. After lunch, I pulled out my foldable wagon, and we headed over to the laundromat, a distance of about three blocks.

The laundromat had a waiting area with a group of post-mature tattooed women sitting on lawn chairs. Mister sat down and looked at them appraisingly, and in an ingratiating Eddie Haskell voice said, "Hello, Mrs. Cleaver, have you lost weight?" He was irresistible that way.

They reminded me of my plan when I was twenty-two. I had been worried that by the time I was sixty, people would see me as irrelevant. It was not a stretch; I saw my elders that way and didn't want to suffer the same treatment. My plan was to get a tattoo right away, so when I flashed it decades later, it would look old and somehow the tattoo would define me as mysterious. In those days, sailors were the only ones with tattoos. I thought it all out. I needed to get it on a piece of flesh not likely to change much so it wouldn't morph into a burst-balloon color slick. And it would be good if it was on a patch of skin that wouldn't scare people if displayed out in broad daylight.

Next, I flew to Los Angeles because, back then, there weren't many tattoo shops close by and I wanted an actual tattoo artist, not that I had anything against local bikers. In Chinatown, a petite Asian woman inked a stand of Japanese iris around my bony ankle as I smiled like it was a spa day. In the next stall, a young sailor was swigging whiskey, pretending he was brave, while his drunk friends made loud, jeering comments. For all the whining and drama, I couldn't imagine where his tattoo was located. But when he stood up, I saw a little redness around a small anchor on his forearm. The group bumped shoulders, hooted like warriors, and then the door closed behind them. The tattoo artist, almost half done with mine, looked up at me and smiled. It was quieter now.

All these years later, this group of elder tattooed women nodded to me and smiled at Mister. What used to be shocking is normal, even common, and yet other things have not changed.

Women still face sexual violence in high numbers and are afraid to report it. We still don't get equal pay and still fight for equal standing in the workplace, even if it's a riding arena. This year, women lost the right to choose. Should I be happy more of us have tattoos and purple hair?

I got change for the only bill I had, and eighty quarters came tumbling out. After loading two washers, we wandered back to the Rancho. A half-hour later, we walked back to the laundromat, put the clothes in the dryer, and got rid of a few more quarters. On our third trip back, some clothes were dry, but most weren't, and I deposited yet more quarters.

On the fourth trip, finally, the laundry was dry, but on the way back, Mister plopped down and refused to go another step. He lost the will to live. I squatted down to debate the value of exercise, but couldn't convince him to walk. So, I picked him up and carried him back to the Rancho and then went back for the wagon. Mister slept past dinner time. I checked for a pulse.

The next morning, we strolled again at sunrise, but Mister brought me right back. He said exercise was for Labradors.

On our last day, we took the wagon for a water run. There was a filtered water machine, two dollars per gallon, over by the laundry. I put my containers into the wagon, and we walked back over. It would taste like champagne and besides, I had way too many quarters.

Just as one container was nearly full, two men pulled up in a golf cart. One was skin-and-bones thin. He hunched over with blueish, pockmarked skin and an appraising glare. He seemed to be the brains of the pair. The other man was the talker. He wore a stained tank top and balanced a cigarette in his teeth while using his hands to talk. They both had open lunch beers. Mister ignored them like cats he didn't trust.

The man gesticulated grandly. "Lemme git that for ya, ma'am."

I said, "*no-thank-you*, I've got it." I could have bench-pressed the skinny guy. By now, the first container was in the wagon and the smoker was still insisting. I repeated my *no-thank-you*. Then he insisted again, then I said *no-thank-you* again. I thought we were clear now. *No-thank-you*, I don't need help.

They wouldn't budge. It took a while for the machine to dispense the next three gallons and I steadied the container, which didn't quite fit on the holding ledge. The men were still watching me but not talking. I didn't know what these guys wanted, but I scanned the area to make sure I knew my escape route. It's a habit most women learn the hard way.

I tried to not judge, to keep an open mind, but these guys were around forty and I was old enough to be their mother, whatever that meant. Was it Southern manners, or did they want something else? What were they waiting for?

As I was screwing the lid on the second container, the talker came around the front of the golf cart, close enough to partially block my way.

"Ma'am, please, lemme git that."

The theme from *High Noon* played just behind my ear. I lifted the water container into my wagon next to the other. It weighed less than a sack of grain, only half the weight of a bale of hay. For crying out loud, why does he care? Straightening up, I looked him in the eyeball, and enunciated, "*no-thank-you*, I've got it." Even slower, more deliberate this time. He didn't move, still standing in front of my wagon. I wanted to scream at him to get out of my way. Instead, I stared. I tried to make my face garish. A Halloween mask of no.

After an eternity of five or eight seconds, the skinny man still in the golf cart said, "I know your problem." I can't wait to hear. He continued in a tone that was half angry and half sarcastic, "Well, you're that independent type." Like it was a crime against *his* sex.

I almost laughed. This would be news to no one who had ever met me. My mother would have thought he was marriage material. It was an unintentional compliment but meant as a personal insult from these two strangers. Dang, it felt like the airplane window seat again. I was cornered between the building, a golf cart, and a man who refused to hear me.

I took the wagon handle and made a sharp reverse turn without an inch to spare. Walking away with Mister trotting beside me, I was mad. What just happened? I took an alternate route, as we truckers say, back to the Rancho, looking behind me at each turn.

Sometimes it felt like I had been defending myself for as long as I could remember. A life of refusing unwanted attention. Blocking a sucker punch. Butting up against the notion that I should shut up and do as I was told. Pressured to care more about being polite than being honest. I thought that maybe at some age, it would stop.

Mister reminded me that neither of us can outrun anybody. He's right, but what the hell was it about saying *no-thank-you* they found so infuriating? Was it that I didn't acquiesce? I even hate the word.

At the Beach

Back at the Rancho, Mister enjoyed a cool grass sploot while I stored the water. All the short, gory monsters, purple princesses, and masked superheroes survived. There were no golf cart drive-bys, and except for a few moments, our time here was mostly restful.

On the last morning, we folded down and drove back east, the same road we'd driven back and forth on the first night to The Outer Banks. This time, we turned South on Highway 12 toward Kitty Hawk, Nags Head, and Rodanthe. There were miles where the land was so narrow that you could see the ocean on one side and the sound on the other, not all that much wider than the highway. The land must disappear entirely during storms. Every couple of miles, there was a turnoff, with a parking area for beach access. Fishing seemed to be the draw. No sunbathers.

This was Mister's chance. We'd driven half the West Coast and had never gotten our toes wet, just close enough to roll in seaweed and eat a dead crab. Today was the day, and this was the last ocean on our trip, so I pulled over. We started over a dune toward the beach, but the sand was dry, which made it deep. I know how hard it is for horses to work in deep arena footing, but this was ridiculous. I needed snowshoes. Picking up my foot for each step was a serious effort.

I lumbered on and Mister was slogging along just behind me. I marched, intent on making it to the harder sand by the water, but then the leash was tight. I turned to see why he had stopped. Mister was high-centered. He had no traction and when he moved his legs, he sank a little. Corgi quicksand. I supported his front end, and he kicked behind. We lumbered the short distance to the beach, bent over and flailing, exhausted, and hoping the sand closer to the water was easier to walk on.

When we were close, I could see thousands of God's jellyfish washed up on the beach. Maybe more, it was hard to tell with jellyfish. Hurricane Ian had battered Cuba and then traveled north recently. I worried that somehow Mister would get his tongue stung or that if he rolled on them, well, then what? Jellyfish guts might be a problem. I didn't even know what to worry about, but Mister wasn't interested. He completely ignored the ocean. Ignoring the obvious was one of Mister's most clear signs of stress. It must be bad, so I took him seriously, and we turned to head back.

Maybe there was a better path to return to the parking lot. I'd never seen sand so deep. We headed to a place that looked more stable, but I was wrong. The sand was just as deep, and this time there were cacti at every step. Really, at the beach? My Crocs were zero protection, and my feet screamed. Mister had several cactus quills in one paw. He sat down, refused to take another step, and looked away with closed eyes. He was right; it had been a lousy idea. I'd forgotten he wasn't really a dog.

One by one, I pulled the quills out with my fingernails as

Mister held his paw out for me. I didn't even try to clear my Crocs. Then I picked him up in my arms and carried him the entire way back. Thirty-seven pounds isn't too much to lift, but he's long and awkward to carry. I lost my balance, stumbled, caught myself, and floundered on. It wasn't that my feet felt as if needles were poking me. There were visible needles and small drops of blood smeared from ankle to toe. Mister let me know it wasn't a comfortable ride, and I promised not to mention the ocean again.

Hatteras Island

I first started writing my blog in early 2010. I kept to my schedule and wrote a blog to post every Friday morning. My first blogs weren't perfect, but I worked at writing better, using more descriptive words, and as much as I disliked doing it, I practiced editing. My readers weren't critical, maybe more embarrassed for me. They emailed me the edits I missed. It takes a village to birth a writer.

There was a small group of us writing about horses and we signed up for each other's blogs and commented on posts. We encouraged each other and posted each other's blog links on our sidebars. It was a welcoming place to start, and for months that's where I stayed, comfy with bloggers like me. My following was in the double digits. At the end of the first year, I had thirty-seven subscribers. The number leaped up to forty-three in the second year. Success was mine!

It had taken superhuman strength to move the mouse across my screen and hit the publish button on the blog each week. Now, I worked my courage up to post my blog on social media. It would take the equivalent strength of lifting a car off a kitten.

After all the hyperventilating, all the twitching and head shaking, and all the drama, no one noticed me at all. Of course not, but I wrote my way through it. That was my answer to every question or dilemma. I still write my way through, but sometimes, I was nostalgic for that early camaraderie with other bloggers.

We drove farther south to Hatteras Island to meet an equine blogger from the old days. Most had laid down their pens and lost touch, but this woman still appeared randomly. She commented on an essay from time to time. I knew her horse from videos and her dog and cat from Zoom meetings. She was a tough, smart, funny woman, and we stopped for a visit.

Hatteras is a toenail-shaped island forged by weather. The trees grew at an angle away from the wind, the roads crept through narrow gaps in sand dunes. Birdsong was everywhere. Gulls cackled and pelicans squawked. Stark-white egrets posed like supermodels in the swampy areas.

We visited a photogenic black-and-white spiral-painted lighthouse, crisp against the blue sky. The quaint historic site had several of the original buildings intact. We visited on a day when a busload of Amish people was there. It was like a rare bird sighting. I had never seen farmers on vacation before.

There was a wonderful small-town feeling in Hatteras, where all the locals knew each other, and you could rent a horse to ride on the beach. The blogger owned a small business and her beautiful home had taken years to build. She had made an enviable place for herself in the community.

Her horse was a stately twenty-year-old gray Thoroughbred. She worried as winter came. Her gelding had experienced some health issues, but he was looking good now. She had done a fabulous job, but I could imagine the layer of anxiety she must have felt as he marked each passing year.

There have been some powerful storms on Hatteras and no doubt there will be more to come. It was a challenge keeping horses on islands. It was hard enough to get normal veterinary care, but emergency services were nonexistent. The same with farrier care, but she had learned that skill and filed between visits. She'd had a plan for her gelding's retirement for years. He would go to a sanctuary in Kentucky and live with a large herd of geldings on green grass and open land. She had a reservation for him, but when?

You can't ignore the climate changes here on the coast. Neither of us was getting younger, and we both wondered about an exit strategy from lives we didn't want to change. There are no simple choices. Her love for this gentleman gelding was visible in his daily care, in their soft interchanges. No one wanted the separation time to come, but when it did, I knew she would honor her word to him. For now, they share precious, bittersweet days.

While in Hatteras, we saw the sights, went for walks, and spent time with her dog and horse. She made wonderful dinners, and I begged off too early. It wasn't just that my brain shut off at five p.m., it's that I needed to keep things on schedule for Mister out in the Rancho. I needed to spend evenings with him. She brought dinner to the Rancho one night and joined us there, but the planning was getting stressful.

I was being a bad guest again. I slept in the Rancho because I could never stay in her guest room, even though it was lovely. Mister would never do well with her animals. He was being a bit more protective of me, and I knew he was anxious this week. I tried to do more, but I could tell I was saying *no-thank-you* too often.

If it would change anything, I'd be glad to take the blame. I could tell I wasn't being the friend she'd hoped for. Breaking my own rules, I gave more than I had, but even I could tell it wasn't enough. Falling short every day made me even more introspective until I shut down. We both hoped the other would understand us, but it didn't turn out that way and I couldn't fix it.

Visiting people I don't know well felt like a clinic day in some ways; I was still expected to be their version of who they thought my work persona was, but that's not me. Or maybe I'm a different depth of tired. I did some unqualified self-diagnosing after listening to a podcast interview with a Baptist minister. He shared a story of trying to hold a fractured congregation together through the pandemic. I related way too personally to everything he said.

Then he talked about his breakdown, caused by a kind of trauma I'd never heard of before, a condition called Cumulative Stress Disorder. The words were a lightning bolt of explanation. I wondered if I knew anyone *not* struggling with this malady.

Like him, I spent untold hours reinventing my business and working to build an online community during the pandemic. Would you call it a barn congregation? In some ways, a clinician wasn't very different from a minister. Clinics are a bit like tent revivals. Some of us preach fire and brimstone toward horses and some of us take a more peaceful path, but that just means we are even more like pastors. Neither job has many days off.

"Never meet your heroes" echoed again like a theme song. Even at that moment, I knew I was failing to be the kind of emotional rock she wanted me to be. I was just an ordinary piece of granite. Any hopes of saint-like holiness fell short. Had I turned into one of those bad boyfriend types who are never emotionally available? Has this work changed me so much that I don't recognize myself?

I looked at Mister, knowing I managed my needs about as well as Mister climbed sand dunes. We were both too much like flat jellyfish out of water. Maybe we should just stick to RV parks. As we drove away, I felt more exhausted than before, and disappointed in myself. My hand crawled to Mister's head to rest.

Itchy Carolina

Back on the road, we traced our way back to Nags Head and headed across North Carolina. I could tell we were heading west because it was morning, and the sun wasn't in my eyes. It was not quite Halloween yet, so ghosts and goblins were lurking, but now they're all God's deer. There were copious highway warning signs about deer, but I didn't expect them all to be dead. Those thin legs are no defense against a bumper. When a fawn was killed, its skin shriveled like a fallen leaf.

The Albemarle Inland Waterway was rich with tall fronds of swamp grass along the edges of the road. The fall colors were catching up with us now and the velvet-moist forests had a few trees turning lemon yellow. All morning, we traveled through land and water that barely separated themselves.

A road turned into a bridge and back, without fanfare. Then over a larger body of water, there was a sign warning of a draw-bridge. This would take some extra time, but I didn't see a thing up ahead. There was a stoplight, a small building, and a few boats stopped but no bridge. The light changed and a section of the road turned perpendicular. It happened surprisingly fast. The boats went through the opening with room to spare and the next moment the road ahead was open again like nothing happened and we drove on.

There were more and more of God's deer at the side of the road, as plentiful as the raccoons had been. But now God's groundhogs had taken the raccoon's place in sheer numbers. There were so many kinds of birds in the sky, trees, water, and everywhere else that it felt like a sanctuary. This land and water combination was swampy enough for alligators, I imagined. Maybe close and watching us. Mister didn't want to stop to check.

Besides, Mister was duck-biting his backside, nibbling ferociously at the skin above his tail. I had patches of tiny bites on my ankles and elbows that were driving me nuts, too. Chiggers, maybe? What a name. I used some eyeglass cleaning papers to soothe mine, but there wasn't as much alcohol on them as you'd like, and they wouldn't help Mister at all. We scratched, tried not to scratch, and scratched some more. As usual, we did most things together.

By noon, there was less swamp water and we passed through land as picturesque as the Ohio farmland. Huge pillared white homes with acres of lawns. I wondered if they were plantations. It was a guess, but there were cotton fields on either side of the road. Until Colorado, I'd always lived near the Canadian border and this land felt almost foreign. Sometimes, a thick pelt of kudzu vines strangled a small unpainted wooden shed. Many buildings were so overgrown with bramble that you only saw the shape of a green chimney and, more faintly, perhaps part of a roof. History lived there.

Then the road curved and revealed a small white church with a slightly larger cemetery behind. These churches seemed to be the community's heart, like the ones in the north. There was a sweet stillness about the place. I was reading *The Book of Lost Friends* by Lisa Wingate. It reminded me of all that churches have done for all kinds of lost souls, including the living. They hold communities together.

I was about to fall in love when a hot rod truck passed me too fast. In the truck bed, loose and darting from corner to corner, was a small Golden Retriever puppy. Almost God's puppy, I warned the church.

We were close to the first clinic location and low on propane, so we took what turned into a forty-minute detour on even smaller back roads. Each of the three locations GPS Woman sent us to was closed and looked like they had been for years. There was another nearly impossible single-lane turnaround between cotton fields. For the hundredth time, I thought about leaving GPS Woman at the side of the road. Instead, we did without the propane.

Two one-day clinics were scheduled at separate locations in the same city. It would have been good to combine them, but that hadn't worked. The first stop had been a challenge to plan and the other easy, but I couldn't tell why.

The first organizer told me she didn't have room for a clinic day, too many horses and trailers. She just wanted a few people in for lessons. Which was a little like saying I know you're a French chef, but I'd like you to make me a peanut butter and jelly sandwich. I can do it, the sandwich would be fabulous, but it wasn't on my menu.

Rather than a group learning experience, a lesson was an hour of private time. I can suggest what the horse and rider should do, but there wasn't time to explain why. No microphone, no auditors, no sharing. A private lesson was most effective after a clinic, to dive deeper into horses from the clinic. Meeting before meant there was no context. But after too many emails explaining why I did it that way, I gave up and agreed to lessons. Then, as I was almost there, she messaged me that she'd changed our agreement to include auditors. She didn't ask me; she told me.

I wanted to drive right past her farm, not because I was mad. An ex-husband used to say I had an exaggerated sense of truth. I still don't know how that was a problem but now there was a break of trust and I was uncomfortable. It was the thing that usually happened between a horse and rider. Not a good starting place for me, but Mister and I pulled in, unfolded, and set up.

The lessons started early the next morning, and I did my job well. There is a zone that exists in an arena with a horse and rider and me. Time slows down, externals fall away. The three of us find each other in the infinite present moment. It's sweet focus on each stride, each cue, each breath. Whether the rider is a beginner or advanced, the thrill is the same. Giving a riding lesson is an adrenaline sport of stillness, a conversation in the hurricane's eye. It's intense and personal, although somehow, it's not to be taken personally. Anyone can bludgeon a horse into dread-filled submission. It's an art to find a rhythm with a thousand-pound animal that will never be entirely tame. It requires each sense and all body parts to partner with light and energy, muscle and bone. Riding is a dance where control isn't an option, but in that stillness of our three minds, we can find oneness.

That was what riding was like for me. Each time I was in the saddle, I ceased existence anywhere else. I craved the moment my leg went over the horse's back, and I got to lay my puny, troubled self down and rise to meet a horse. In my mind, I knew we could never truly train horses to conformity, but I could give myself up to their movement. I could get along with them and they would carry me. Riders say horses give them freedom, but I think it was a choice we made to be less earthbound, a leap of faith beyond our limited minds.

I didn't think I could love anything more than riding. But being a tour guide to that ephemeral place was a close second. This place of oneness could be as solid as a brick. It was always available, but success in the lesson had to do with the willingness of the horse and rider to surrender their fears and restrictions. If I could make it safe enough to try.

I loved my job more than I hated how the organizing went, but there was no heartfelt sharing. We left as soon as the last lesson finished. Months before, when trying to encourage me to come, the organizer told me about a male clinician who had a clinic at her farm earlier in the year. There were twelve participants, four more than my usual number, and she said it had been a great success. Just to say the hardest part of this job has nothing to do with horses.

Horses Taught the Clinic

When we found the second facility on the other side of town, it was already filling up with horse trailers. There were co-organizers here. I'm not sure if that's a title they would use, but this couple pulled like a team. It was wonderful to see the two of them enjoy each other as their dream was unfolding. They had been building their farm from scratch, starting with clearing some forest behind the house. To make room for participant horses, they had moved theirs to a friend's farm. Participant horses were settling in turnout pens with room to move, and the activity level was bright with excitement and laughter.

I did a presentation a couple of hours after I got there to a crowd of participants and auditors who laughed and asked intelligent questions. We shared dinner and bantered through delightful smells and tasty food. Working with horses and humans was a roller coaster ride.

The next day, there were auditors, blog readers, and others who didn't know me at all. Everyone was positive and there to learn. There was much laughter; it's the best thing to hear because it's a human calming signal. It means people are relaxed and learning can happen. Even with a crowd, I didn't have to worry. I knew the horses would speak up, prompting me on their important topics. I trusted them because horses were reliable and honest.

Sometimes when I'm teaching, I like to use human demo horses. It works because humans respond to most things like horses do. We do share similar autonomic nervous systems. I noticed humans learn better when it feels more personal. Plus, if I chose the right volunteer, it would be big fun.

I wanted to show passive domination compared to affirmative training, so I asked the he-organizer to join me. He was a tall, muscular firefighter. We'd already talked about the affirmative methods he used in his job, often first on the scene with paramedics, in emergencies. We'd compared our jobs, laughed a lot together, and I hoped my idea would work.

He cautiously walked over to join me in front of the auditors. He didn't know what was going to happen. Okay, neither did I, but control is overrated. I asked if he would waltz with me. Holding my arms up in the dancing position, he joined me, inches taller. I counted to three and marched over him like a steamroller, tilting him to one side and then the other. I didn't just lead, I overwhelmed. His eyebrows were priceless.

Everyone laughed, and then I said let's go again. I made eye contact and softened my body. I exhaled to steady us and matched my breathing to his. Then, on the next inhale, we both began to waltz together. It was intuitive, we both let go of trying. And for a moment, we were Fred and Ginger. It was exactly what dressage meant. What partnership meant. His willingness to go along and let it happen without peremptory correction was also where possibility existed with a horse. It was a positive softness, a breath of affirmation that gave us that chance.

***

Sometimes, getting a horse to a clinic (or a show or a friend's house) was about all the horse can manage. If the horse was a youngster, under eight years old, travel and being away was exhausting enough. Now they were in new surroundings with no idea if they would see home again. Youngsters were there for the experience. It was my hope they had a light, happy work session, lasting hardly any time at all, and then an easy trip home.

And I wished the same experience for every horse, at every age, and every breed. Clinics are not boot camps; they are for the experience of being out together, with both partners getting their brains exercised. If it went well, I hoped the owner was happily repacking everything she had just unpacked, and the horse thought the world was okay. For a prey animal, survival was the win. Humans need to lower our expectations. And maybe watch fewer horse movies.

Lena was elegant in that special way that Thoroughbred mares can be. Her face had long planes and gentle curves with a classic simple beauty. She made her bay color look like melted brown sugar. There was no question about her intelligence, but her flank was tight, and she was in pain.

Lena's owner did everything right. The horse had a health issue earlier in the year, but her owner worked with a vet and the condition had improved and was under basic management. She had trailered Lena short distances several times and even stayed at a friend's farm nearby. To tell the truth, Lena was better prepared for this clinic than many other horses.

Then Lena's owner planned for a double trailer date with Kiefer, an older Quarter horse gelding, and his owner. The two horses traveled well together, and the owners got along, too. Once they all arrived at the clinic location, Lena and Kiefer were given grass pens next to each other with room to trot. Everything was just the way you'd like it to be. Except it wasn't.

As Lena's lesson time came, her owner and I stood just inside her pen. Lena froze for a moment, a calming signal to let us know she was no threat to us. Her owner said Lena hadn't eaten her dinner or her breakfast. The mare was visibly dull, a bit too still, and was throat breathing, all signs of stress. Originally, she'd planned to tack Lena up and ride, but now she knew she couldn't. It was disappointing, but she put her Lena first. I respected that. And I don't like it when a participant doesn't get their ride, but that doesn't mean she doesn't get her time.

I was breathing deep and regular, steady and quiet in my emotions. I believe Lena's owner did the same because the mare softened for a moment and then dropped her head to graze. Simple acknowledgment is always a profound tool. The gelding on the other side of the fence was eating from a pile of hay. You could say he was keeping her company, but it was more than that. He was giving her calming signals, too, as horses do.

Sometimes one horse will eat if another horse was eating close by, so I suggested we toss some hay into the mare's pen next to the fence line where the gelding was eating. Both owners scurried to give her hay, but before they could, Kiefer used his nose to shove half of his hay under the fence to Lena, who tucked right in.

There was general relief. An auditor said it seemed like every time I said something, the horse did it, not just then but throughout the day. It's enough to make me look like a walking party trick, but that's not it. If we breathe and clear our minds of human agenda and related trash, our bodies say everything, just like a horse's. Horses aren't psychic and they surely don't speak English. It's us. Humans are transparently easy to read, and horses are more aware and intelligent than they get credit for. Nothing mystical about it. It's communication as literal as reading these words. It was the horses being in our conversation all the time.

Soon Lena walked to the water bucket and had a deep drink. Half an hour later, she stepped away and urinated, of a sort. The trailer ride with this old gentleman brought on a heat cycle. With mares, hormones were always part of the puzzle. The owner and I got to shrug at each other. Lena grazed through her two missed meals. After that, I saw her roll, stand up, and shake, a full reset of her nervous system. I knew she was fine and if it had been a two-day clinic, they could have ridden the next day.

The owner asked me if it was unethical to bring her, but truly, I don't think so. You can't train horses to travel by staying home. How horses got familiar with going to do things was by doing them, while we stayed consistently affirmative. Habits needed to be formed, but even then, there was no guarantee. Every day was brand new. We were supposed to learn to like that part.

We take baby steps, asking for just a little. The horse may give us a different, better answer. We grow patient by letting the horse make a choice and rewarding the result. Lena needed self-assurance to progress, and because change was inevitable, it was best to steer that change in a good direction. It wasn't our job to demand obedience or answer for her. We just listened as the horse told us something about herself.

The secret is not caring about the answer before we ask the question. "Can you take one more step (or eat, or breathe and self-soothe), not that I care?" Then we wait. We give horses space to answer when we lay down our chatter, the defense of our shortcomings, and stop telling our own story. Profound listening means being quiet long enough for the horses to feel safe to answer without us interrupting or repeating the request.

Earlier in the day, Kiefer's owner had her lesson. She wanted to tack up and get my input on what he might have felt during the complete process, rather than ride. He was mainly retired and had been a lesson horse previously. She wanted to understand him better. Kiefer and I shared a great conversation with the halter, and he told us all about himself. The horse is always the expert, regardless of what we think we know about them. Kiefer was stoic, his answers plain but quiet, so we had to become still to hear. Always an excellent lesson.

Every horse offered more than we asked. It was that kind of humbling day where we understood the debt we owed to all horses. Lena and Kiefer took the lead. When horses can't "do" the clinic, they teach it instead.

Sometimes people think I am a horse whisperer, whatever that was supposed to mean. But it was all the horses. I'm just a hand puppet. I know it sounds creepy, but if you can focus your senses and let your own busy thoughts rest, that's just how it feels. More intimate than riding, it was sensing what they meant. It was the horse communicating inside you without words, but as plain as day.

By the end, we were a happy, tired bunch. I acknowledged the horses. It was always unavoidably easy to thank horses. We had fallen in love with them all over again for the first time. But there was a certain magic about this group of people that added an exceptional quality to the day. They wanted to be there and chose to be vulnerable and open to ideas. Willing to dive deep and willing to laugh. We became a herd, not as graceful as those with hooves and manes, but a group of like minds and kindred spirits. Clinics were no more controllable than a horse, but days like this renewed my faith. I wanted us to get it right with horses; we owed them so much. I owed them so much.

The organizers helped all the participants get loaded and on their way. I offered them and their helper a free lesson the next morning. I wanted to thank them one more time and the next day was a short driving day.

Finally finished for the day, I walked to the Rancho to let my breath out and became me again. Mister took me for a walk. The sunset dazzled the leaves, and the leaves winked the same colors back. I closed my eyes and had a slow dance ride on my Grandfather Horse.

***

The next morning was filled with horses and laughter, and genuine thanks on all sides. The organizers invited me back the next year, and I agreed, thanking them. In a world of one-time stops, return visits are golden.

My mind went back to a great clinic a few years earlier. It had been a fabulous weekend on the West Coast, well attended, and a complete success. Meaning I was exhausted from sprinting the distance, and the organizer was giddy that everyone was so pleased with the clinic. She asked me who she should invite, clinician-wise, because she wanted more clinics like mine had been. I waited, hoping she heard herself. She asked again, impatient for my advice about who she could hire. I'm sure my face was as flat as I felt. You hire me, I told her. Her embarrassment silenced her, but I knew I wouldn't be going back before I said it.

At noontime, Mister and I were driving west. I was thinking about all the horses and all the perfect moments. There were bumps but I had kept my eyes on the road and my mind on the task, and Mister had avoided getting his feet wet in two oceans. We were not just doing this thing; we had almost done this thing.

After driving less than three hours, we landed at our stop for the night in a wooded RV park. They all have trees here. In many areas, the RV parks were paved lots next to a freeway, but this place felt like camping should. Then we lounged, snacked, and listened for varmints. Mister was always patient for his day to happen, patient about most things.

He liked quiet days when he saw himself as an only dog. Or

me as an only person. We are utterly comfortable. Our lives have dove-tailed together and when an idea came, it was hard to tell who thought it first. Mister wasn't the only dog to fill my gaps so well, but he was the first in a long time. I will regret none of the rescues that have come, the dogs I have altered my home and remodeled my life to suit. I am too much of a lost dog myself to turn them away. But Mister needs nothing from me. Beyond that, he holds a unique place in my life. Mister takes me as I am without complaint. He asks for nothing. He's the only one.

We slept forever and then slept some more, deep in the forest. Languishing and loitering, we folded down minutes before checkout time, the day half gone.

Puppy Mill

It was a quick hop to see our friends at Proud Spirit Horse Sanctuary today. Like all good horse homes, the sanctuary was on an obscure dead-end road where there was spotty cell service. GPS Woman may or may not know the way. Her voice does not betray her intent, which was why I continually fell for her tricks. I looked at the pretty trees and went where I was told. For someone who considered disobedience an art form and had "Question Authority" t-shirts in four colors, you'd think I'd be more suspicious.

The beauty in the woods of North Carolina was like being in a virgin forest on a normal day. Not a rare event, it was relentless primeval glory. GPS Woman told me to turn, so I did. The road bent and curved, and her directions didn't always match the land, but then they did sometimes. Slowing down even more to look for roads, I checked the supplemental directions from my host. I was going to a place I had never been, and it was well off the beaten path. Just like usual, but I never got used to it.

Take the first gravel road on the right, GPS Woman said, and I did. A few hundred feet in, there were a couple of wrecked cars back in some trees. It looked like someone was living there. The road was narrow and steep, so I had my four-wheel drive engaged. GPS Woman seemed to say I was not quite on the right road, but not wrong either. Or maybe we were in a dead spot for cell service. There's a thought. I rolled on slowly around blind corners on a road that was as old as the trees. It was more of a hike than a drive. There were no clearings, but off the road, I could see an old plastic kid's slide and barrels. No house, no cars, but leaves so deep I wondered what else was buried there.

Up a steep hill and another curve, and GPS Woman encouraged me on. A flicker of confidence, but the dirt road had a strip of grass down the middle, like parallel footpaths. Then I saw numbers on a post, but they were all wrong. Now the road curved sharper downhill, but the trees were dense, and it was hard to see. It looked like a fork ahead, so I tried to guess the least awful choice. One side of the fork got too narrow for my truck, so I turned into the other, which was slightly less narrow but just as steep. There were no more numbers, but I didn't think mail got delivered here either. I checked my rearview mirror and sure enough, I was still pulling a trailer.

Then the road got wider, but for the wrong reason, and the theme from the movie *Deliverance* twanged in the distance. The road dead-ended and dropped us into a large dirt yard with a broken-down house that didn't look like it had ever been painted. We were blocking the entry, which was already partially blocked by a tractor and a low-to-the-ground mower. They looked like they hadn't been used in a decade, but tractors can fool you. But a mower? Who even had open space here to mow? There was a mash of sheds and barrels, along with seven or eight vehicles in various states of rusty decomposition scattered around. It looked like a parking lot, except vehicles were all pointed in different directions and mixed in with spare parts that were unrecognizable. And the one newish truck that was probably only twenty-five years old.

There was a no trespassing sign. Of course, there was. But it was already too late. I was in and it was so tight that I couldn't get out fast. Should I go to the door and apologize? It felt like I was being watched; someone must be home.

Then I saw beagles in small chicken wire pens of different sizes arcing around the yard to the house and beyond. The dogs were silent. One beagle was on the front porch, sitting watching me. Beagles were looking from the house windows. How were they quiet? If beagles aren't barking, they aren't breathing.

I began turning, nosing my truck close to a rusty wringer washing machine, then cranked the wheel and backed a few inches. Then cranked my steering wheel and rolled forward a few more inches. Then repeat that a few dozen times, nervously squinting into my rearview to see if anyone was there. I had no choice but to escape as quickly as I could, but we only gained a few inches at a time, then gave them back. Again, straighten the wheel, back, crank the wheel, and roll forward, then peek into the rearview. When I was younger, my fears revolved around my physical safety. This was the first time I thought of the value of my truck. My shoulders were nearly touching my ears.

Reverse, forward, reverse, forward. I had made some progress. Now I was pulling forward a tiny bit more each time toward the old tractor, but I couldn't see the edge of the mower over my hood. It was low and sharp, and I just wanted out. I'd lost track of the number of times I'd shifted, won a bit of ground in the direction I wanted, and shifted, only to gain an inch. If I tore a tire open on the mower, oh, don't think about that. Don't look at the dogs and don't be impatient.

All forty-four feet of my rig are inching their way to reverse in an area not much bigger than that same forty-four feet. I had spun my steering wheel all the way over and all the way back until my shoulders ached. Each time I shifted forward, I wanted to floor it and go over the top of anything in my way, but I didn't.

Finally, I cranked extra hard; I cleared the mower by a hair and bumped through a ditch back onto the steep incline to the road, grateful for my granny gear. I needed it for my slow-motion escape. GPS Woman was mysteriously quiet because it heightened the drama.

Melanie Sue and Jean: Proud Spirit Horse Sanctuary

We made it back to a proper two-lane road where the cell service worked again. I felt very relieved and very ancient. I'd love to say these dead-end adventures rolled off my back, but this one left me shaky. We were still trying to get to Proud Spirit Sanctuary, with Melanie Sue and her husband, Jim, at the helm. I called and after trying to describe landmarks over the phone, Mel came and found us. We followed her back to the Sanctuary, feeling as lucky as the horses who had come through those gates.

Mel knew about the beagle farm and grimaced. It's the same where I live. There wasn't much to be done about animals on private property. It wasn't a crime to own a pack of dogs or a herd of horses. But when there's a sanctuary next to a puppy mill, it might count as making progress.

Later, after unfolding and setting up, we went to check on the herd. The barn was on a rise, with a long sloping meadow, edged by trees turning color and a heart-stopping view in all directions. This was a new location for the farm, but the sanctuary had endured. So many horses had lived in peace over decades at Proud Spirit, but the herd was smaller now, always by attrition. The sanctuary stopped taking in new horses a few years earlier, but the herd was all the sweeter for it. Mel and I remembered Polly, a small mare I had known in Colorado. She died earlier in the year and looking around, I couldn't feel sorry for her spending her last time in this beautiful place. It was good to be with old friends, two-legged and four.

Mel is a writer who just published a young adult book called *Liberty Biscuit*. The engaging story captured my less-than-young mind, and the hook was visible to someone with our shared background with rescues. The story was a kind of primer for recruiting young horse advocates. Maybe the book needed a warning label, and I smiled to think of it. We were proof it was dangerous to let horse-crazy girls read about donkey friends and horses in trouble. *Black Beauty* had left a mark on generations. I hoped Mel's book would do the same.

In the morning, we folded down, and both Mel and I drove a couple of hours west to a book signing and a visit with our mutual friend, Jean. It was a little cooler outside and with each mile, the colors became more intense. The road pulled us deeper through rolling hills and thick forests until we crested a hill and I saw what could only be the Blue Ridge Mountains. They looked exactly like their name, only more beautiful. They were so unexpected I wanted to slam on my brakes.

How can it be possible to have this view be at the rise of a hill, or just around a corner? But it's happened more times than imaginable on this trip. The beauty of our country defies photos. When a panoramic view like this opened in front of me, horizon to horizon, it always took my breath away. Also, my words. I took photos, but they were only a poor place keeper for the memory. Cameras are weapons of cellular destruction, squeezing the infinite to fit into a tiny frame. When I tried to express the beauty I'd seen during this year of travel, I felt like a toddler bouncing in a car seat, pointing a sticky finger at a car window, chanting ou-ou-ou! A wordless smear.

We arrived the afternoon before the book event. Mel drove on to Jean's home on top of a nearby mountain. Mister and I unfolded and set up at a local RV park, and then left to meet them for dinner at Jean's, about a half-hour away. Her home was up a steep, winding road through some of the most breath-taking fall foliage so far. It was an older community, lush with trees and vistas. The houses had a sparse simple beauty, nested in old growth. The road got narrower as we climbed higher, but I had good directions from there. Jean's home was at the top of the mountain, and I parked as instructed, thrilled to have no trailer attached. An easy turnaround to be headed in the right direction later.

We had one of those glorious visits with dogs and dinner and good company. Her home was also a sanctuary, the kind of place that made you feel like family. Even the wood said welcome. There was so much to see and talk about. We all had horses in common, and our friendship had grown from there.

Naturally, I stayed too long. I try to not drive after dark in places I don't know, but it took a while to say goodbye and start back. It was just past dusk when I started down the single-lane road. There were no streetlights, of course, and the trees obscured the sky. We went slowly, got out of the security gate, and drove on. By now, GPS Woman worked again, off and on. Things didn't look familiar, but it was dark. What did I know? I drove where I was told but felt more bruised than I looked.

In the first town we came to, there was too much light, and too many numbered highway signs. Each state was different, and in this town, they stacked highway signs on light poles, a dozen at a time. With traffic behind me, I couldn't confirm what GPS Woman said with the signs and turned too late a couple of times.

I recognized nothing. There was construction that I hadn't seen earlier, but I came here on a four-lane divided highway, with the other half out of view, so maybe that was to be expected. GPS Woman barked one turn after another. We'd been driving for over forty-five minutes and should have been back at the RV park. Instead, we were on narrow back roads, and it felt like we were inching forward deeper into the woods. Not again.

I was hanging on every word GPS Woman said, but the map showed we were still forty-five minutes away. How was that possible? Then I was told to turn on a road I thought we had turned on before. But how could I tell? Two-lane roads in the woods after dark all look remarkably similar. Cell service had cut out, so I didn't know what I had missed, but now I was talking to myself. I was trying to breathe my way out of panicking, but if I wasn't panicking already, I wouldn't need to try.

A half-hour after that, GPS Woman chirped that I had arrived at my destination. We were not at the RV park, but I thought I could find it from there. I swore to never go that far after dark again. We barely made the park curfew. Yes, some RV parks lock the gate.

Mister would like to mention that his dinner was very late, thanks for asking.

The next day at the book talk, I asked Jean about the definition of a word I didn't know. "Bespoke" was on a sign and I thought Jean knew all the words. She flashed a wry smile, and with an easy laugh, said she had no idea. So, we made up definitions and had a wine and cookie afternoon. I looked the word up later. It means tailor-made, and it suits Jean, truly a one-of-a-kind. These were precious moments in stacks of books with women I cared about. It was a feast.

I'm quite in awe of Jean living in such a remote area. It had been her summer home for decades and she was not giving it up now. Part of me worried she was in such a remote area, and part of me hoped she never had to leave it. I don't underestimate women, especially those older than me. She wasn't living wild on her mountain; she had wonderful friends. There had been losses and impracticalities, of course. May we get less tame with age, and closer to our truest selves, like the nearly transparent delicate wildflowers that have miles of root systems underground. I like to think of Jean that way.

An Extremely Nice Dog House

We were finally leaving North Carolina. I had worn out my welcome staying here for two full weeks with only two paid clinic days. The sting of the last-minute cancellations was real now. Worse than that, I'd been myself, not the role I play as a clinician. And my ordinary self was not all that appealing. I can't indefinitely hold up people's ideals of who they think I should be. Eventually, I started to smell fishy.

Back on the road west, the leaves were in deep color now. It stayed dusk for a longer time in the evening and the sun was slow to rise in the forest. Many trees had empty branches, and the ground was inches deep with leaves. Crossing the border into Tennessee, the roads immediately got wider and smoother, but apparently, the state roadkill species here was God's opossums. The trees receded and a little more sky became visible. Open land and stands of trees leapfrog in front of us, the view looms large, letting us know we're insignificant gnats. As beautiful as these changing leaves are, we'd been in the woods since Pennsylvania. I was looking forward to the open prairie and being able to see what was coming at me.

GPS Woman confidently directed us to our RV park between two Barn Visit locations near Manchester. We exited the freeway and drove past a Starbucks on a frontage road. Turn right, came the command, and it was a dirt road. I got squinty-eyed with anxiety, but to my relief, there was a sign and a passel of trailers nestled in the trees. Thanks, GPS Woman. I was already planning a coffee stop the next morning.

We set up, and I started a load of laundry in the machines there because I still had too many quarters. I was pulling my wagon with clean laundry back to the Rancho when a doddering old dog who had just finished her business, gave me a mumble-bark. Cloudy-eyed and stiff-backed, with a lump on her side. I doubt she heard or saw me. It was probably the random *just-in-case* warning old dogs use to let us know they were still on the job. She was a tan and white Lab-Mix who weighed half what she probably did in her prime.

I greeted the man holding her leash. He had a bushy gray beard and a T-shirt with writing that was old enough to be illegible. He was about my age and looked better suited to a Harley Davidson. Instead, he stood by a large Class A, the type of RV that looked like a tour bus.

Solo? he asked.

I nodded. Before leaving home, I'd read that almost a third of RVers were traveling alone but I hadn't seen it.

He smiled in a familiar way that made me think I knew him and asked about the Rancho. I told him I worked on the road, but the Rancho was nicer than my home with a good bed and air conditioning. He agreed his rig was nicer than his house, and worth more, too. He had a soft laugh at this notion, and his good old dog took a step to sniff my shoe. Mister couldn't see me, but he'd know soon enough.

The man said his dad had taken him and his brother camping often when they were kids. His father worked hard all his life, and being tight with money, had left more in his will than his gray-haired son expected. He figured spending his inheritance this way was a fitting tribute to his father's memory, and now they got to be part of their grandchildren's lives.

He and his wife lived in Massachusetts, but their kids and grandkids lived in this area, so they were staying for a couple of weeks. It was their second trip down. The drive had gotten easier because they finally decided it wasn't a race, he chuckled. Now they drove shorter days and took more frequent breaks. Once they arrived, they stayed on their own, but joined the family to do ordinary things like go to the kids' soccer games. It would be great to see his smile from the sidelines, I thought.

They traveled more than they expected they would. He said it was like living in a newer apartment that allowed pets. The best part was being able to bring the old dog, who gave a faint wag, and the Chihuahua, who was inside. There was also a cat that needed medication every day, he added. He wasn't sure he could trust them to pet sitters, but traveling this way, their animals got the care they needed. His RV wasn't quite the size of Noah's Ark, but it was an extremely nice dog house.

Giving him my very best smile, I told him he was my hero. His self-deprecating laugh came from deep in his chest, his heart maybe. He leaned over to let his old dog know where he was. She was looking slightly disoriented, but she settled at his touch.

Back in the Rancho, Mister eyeballed me suspiciously. He

knew I'd cheated on him again. I carried the stink of betrayal with the old dog. I packed away the laundry and made his dinner. We didn't see the next-door dogs outside again, but he still avoided their site as we passed it on our walks. Not to worry, Mister. I promise we will never upgrade to a tour bus. They don't look easy to turn around on a dead-end. It certainly couldn't be the $250K plus price tag.

Just Golden

The sun and I both moved slower in the mornings now that it was late October. The first coffee got stronger. Reading the overnight emails, there was a note from a participant at a previous clinic. I'd loved her dark horse, full of bravado, meaning his insecurity was dramatic, not hidden. He was handsome and charismatic. And he could be a bit intimidating. She wrote to tell me she'd realized something fundamental after having time to process the weekend. She wasn't actually afraid of her horse as she had thought (and then felt shame about.) What a bold breakthrough. Those were some sweet words so early in the morning. She said what she was really afraid of was doing aggressive training methods because they seemed dangerous to her and her horse. Right again, I thought. She found an internal integrity that had been hidden and it gave her new enthusiasm about both of them. Hallelujah!

It seemed so obvious when she put it that way. Not just common sense, I thought, but a life-changing shift of perception. I had seen similar anxiety often, and I wondered how many would agree. A cleaner definition of what the fear was would help me drag it out into the sunlight for others. Then we could watch it shrivel up together.

She continued, sounding confident. She said when she'd stopped fighting with her horse, she began experiencing genuine relationship and trust. Her shift changed her horse, reciprocity was that simple. She must feel such relief. When I got notes like this, I dined on them for days.

A couple of hours later, we headed out to work, with a stop at Starbucks first. I was shocked Mister knew exactly where we were. All this time, he never looked out windows or sat up tall, but he surely was now. We got to the window and his best friend in the world took my order and asked if my dog would like a Puppuccino. I didn't quite understand what the server said, but Mister clearly did. He was stretching, his ears on high alert, trying to stand on the console, but his seat belt didn't reach. Was he doing his George Clooney impression? This was not his first Starbucks, that was for sure. We got our orders and pulled ahead to park until Mister finished his. Whip cream, I'd hop on the console, too.

How had we gone this far without me knowing this? It had to be over a year since his last one because he'd been with me that long, but it was only yesterday to him. Noted, and we drove on. I wondered how to work his recognition skills to replace GPS Woman, but immediately gave up the idea. Her one advantage was that she didn't nap as much.

It's our last Barn Visit of the trip, stopping with a long-time client for three days. We'd be at the client's barn each morning and then on to a nearby facility with her local trainer in the afternoon. It was a small group of horses and women. We shared a camaraderie of like minds, and we enjoyed the minutiae of calming signals. There was a photographer in the group, always a pleasure. We had the luxury of time, but somehow, we still ran late every day. Mister reminded me of his sainthood, and we stopped for guilt Puppuccino's every morning. As one does.

I was working with River, the organizer's beautiful Morgan gelding, doing some groundwork, asking him some questions. He had been considering his answers when, just like that, he decided he needed a stroll. It wasn't that he was unable to do the task, and he certainly wasn't quitting. We had been encouraging his confidence, listening to his anxiety, and this was a clear decision on his part.

River took me for a walk. It wasn't a refusal of any sort, and he wasn't trying to escape me. Maybe he needed a moment to walk it out. We should all like it when a horse takes time to think and process. Pressuring horses for quick answers was just human impatience. Time isn't real to horses in the same way, and we would do well to slow down ourselves.

The two of us walked away from the group at a good speed. It was a beautiful morning, and the pasture had a border of golden trees. The leaves were so thick on the trees, a wall up to the sky, and deep on the ground. They seemed warm and River looked even more golden than his usual rich Palomino color in the light. Or was the light golden, too? I soaked it in, knowing he would read it in my body. At the foot of the pasture, we turned and maintained that good walk back to the barn. I came to his side and looked at his face, refreshed and brand new. I felt the same way, warmer inside. So glad I trusted his idea, and my reward for listening was a horse who had become more willing. We must learn to trust that horses know what they need.

If we spent the time being affirmative with horses that we spend thinking the horse has failed, I can't imagine where we would be. We have to learn to trust their intelligence. Then River picked up just where we left off, without a cue, and did what I had previously asked, as perfect as a horse could be.

After lunch, we traveled to the other barn. I met more horses, and the conversation went to handling horses with anxiety. I always felt my father's glare from beyond the grave when I talked about anxiety in horses. He was old school and thought horses didn't have feelings. My methods would embarrass him even more now. When I was little, he accused me of training like a girl. It was and has been since, meant to be the ultimate insult.

Now, my job helping damaged horses all came down to their feelings. Domination was easier than trying to understand a horse. It was always a struggle to let our egos rest long enough to listen. I can quote all the science, but it was a good feeling to know after all these name-calling years, training like a girl was in alignment with how horses learn. Science had become my best friend.

As I continued doing this work, I realized that the root cause of most non-pain-related training problems in horses was their initial training. Like us, their earliest experiences color their entire lives. We can't ignore the trauma of a harsh start for them or us. Whether the horse was stoic or reactive, it all started by letting them tell us about themselves. It takes patience at first. You might take some unplanned walks like mine, but once that anxiety softens, trust can begin. They need to lead us into the past before we can lead them to a brighter future.

In the meantime, I looked like a bliss ninny while I stood around and breathed. It's how you can tell I'd been listening to horses instead of humans. We humans were more judgmental and result driven. Horses existed in each precious moment of the natural world. We think the end justifies the means, but horses think we miss the point.

White Lies

Every clinic day, the alarm on my phone went off at five p.m. and people knew the day was over. Then the conversation continued for a few moments while I packed up. I told them Mister needed his dinner, but one more question, please. They just couldn't let me go. Not every stop, but often enough that I dreaded that ending time. I tried to come up with an inspiring idea to end with a dramatic mic drop moment, but that seemed to make things worse. The five o'clock line in the sand shouldn't need to be negotiated, and most of the time, I didn't want the day to end either. But my tight rubber superhero-clinician suit chafed. In daydreams, I thought it would be so much easier if, like a factory job, someone else sounded a horn to mark quitting time. That was why I set my alarm.

Most of us have had years of our lives under the control of alarms and calendars and hours on the clock. Some of us will always rebel against the notion of boundaries, not liking to be held to restrictions. I love the boundaries I set for myself. Or maybe I love telling myself what to do. The discipline of being on time is a beautiful freedom that means I have less anxiety about being late. And I made a time schedule that gave me hours for my passions. My horse education and riding skills were thanks to years of walking out of my house at 6:30 every morning and heading to the barn to ride before work.

I enjoyed having rules about what to do in stressful or unfamiliar situations. If a heckler appeared or a participant at a clinic was unhappy, I knew what to do. Setting boundaries gave me the confidence to solve problems calmly. I could break my own rules by choice, but most of my stress was relieved simply because I had a plan, even one I rarely used. Discipline was freedom once you got on the right side of it.

Truth-telling is a discipline that gave me confidence. It's remarkable how much being taken at my word mattered to me as I traveled for work. I needed that after growing up not knowing who to trust. I wanted the boundary of saying *no-thank-you* to hold. Like spitting in my hand and shaking on it, I was old-fashioned that way. I took others at their word and didn't like having mine doubted. It seemed to me it should be a simple trust.

After sharing these thoughts with one client and whining about needing to nearly throw a fit to be heard, she had an interesting answer. She wondered if women told white lies so commonly that we coaxed others to give them the option to be truthful when it was not our public habit. It sounded upside down, but my client continued. We were all raised to smile and be agreeable, she said. We grew into women who told white lies to the world because it made us more acceptable. Certainly, we found lies more expedient than admitting the real reason that might hurt someone's feelings or lead to judgment. It was a small step to assume other women used white lies to appear more agreeable, too. In that light, double questioning was a way of saying it was okay to tell the truth.

As she explained, it almost sounded reasonable that we wouldn't believe 'no-thank-you' by unspoken agreement. I hated to think women had a white lie pact. Telling the truth was a moral duty to me. It sounded stuffy when I said it, but was a lie routinely expected and just good manners?

If that was true, it meant the feelings of others took priority over our own. We are people-pleasers, not by choice, but by obligation. My mother would agree it was better to lie than to ruffle feathers. Peace through deceit was her golden rule. It might be why I'm so touchy about truth-telling. How do we look past all the pain and distrust caused by white lies? Did we even notice when we lost our integrity and authenticity?

Then do we induct girls into our white lie cult when we teach them to be respectable, which sometimes means being unexceptional and other times deceptive? It may all be done with love and the best of intentions, but it will always be a loss if we take their honest voices away.

Excuse me if I sound like someone who spent two decades in therapy, but no. *No-thank-you.* Please stop trying to control everyone's emotions. Instead of trying to soothe everything to a pale tan color, could we at least experiment with telling the truth?

That's where horses come in. We love their beauty, constantly in awe of their strength and intelligence, hailing their boldness and sensitivity. But then we immediately try to corner and trap horses, literally and figuratively, forcing them into Breyer horse molds. While working to tame them, too often we shut them down, with fear of pain, or the massive force of our cloying love. We try to manage their behaviors and deaden their instincts. Asking for obedience while imagining it's a partnership. This kind of training should sound both familiar and dangerous to us.

How could a state of subjugation be anyone's highest calling? Hope drowned out by a list of hollow beige rules. Are we still being crowded into that cursed window seat with a view outside, but with no way to escape?

The Oxford Dictionary defines domestication as "taming an animal and keeping it as a pet…" Is that what we have become? Or we could let our capability, compassion, and intelligence shine, with no false humility or apology.

It matters because when we consent to limit the expression of our lives, we live in cages of our own making. When we pretend to be less than we are, we damage our confidence down to the soul. It matters because even horses can read our self-deception. They don't know the details of our lives, just that we are not who we seem. They read our incongruity, as counterfeit as the face-talker.

But horses are also the antidote. They are the haunting temptation we couldn't shake from early childhood. We heard their hooves on the wind, a sweet reminder that encouraged us to loosen our bonds and run with them. It might have taken years, but when we finally answered their call, it was with an authentic, undomesticated voice.

Music City

This three-day Barn Visit, with its advanced participants and fantastic and complicated horses, had given us an opportunity to stretch. The line between how we train horses and how we live our lives was flimsy, and that was just how it should be. Each of us was left with more questions than answers, but hopefully more confident to trust our own voice in the conversation.

Mister and I had four nights in this wooded park and the sun seemed to rise a bit later each day. The dew was heavy, and it felt like fall had fully arrived. We hooked up the truck and packed up the Rancho, ready for the road. I gave our neighbor and his old dog a wave as we pulled out. Two minutes later, Mister sat tall for his Puppuccino, every server at that Starbucks was besotted with him.

We headed northwest, and in an hour, we were crawling through Nashville traffic. The downtown skyline was beautiful with elegant bridges and contemporary architecture. Nashville had a brown cloud, and more air pollution than we'd seen in a very long time, but it also had an Americana Radio Station at 89.5 that made us want to drive slower to listen. Linda Ronstadt belted out *Different Drum*, one of my first battle cries. Then Bonnie Raitt with *Nick of Time*. Just when it couldn't get better, Willie chimed in with *Always on My Mind*. I nearly had to pull over when Dolly crooned *Jolene*. Really, Nashville, you've got to let me go.

We crossed from Tennessee through Kentucky to Illinois and within a few miles, we were back on farmland. The trees had lost all their leaves here. The farmers had stripped crops from the fields, and we were deep into fall. It was visible proof that time had passed with the miles, an affirmation of the reality that edged this road trip. Driving was an experience of unstuck moments shifting between new experiences and treasured memories, tethered to a calendar.

By the side of the road were more deer, new roadkill, their frail legs akimbo. Highway workers must regularly pick them up. Did parents hide their children's eyes from the gore, or was it a lost cause? Soon, more deer would wander too close, sacrificed from an abundant supply. But the circle of life was off-kilter, it was a one-sided fight, and they had no defense. These deer, every few hundred feet, looked healthy. They were grazing in the sun, and an instant later, fresh road meat. They were God's deer, at the moment before and the moment after it happened. I tried to comfort myself, but just like the wolf kill last spring, they died with bloody bodies and broken haunches. I'd call humans road wolves, but we're worse. Wolves would eat their kill. We leave destruction in our wake. Earth was watching.

A little after three p.m., we pulled into our RV park and, like every Thursday night, I started writing my blog. People ask me why I don't have a few of them stacked up, written ahead of time so that I don't have to get up so early on a Friday. The answer was simple; I like my habit. Readers say they like to have coffee with me and the blog on Fridays, and I like Thursday nights baking my words like fresh bread.

Some have told me that reading my blog changed their relationship with their horses. In the futuristic world of technology, we use the time-honored written word. I like it better than YouTube videos because instead of seeing me with a perfect horse, you imagine yourself starring in a home movie with your own horse. Visualizing was the important thing, and the written word encouraged that.

I felt sleepy after posting in the morning. I had two cups of good strong coffee before dawn, but just the same, maybe a little nap. It was 6:30 a.m. when I pulled the covers up. Usually, Mister was happy to roll over and fall asleep again, but no deal today. He wanted to play, but my eyelids were impossible to lift. For a while, I tried to put his plush pull toy under my backside and trick him into thinking I was holding up my end of the game, but it didn't work. Then my hand found his belly. It worked like mesmerizing a chicken. He melted belly up and arced over my chest. He never made eye contact, but I scratched under his chin, and he melted slowly until all played out, he dozed off and so did I.

It was a short drive today, and we started late, just before checkout time. We blew into St. Louis, a bright, beautiful downtown area with the Gateway Arch. Google told me it's the tallest monument in the US, but my favorite was the Stan Musial Veterans Memorial Bridge, which spanned the Mississippi River and connected Missouri with Illinois. From a distance, it appeared to be made of string so delicate it would tangle in the wind. I loved the idea of creating a thing as stalwart as a bridge to be so filled with air. Earlier on the trip, I read a Willa Cather book called *Alexander's Bridge, and* I thanked her for helping me appreciate bridges more.

Not far beyond, there was a large sign that said, "Wages of Sin is Hell." My inner editor cringed. Where were the grammar police when you needed them? Should that be plural? "Are hell?" I checked and the actual quote was "The wages of sins are death." Okay, sounds a little better but maybe I missed the point.

The world was a place of wonder and horror, existing right next to each other, and left for us to translate into understandable messages from beyond. We are always looking for signs. Like training horses, there was a choice between fear or affirmative thoughts. It's true in our lives as well. We can worship threats from a vengeful god on a billboard, or marvel at the beauty and possibility in our lives and try to do better. Because Earth is the real church.

Acknowledging a Mare

One last RV park and, the next morning, off for the last clinic of the trip near Kansas City. I pulled down the drive to a farm for a Calming Signal intensive. Meeting new horses and people who care about them was always special. I was excited for days like this because honing our listening skills should always be our goal. I parked my trailer near a pen with three horses close to the barn. One horse was a gray mare who was quite thin, visibly lame, and showed pain in her body. This was the part of my job that I didn't talk about much.

Sometimes I get to a clinic stop and the trainer will let me know that someone in the clinic should consider retirement for their horse. Sometimes I see it for myself and mention it as kindly as I can, knowing that I have fresh eyes. Besides, I knew it was on the owner's mind already. It can be easier to talk about hard topics, even death, with someone they don't know.

The farm owner came over and we greeted each other and exchanged a few words. I didn't know the mare's situation, but she was right there, the elephant in the room. Count on me to speak up. I asked if the mare was older. The owner related the horse's history and her present condition with concern. She told me I couldn't see the worst of it. The mare had a large tumor on her far side, and she had already had an appointment for euthanasia the week before. But the vet told her that the horse was not in pain. I said the mare looked pretty uncomfortable to me, or maybe exhausted. Sadly, our conversation was almost good news to the farm owner, who said she didn't agree with the vet, but she loved this mare. She didn't want to believe her eyes, and I can't blame her. We had an intense first conversation about horrible things. But horses were a shared passion and even this hard topic ended up aligning us more than separating us.

The clinic began early the next day with my Calming Signals PowerPoint presentation, complete with photos and videos. I have a library of PowerPoint presentations, not usual for horse trainers, but a great tool to introduce whatever I was talking about. Most of us are visual learners. We could have a start with pictures and videos, along with words about what we'd see later with the horses. Having a clinician visit was like a good news/bad news joke. I acknowledged everything that was going well but also listened to the horses and shared ideas for improvement. Clinics were a vulnerable time; people wanted to get it right, but that wasn't always easy to figure out.

Then we went outside where we took turns haltering the horses for the rest of the day. If that sounds boring and slow, then you aren't listening. Perhaps it isn't too late to take up something that might interest you more. Like needlepoint or fence painting.

Haltering is how we greet horses, our first interchange. Every time a halter goes on, it means that the horse surrenders to us, so we're polite. To be clear, everyone, horses and humans alike, totally knew how to halter before I got there. Think of the halter as a conversation starter. It wasn't about getting it done so much as letting the horse tell us something about themselves. Haltering was a language lesson for us. We had always been told to listen, but did we know what we were supposed to be listening to?

The first horse was a snow-white mini who showed some muzzle anxiety. Horses do this for a few reasons, but it wasn't about us making up a story about him. It was about listening to his story straight from the one who was telling us. We talked about ways to alleviate his stress and the participant changed her position slightly. We crowd horses too often. She took a step farther from his head and his countenance visibly changed. It was the right answer. The mini inhaled and stretched tall, filled his space, and transformed into a Percheron draft horse in his mind.

We continued from pen to pen, and each horse and participant had thoughtful exchanges. Some of the horses were complicated elders and others were young draft horses as curious as kittens. Some horses tried too hard, and some said *no-thank-you* with profound kindness. Some horses needed extra time to speak up.

Horses use calming signals when two conflicting thoughts or feelings happen at the same time, so we waited, letting them sort it out. A considered response from a horse was always the goal. Sometimes we don't get the answer we want and instead, we get a better one.

The last horse of the afternoon was that gray mare. Everyone in the group knew what was going on with her; they had all loved her for a long time, knew her care had been impeccable, and her time was near. The mare walked along the front fence line of her pen, passing in front of the group, and showing her tumor. She moved slowly, her body stiff, her stride uneven. Not that she was lame on one hoof, it seemed like pain on all four. Her eyes were small and half-closed. Slowly, she came to a stop in front of us and dropped her head lower, gave a couple of small licks, and exhaled loudly. These are signs of self-soothing, a release of stress. That's good theoretically, but it would not get her out of the condition she was in. The mare continued after a moment, moving along the fence line through a corner, and stopped, facing up the hill, looking away from the group.

The participant who was going to halter the mare entered and walked to the center of her pen. The idea was to begin the conversation away from the gate, not pressure the horse, and show the horse you were listening. We gave them space and then played the children's game, Mother, may I? Taking the cue from the mare, halting when her calming signals showed more anxiety. Then coming closer when the mare gave a release signal. The participant changed her position patiently twice, but the mare showed no sign of acknowledgment at all. She was frozen, and that's unusual.

When something isn't normal, we go even slower and listen even closer. If we concentrate too much on the task, we might miss the message. Being frozen was a message.

I saw this mare's response in her body and asked the participant to forget about haltering the mare. Instead, I asked her to move to the mare's shoulder, facing away toward the mare's rump. Then I asked her to put her left hand on the mare's chest between her front legs and breathe. I didn't want to confuse the moment by explaining why just then. The participant did as I asked her. Behind her back, the mare relaxed, and her eyes got larger and softer. Then I asked the participant to step away. At that moment, the mare turned and walked back along the front of the pen, but now her walk was lighter, with more rhythm and a little more swing. Her body had softened.

Nothing mystical happened. We listened to her resistance to the halter, as quiet as it was. The participant simply and silently acknowledged the mare without being confrontational in her body position. There was no cure for the mare's pain that was not an illness or injury. But there was relief in being heard and the participant felt the shift in the mare, as we saw it visibly.

If we felt too much sympathy or pressure to save her, it would just add more anxiety to the mare. What horses want from us was often no more than simple acknowledgment. "Yes, we know you're in pain." The mare showed relief immediately. She was crystal clear. When a horse gets what they ask for, they stop asking, and the mare walked away.

There couldn't have been a more eloquent closing message to our clinic. This beautiful and decrepit gray mare was just a horse. There have been several similar sad conversations about euthanasia recently. But rarely such a visual affirmation of the power of simple breath. We listen to the horse by standing and breathing, touching them or not, as they choose. Breath is peace.

Some people approach horses like a swat team breaking down a door to save the world. Like a rock star greeting adoring fans. It's all about them.

When we wait, we let horses express their emotions. There is no finer gift than acknowledgment, just as they are. We aren't here to cure them of being horses. We're here to listen to nuance.

Travels with Charley and Mister

We studied Steinbeck in high school, but I took it farther on my own, reading everything he wrote, one book after another. Well, not quite everything. *Travels with Charley* was the lone stray. I waited an extra fifty years to crank it up on Audible.

Steinbeck inspired me by writing about everyman, poor Americans, my people. He made us seem heroic. My parents grew up in the Great Depression and we lived in that shadow, partly from memory and partly because we lost our farm and moved west in the sixties.

But when I tried to recall Steinbeck's writing, I wasn't sure of my critical discernment of literature at sixteen. A crush on a character was enough for me to defend an author forever. Well, I've grown up and I'm not that easy now. Not only a book report here, I have the audacity to compare myself to Steinbeck. My favorite English teacher would sit back, peer over her glasses, and smile.

Steinbeck said the country was a memory if you lived in the city and he wanted to go back and see it all again. He was fifty-eight, and his health was failing by then. I was sixty-seven when I started my trip. Seven years older than him, but likely in better health. He was a smoker and I lived in the country with horses. But I suspect he didn't take advice any better than me. We're both stubborn and liberals in staunchly conservative families.

Steinbeck's truck had a special custom-built camper, a "turtle shell." It was a fancy rig for the time, with a lovely knotty pine interior. He described it in more humble terms than the photos revealed. He named it after Quixote's horse, Rocinante. I had to like the horse reference. Steinbeck may have seen himself jousting with windmills, but neither of us finished college. I wonder if he homeschooled the classics like I did.

My rig, one of the smallest and cheapest available, carries the first farm sign I bought twenty-odd years ago: Howlin' Cowgirl Rancho. When I turned pro, I renamed my place Infinity Farm to feign some respectability, but this rant-at-the-moon name fit my new A-Frame. I screwed some hooks into it to hold coats. It reminds me of home and good horses gone by. It reminds me to stay in a strong voice. I joust for horses.

Steinbeck laid in an impressive supply of hard liquors and cans of chili but often ate out in restaurants. He brought a wardrobe of hats, including a yachting hat for disguise, he said. And he brought guns, of course. While on the road, he bought more liquor and guns.

I laid in horse training equipment, dog toys, and some tiny box wines. I ate as fresh and healthy as I could, preferring Mister's company to restaurants. Hats in the horse world are like gang colors, so I wear an environmentalist's hat, a brimmed cloth one with UPF protection. I have no guns. Perhaps I should have one to release injured animals. I wrestle with some questions that Steinbeck didn't. And I probably have more pillows, but he didn't mention his.

We are both writers. We curate the stories we tell, and road trips are fertile ground. In 1960, the country was at the height of the Cold War, and worried about nuclear weapons. The Civil Rights Movement was in full swing. Not so different from today.

Steinbeck went through his trip routinely getting lost, with the luxury of no time constraints. He made it seem endearing and self-deprecating, playing a ne'er-do-well wanderer, like a character in one of his books. Women don't have that luxury and it's never endearing to feel unsafe. I want to think GPS was an advantage, but maybe not. And I needed to keep to my work schedule. No one told Steinbeck he was brave, but I heard it often. The reasons for that haven't changed in the sixty years between our trips.

Steinbeck talked to men mainly, describing them with rustic romance. He loved men, praising their stalwart shoulders and honorable natures. They were each heroic in ordinary ways, a common theme for him, undeniable and sacred. This isn't a hard secret to discern in his writing, it's literal hero worship.

"*There is absolutely nothing to take the place of a good man.*" Said Steinbeck as he traveled with Charley.

He seemed to write about women as an afterthought, set dressing. Never the lead. Steinbeck's women, who were often waitresses, only bit characters in his book, described as cranky (more likely tired or unimpressed), or cheerfully subservient (as if women lived to pour men's coffee). The commonality was the women were all in some state of *bustiness*. He used the word "bust" (my head explodes at the word) as if our breasts were his to weigh and judge.

Steinbeck attempts to be fair in his writing, but he is aware he falls short. He's good-natured about it, apologizing along the way. It's white privilege at its finest, with verbalized respect all around. But it rang hollow to an elder African American hitchhiker who called him Captain Sir and asked to be let out of the vehicle before his destination. He didn't feel safe with Steinbeck. I'm not sure I would have either.

I'm not as interested in men as Steinbeck was. Saturated, I've read my quota, and more, of the male experience. I want to read and write about women and give top billing to those I see as heroic, out of step with their time, or ahead of it. I use the lens of horses because it's the world I know. Because just below the surface, women and horses have much in common. Each woman I meet has an interesting story, stranger or friend. It would never occur to me to describe anyone's breasts.

I wonder if Steinbeck would have made the connection between civil rights and women's rights, both long on the political landscape by then. It was a blind spot but with more years, maybe that would have changed. I would like to read that book.

Steinbeck wrote about a holiday stop in Texas for a large party. The hosts and other guests were wealthy. Steinbeck avoided mentioning his financial situation, but he flew his wife in for a holiday meal. There was a well-written exchange in this chapter about the freedom that comes with having money. Wealthy Texans wore jeans and expensive boots to events when someone of low means would dress up for fear of appearing dirty or poor.

My pedigree has always been visible. Before leaving for my month-long stint as a scholarship kid at a private college, my mother scrimped and bought me a cheap leather coat. She said everyone wore jeans but with this coat, I could pass as one of them. One of the rich kids, she meant. Even now, I can't pass.

Steinbeck traveled between classes almost invisibly. I do that but between horses and humans. Steinbeck was a privileged voyeur, watching from a safe distance. Or was he invited because of his celebrity in that circle, as I sometimes am?

Steinbeck's trip was 10,000 miles. Mine was over 14,000 miles. Scholars believe his book was heavily fictionalized, especially Charley. What do you expect? Steinbeck wrote fiction. He had a story of America he wanted to tell and needed a bit of humanity in it. Dogs are the obvious choice.

Charley, Steinbeck's dog, was a black standard poodle from France. He had a short clip with a bun of longer hair on top of his head. He looked a little more sophisticated than the scruffy Steinbeck. Mister says poodles are very intelligent and, lacking a worthwhile job like herding, can seem effete or even pretentious. But Charley loved trees and didn't seem to own a leash. Steinbeck encouraged him to wander off to make friends, easing the introduction for Steinbeck.

I have a mortal fear of seeing Mister crushed and bloody, so I don't send him anywhere alone. Besides, he is not willing to pander like a poodle. Mister cautiously enjoys the environment but doesn't search out trees. Maybe he prefers flat for ease of leg-lifting. Less willing to please people, Mister is a disaffected dog, proudly indifferent, and as conservative as a donkey. Arguably, I'm as scruffy as Steinbeck. Maybe I should look up the definition of effete.

Charley had two urinary infections during the trip. Mister understands the difficulty of navigating personal dilemmas of this sort while traveling. During the second infection, Steinbeck left him boarded at a vet he described with manly praise and went to that wealthy Texan's party with his wife. I would have camped in the vet's parking lot. How do you leave your dog and go to a party?

Steinbeck gave off the appearance of Hemingway, with a poodle. A literary man, rich or famous enough to dress shabby like the Texans. He was a man of casual and undeniable position, playing possum, doing undercover work for a book. He was a loner with a turned-up collar, until he brought out his whiskey, stayed up late, and got men to talk.

Meanwhile, I am working the longest hours of my life, squinting my eyes to focus, and talking non-stop. I play the part of a charming clinician delivering messages people might not want to hear but are dying to know. By the time everyone is basking in the afterglow, I'm a dying ember. No late-night whiskey fests for me and he probably held his liquor better. We both hide in plain sight.

Steinbeck had a romantic struggle with his writing, comparing it to a fickle lover who teased and threatened to leave him. He feared her betrayal with each sentence. For better or worse, me and my words are like an old married couple comfortable in our quirky habits. We complete each other's sentences as easy as coffee with cream. Zero artistic struggle. Do writers need to suffer overtly, to cut their ears off like Van Gogh, smoke and drink the hard stuff, I wonder, swilling a seltzer to the bottom?

I thought it strange that Steinbeck described his body early in the book, but he did, and in the way you would expect. Manly, masculine, and all-male. He was nothing if not a man's man with a translucent veneer of humility. I accept the challenge.

My body is my fortress, crowned with hair gone white as mid-winter snow, not a sparse fall frost. My hair drifts erratically because I cut it myself and then let it storm its own way.

I am eroded soil, not as tall as I once was, not as thin. My left foot has been mended like a fence, with a few screws, a lever, and a bent staple. It's thicker than the other, so I wear bulky shoes that match my ankles, sturdy as tree trunks.

My skin looks like miles of Navajo reservation land dried by the sun. In the moonlight, my heels have a shadow edge like the mesas and arroyos of the great Southwest. My heart is the Rocky Mountains, scarred and bruised, purple and blue, but standing all the taller for it. I fill my lungs with the endless prairie wind.

I am held to this life by slow-moving streams of muscles that are visible through transparent wrapping. My breasts have migrated to a protected cave under my arms and my belly has become a dog bed in the sun. I'm happy it's soft.

Steinbeck said he wore a beard because it was the one thing he was sure a man can do better than a woman. When I find a few thick hairs growing under my nose or on my chin, I hope I'm turning into a horse. Barring that, I hope to give Steinbeck pause.

He began his book by stating his intention to not surrender to becoming an elderly baby. Amen, he was right to worry. That's a chronic issue for men. I am fearless on that account, proud that I have never been a baby in life. Even as a child, it wasn't an option. I am proud to have survived to be a woman of a certain age, a gray mare. Proud to be out on this highway, making a living by my intelligence and wits. I'm especially proud of my dog.

Steinbeck and I probably hear the same soundtrack. It isn't *America, the Beautiful*. It's Woody Guthrie singing, *This Land is Your Land*. The volume swells louder right about now.

In the end, we write, one of us famously and one of us without asking permission. Never truly lost, each of us found just what we looked for. We recognized our deepest beliefs in the landscape, in the companionship of good dogs, and in the ordinary honor of the people we met along the way. We each create our worlds and then stand back to see who we are. We are America, of course.

Sprinting

Preparing to leave Kansas City, we were up early, eager to be headed home. Parked in the site next to us was a huge fifth wheel on a pretty cobalt blue Chevy Dually. They were an older couple from Canada. She took a few small steps toward me and offered to help check if my blinkers were working, just as she does for her husband. They traveled from British Columbia in the summer to Texas and Arizona in the winter. She said they were on their way south right now, but obviously taking an alternate route.

I bragged about my mileage this year. She confirmed theirs with her husband; they had gone over 100,000 miles so far. She didn't move as well as I did, probably had ten years on me. She said they planned to travel as long as they could, and then sit back and remember it all. I like to think I'm not like these RV park elders, but the truth is, I am.

The road ahead of me is shorter than the road behind me. I know working this way is not sustainable forever, but it's the very best work I've ever done and the most challenging. There is a price to pay for pretending to be someone else, even if you do it for horses. I have no regrets.

I was a contrary child, quitting Brownies because they were sissies, and I'm no different as a gray mare. I swore I'd never change to please others, not submit to rules meant to keep me cornered. I would not be trapped in that window seat of expectations, pressured to fit into a life that kept me muzzled and hobbled, like an animal held as a pet. I am the one who refuses to be "cute."

Averse to my kind from the start, but inexplicably drawn to run with that herd, I gave myself over. Anything for a horse. I'd turn myself inside out, give it all away for a horse. But even that was not enough. After I changed for my horses, I changed for yours.

There was so much misinterpretation. I wanted to listen to the depth of horses, and truly learn their language, and to ponder their mystery beyond our use of them. To give them autonomy in return for the freedom they offer women like me who don't quite fit. We were always meant to carry each other, neither of us being a beast of burden. A small voice deep inside affirms it, saying "I am your equal." I can't tell if it's theirs or mine.

I am the proud legacy of my ghost herd. They carried me until my back grew strong enough to carry others. One day, I will have paid that debt and I will sit back and remember. Exhausted by my ruse, unfettered in my skin, but still kept by a dog unimpressed with fame. I'll stay home to watch sunsets with old horses. But I'm not ready for that just yet.

Then, I asked Mister if he wanted to get in the truck. We have an agreement, Mister and me. I only ask him questions that he'll answer with yes because it's the only answer that works for both of us. Yes, because he's the best dog. Yes, to barking at cats and being slow to find a place to pee and wanting his dinner now, please. Yes, the only answer he hears from me and so it's his only response, too. Yes, in the truck for another day. He stood on the running board and gave a little jump. More of a bounce, really, but I hoisted him the rest of the way into his safety seat. Clicking his harness to the headrest, I pray he is safe always and thank him for being my dog.

Then I walked the lap and checked the connections before climbing in. When Virginia Woolf spoke of *A Room of One's Own*, she said in order to write, a woman needed a private place and money of her own. She didn't imagine my Rollin' Rancho, but it's the place where I coil my strength and find my words. It's a room the size of my imagination. I'm amazed the truck can tow it.

Checking both directions, with no Starbucks in sight, we pulled out into traffic. I gave GPS Woman the day off. I can find my way from here. Driving across Kansas on I-70 was a straight shot. We were on the road with the sun barely over the horizon. We slid in behind a fast-moving eighteen-wheeler, patient to sit here and let him draw us home. There is a familiar thrill to starting a day driving and on this last day, it still kicks in full strength. Going up a long hill, just off the road on the right side, I spotted a huge buck with a massive rack of antlers standing in a hayfield. Honey in the sun, he was a healthy and slightly portly reminder that everything dies, but not all at once. Still alive, God's tubby deer.

It was near Mulberry Creek that we saw the edge of the first white blade. It took a few minutes to get up the long rise, but as we crested the hill, the road opened onto a tallgrass prairie. Wind turbines surrounded us as far as we could see, like a great flock of herons pecking for water. Some were so close to the road that I heard their whooshing calls.

The cracked ground said the drought had been relentless.

The land was dry, the sand color visible through frail grass. This is the high prairie I live on. It's a hard land, a bit more forgiving than farther southwest. Cattle can graze if there are hundreds of acres to rotate them, but the soil is not good enough to grow crops. A few cattle loiter by a water tank, their backsides to the wind. There were sparse bits of yucca warning a desert was near and a few shade trees around older farmhouses. Stick-built, we call them, not as common as single-wides, or double-wides. A modular home is the commercially preferred name, but they will never be mistaken for a farmhouse with a big fat porch.

An arms dealer has set up in an aluminum building next to the road. Pickups like mine are parked in front. A fluorescent sign yells Ammo. I wonder how many assault rifles the hunters are buying. How much ammo they need while waiting for Armageddon? They keep their flag at half-mast, so we will all know they're mad.

The sky was full of Canada geese, dozens in wedge-shaped arrowheads flying high above the tan prairie. Now and then, one fell back, and another came to the tip. They work together to ease up the pressure of leading, of cutting a trail in the air. I pulled ahead of the semi now. We're almost there. We cut across back roads, the last stretch. I can see the front range of the Rocky Mountains now. The peaks are a long directional marker. You know where your home is by locating your mountain. Mine is Pikes Peak. Mister rolls to adjust his belly for the air conditioning vent and dreams on.

Home

It was late afternoon when I drove along the front of my farm to the gate. A bumper crop of tumbleweeds shrouded the field fence. Some of the arena perimeter had blown down. It was one season when I left and another now. Only the wind hadn't changed over the weeks I've been gone.

We came through the gate, and I cut the engine. Twisting sideways in the driver's seat, I dangled my feet and made the drop to the ground. I walked to the passenger door, un-clicked Mister, and lifted him down. He acted like we had just gotten home from an agility class, only gone for an hour. Edgar Rice Burro, in the barn on the far side of the house, let out a bray like a foghorn in the sandstorm. I heard the front door open. Home, sweet home. It sounds trite. I didn't kiss the dust and gravel, but this is my land. The place I am all mine.

This farm is nothing special, just over five acres. It has no white vinyl fencing. They moved the house here from a local Army base. No one is sure when. The fence panels don't match, the trim wants paint, and the leach field is partly under the garage. About one month a year, the weeds look pretty good. It's the kind of property they call a hobby farm, but it will always be more work than play.

Here on the flat windy prairie, there aren't many trees. We mourn the four big ones we lost last year. None are left in the backyard now or by the driveway. There is one elm that's doing okay over near the barn, a testament to how often I clean the water tanks. It holds the tree swings in the summer but also has a condition called bacterial wetwood, which means it weeps. Although the bird population has noticeably dropped in recent years, this giant perch of a tree remains. Its cries haunt the night like the mourning doves it sheltered.

This is an arid semi-desert prairie, over 7,000 feet in altitude. When people find out I live in Colorado, they smile, and I know they imagine scenic postcard photos of rugged mountains, pine trees, and alpine lakes. No, I say, not that part of Colorado. My farm holds no romance for anyone but me. I protect my pasture, meaning the weeds that grow there. When I first moved here, I wanted to be rid of every plant that didn't look like it belonged on a golf course. Now I protect the weeds because without them, there is no ground cover at all. The weeds hold us together.

The drought, now being called historic, has meant more fires.

We've been lucky so far. I get the alerts on my phone, but they don't help if I'm working a few states away. We feed our horses year-round. Hay prices are higher than ever and I'm grateful to have a good hay dealer who sadly apologizes when he must raise his prices. His truck isn't new; we rely on each other.

Civilization is stalking us. The town encroaches from the west and north. My view of Pikes Peak is sliced, hacked, and butchered by high-tension power lines carrying the electricity from all those wind turbines we passed out east. They are the visual price I pay for electricity that isn't meant for me. Traffic circles were constructed for the housing developments, along with a new four-lane intersection. I can watch the stoplight cycle to red from my barn door. Stop.

I swear, there are days when Earth seems angry. The light spoils to a sallow color and the ground turns sooty with dread. The trees are black against a white sky. Try as I do to be a good steward of her precious land, I worry we are losing this fight. Humankind is foolish to think we can survive without her. Farmers and ranchers know Earth will never be tamed.

My farm is a gray area between the domestic and the wild. Deer and birds and varmints mingle with horses and llamas and dogs. Boundaries have become blurred, and some change with the seasons. Eventually, I lost track my boundaries and became owned by this land. Then by all her land.

I live this way because some part of me is still a pioneer. Because I can't find a fit for my habits. Here's proof, I get along with goats. I am that dirty insult: independent. If it's a fault, I won't trade it for the night sky.

It's been my extreme honor and pleasure to travel and work with horses in some of the most beautiful places on the planet. The unforgettable red dirt of Australia has stained my skin and the otherworldly botanic beauty of New Zealand gives me hope to continue. The midnight sun in Alaska has kept me on the watch for dawn. The north of Scotland stands me tall in the wind, like a Przewalski's horse, wild and timeless. The diversity of beauty in this country I love has been an astonishing and humbling experience. God's country. With miracles as thick as Edgar Rice Burro's winter coat.

Clients tell me I should move closer to them. There are a million reasons to go. The droughts have gone on so long that the pond has evaporated to a mud puddle, the surface slick with algae. My house is old, but not in a clever, eclectic way. I have fence posts with six inches of cement showing above the soil, but my commitment has not eroded at all.

This farm is like no place I have ever been to before. It's home, that word that quivers on the back of my tongue, that place that I cling to with battered hands. My home, even the word is an exhale.

It's a better choice to stay and protect Earth's wildness, even those parts with fences. It's a better choice to stand with her animals and worship the sunset. For all the farms I've visited, and for this dear farm, I will hold steady and grateful, stubbornly rooted in an undomesticated life.

Acknowledgments

Mister, of course. I could not have gone a mile without him. He completes me. He knows.

I want to thank Sarah, my longtime friend from sophomore French class, who planted the seed of this book in my head at the beginning of the pandemic. You suggested I respond to a call from the New York Times to share an essay about how the pandemic changed how we work, but the essay ran long. Very long. Thanks for being my librarian and giving me a reading list all our lives; the books lifted my writing goals. Thanks for the rare loyalty of sticking with our friendship over all these miles. Having known each other when we were puppies is more precious over all these years.

I can't do what I do without my clients. Thanks for sharing your horses with me and trusting the online courses. Thanks for keeping me working during the pandemic and for buying hay for my horses. A special thanks to the dreamers who organized clinics and invited me. I'm grateful for each invitation, and the leap of faith in sharing my work with your friends. I am beyond impressed at your desire to understand, do your best, and forge a peaceful path of training. It's you who are changing the world for horses.

I worked with three editors on this book, each focused and insightful. Crissi McDonald and Elisabeth Kauffman did developmental edits and Kara Stewart did a copy edit. I learn the most about the craft of writing from editors tweaking my words. Thank you for the direction correction, the grammar changes, and the little notes tucked into the manuscript along the way to cheer me on. A special thank you to Peggy Brown who gave the manuscript a last proofread and managed to find a few strays. Anything that works in this book is because of their diligence, and any fault is all mine.

Crissi McDonald, I am proud to call you my undomesticated friend. The best listener and talker, not just for this book, but for what it means to work for horses. Self-employment doesn't have the perks like paid vacations and sick days, but every five-hour lunch date, Crissi, was a month-long tropical trip for my sanity. You know and understand what others can't. We're horse buddies who have never ridden together, writing partners who type in different rooms, but so closely attached by thoughts and words and the things we love. Thank you for your enthusiastic vision of this book, for being a compatriot in life, and for Lilith House Press, where we practice what we preach. I can't wait for your next book. Let's do this forever.

I can't go *there* without leaving *here*, so a special debt of gratitude to The Dude Rancher for taking care of the herd while I'm gone. You are the quintessential introvert and don't like me to mention you, but I'm not an obedient wife, so that works. We were not young when we met, and your city life and corporate job didn't prepare you for life on a farm or a woman like me. Maybe none of us ever know what life has in store, but I'm pretty sure wrestling goats wasn't on your bucket list. Thank you for doing the weird tasks that make no sense to you but make all the difference to the souls in the barn. Thanks for scratching Edgar's ears and the phone calls telling me what you had for dinner. You're like Mister that way, keeping my toes on the ground.

And infinite gratitude to horses, closer than kin. You have been my safe harbor, taken me in when humans pushed me out. You have brought me an understanding of my complicated species and given me a place with them. You have carried me around the world and back again. You are my family, my language, my financial support, my lens on the world, my truest home. I'm eternally and happily grateful for the place you've given me, not just professionally but as a member of your extended herd on this beautiful planet. My gratitude will never match who you all have been in my life. So, I give you my breath.

About the Author

I'm an animal advocate, award-winning author, born-again RV traveler, old-school feminist, dog companion, unabashed lover of sunsets, and professional horse trainer/clinician. I'm sixty-nine years old. I've done everything and done it damn well. I'm no longer auditioning.

My books include:

Stable Relation,
A memoir of one woman's spirited journey home.

Relaxed & Forward: Relationship advice from your horse.

Barn Dance, Nickers, brays, bleats, howls, and quacks:
Tales from the herd.

Horse Prayers, Poems from the prairie.

Going Steady, More relationship advice from your horse.

Horse. Woman. Poems from our lives.

Road Trip Library

Friend's books that I mentioned:

A Horse A Husband and Cancer by Elaine Kirsch Edsall and Mark Edsall

Liberty Biscuit by Melanie Sue Bowles

My 2022 reading list:

Heartland by Sarah Smarsh

The Story of Edgar Sawtelle By David Wroblewski

Still Life By Louise Penny

Perestroika in Paris By Jane Smiley

The Call of the Wild By Jack London

Stein on Writing By Sol Stein

A Fatal Thaw By Dana Stabenow

Wise Blood By Flannery O'Connor

Hamnet By Maggie O'Farrell

Empire of the Summer Moon By S. C. Gwynne

American Girl By Wendy Walker

Cloud Cuckoo Land By Anthony Doerr

A Prayer for Owen Meany By John Irving

The Good Daughter By Karin Slaughter

The Spectator Bird By Wallace Stegner

The Sentence By Louise Erdrich

A Cold Day for Murder By Dana Stabenow

A Lost Lady By Willa Cather

All the Light We Cannot See By Anthony Doerr

Their Lost Daughters By Joy Ellis

The God of Small Things By Arundhati Roy

Last Breath By Karin Slaughter

The Book of Lost Friends By Lisa Wingate

The Night Watchman By Louise Erdrich

The Book of Form and Emptiness By Ruth Ozeki

The Return of the Native By Thomas Hardy

Alexander's Bridge By Willa Cather

Our Story Begins By Tobias Wolff

Oh William! By Elizabeth Strout

Blink By Malcolm Gladwell

Flight Patterns By Karen White

An Immense World By Ed Yong

Travels with Charley in Search of America
By John Steinbeck

Klara and the Sun By Kazuo Ishiguro

A Ghost in the Throat By Doireann Ní Ghríofa

Missoula by Jon Krakauer

Klara and the Sun By Kazuo Ishiguro

Remembering Laughter By Wallace Stegner

Braiding Sweetgrass By Robin Wall Kimmerer

Horse By Geraldine Brooks

The Master Butcher's Singing Club By Louise Erdrich

The Oregon Trail By Francis Parkman

Somebody's Daughter By Ashley C. Ford

This Is the Story of a Happy Marriage By Ann Patchett

Solito By Javier Zamora

The Sparrow By Mary Doria Russell

The Book Woman of Troublesome Creek by Kim Michele
Richardson

The Elephant Whisperer by Lawrence Anthony,
Graham Spence

Printed in the USA
CPSIA information can be obtained
at www.ICGtesting.com
JSHW011619021223
52755JS00001B/1